Twenty Years of Euro-Mediterranean Relations

The creation of the Euro-Mediterranean Partnership in 1995 was seen, at the time, as a forward-thinking foreign policy which would strengthen ties between Europe and the Mediterranean Arab states. Since that time, however, almost none of this initial ambition has been translated into positive, successful policy.

Twenty years on from the creation of the Euro-Mediterranean Partnership (now the Union for the Mediterranean), this book collects some of the most influential articles published in the *Mediterranean Politics* journal since 1995 – and suggests what these articles tell us about the state of relations between Europe and the Middle East. The selection of articles gives a sense of the way in which analytical debate has changed in the journal's lifetime, the two decades in which the journal has been at the forefront of academic study on a variety of issues in the Mediterranean region. As such, the selection is naturally a reflection of the different periods from which the articles are selected, and, taken together, they paint a picture of how the Euro-Mediterranean Partnership has been reshaped over time.

Richard Youngs is Professor of International Relations at Warwick University, UK, and Senior Associate at the Carnegie Endowment for International Peace.

Twenty Years of Euro-Mediterranean Relations

Edited by
Richard Youngs

Routledge
Taylor & Francis Group

LONDON AND NEW YORK

First published 2016 by Routledge

2 Park Square, Milton Park, Abingdon, Oxfordshire OX14 4RN
711 Third Avenue, New York, NY 10017

Routledge is an imprint of the Taylor & Francis Group, an informa business

First issued in paperback 2017

British Library Cataloguing in Publication Data
A catalogue record for this book is available from the British Library

ISBN 13: 978-1-138-10131-9 (hbk)
ISBN 13: 978-1-138-30899-2 (pbk)

Typeset in Times New Roman
by RefineCatch Limited, Bungay, Suffolk

Publisher's Note
The publisher accepts responsibility for any inconsistencies that may have
arisen during the conversion of this book from journal articles to book chapters,
namely the possible inclusion of journal terminology.

Disclaimer
Every effort has been made to contact copyright holders for their permission to
reprint material in this book. The publishers would be grateful to hear from any
copyright holder who is not here acknowledged and will undertake to rectify
any errors or omissions in future editions of this book.

Contents

CONTENTS

Citation Information

The chapters in this book were originally published in various issues of *Mediterranean Politics*. When citing this material, please use the original page numbering for each article, as follows:

Chapter 1
The Barcelona Conference: Launching Pad of a Process
Esther Barbé
Mediterranean Politics, volume 1, issue 1 (Summer 1996) pp. 25–42

Chapter 2
Southern Attitudes towards an Integrated Mediterranean Region
George Joffé
Mediterranean Politics, volume 2, issue 1 (Summer 1997) pp. 12–29

Chapter 3
Destabilization through Partnership? Euro-Mediterranean Relations after the Barcelona Declaration
Eberhard Kienle
Mediterranean Politics, volume 3, issue 2 (Autumn 1998) pp. 1–20

Chapter 4
Reshaping the Agenda? The Internal Politics of the Barcelona Process in the Aftermath of September 11
Richard Gillespie
Mediterranean Politics, volume 8, issue 3 (Autumn 2003) pp. 21–36

Chapter 5
Regional Community Building and the Transformation of International Relations: The Case of the Euro-Mediterranean Partnership
Frédéric Volpi
Mediterranean Politics, volume 9, issue 2 (Summer 2004) pp. 145–164

Chapter 6
The Use of Conditionality in Support of Political, Economic and Social Rights:
Unveiling the Euro-Mediterranean Partnership's True Hierarchy of Objectives?
Dorothée Schmid
Mediterranean Politics, volume 9, issue 3 (Autumn 2004) pp. 396–421

Chapter 7
Imagining Co-presence in Euro-Mediterranean Relations: The Role of
'Dialogue'
Michelle Pace
Mediterranean Politics, volume 10, issue 3 (November 2005) pp. 291–312

Chapter 8
Talking Tough or Talking Together? European Security Discourses towards the
Mediterranean
Federica Bicchi & Mary Martin
Mediterranean Politics, volume 11, issue 2 (July 2006) pp. 189–207

Chapter 9
Converging, Diverging and Instrumentalizing European Security and Defence
Policy in the Mediterranean
Eduard Soler i Lecha
Mediterranean Politics, volume 15, issue 2 (July 2010) pp. 231–248

Chapter 10
The Ties that do not Bind: The Union for the Mediterranean and the Future of
Euro-Arab Relations
Oliver Schlumberger
Mediterranean Politics, volume 16, issue 1 (March 2011) pp. 135–153

Chapter 11
The Return of Arab Politics and Europe's Chance to Engage Anew
Rasmus Alenius Boserup & Fabrizio Tassinari
Mediterranean Politics, volume 17, issue 1 (March 2012) pp. 97–103

For any permission-related enquiries please visit:
http://www.tandfonline.com/page/help/permissions

Notes on Contributors

Esther Barbé is Research Program Coordinator at the Institut Barcelona d'Estudis Internacionals, and a Professor at the Universitat Autònoma de Barcelona, Spain.

Federica Bicchi is Associate Professor in International Relations of Europe at the London School of Economics and Political Science, London, UK.

Rasmus Alenius Boserup is Senior Researcher of Foreign Policy at the Danish Institute for International Studies, Copenhagen, Denmark.

Richard Gillespie is Professor of Politics at the University of Liverpool, UK, where he is co-Director of the Europe and the World Centre. He is the founder of the *Mediterranean Politics* journal.

George Joffé is a Senior Research Fellow at the Centre of International Studies, University of Cambridge, UK, and Visiting Professor of Geography at Kings College, London, UK.

Eberhard Kienle is Director of the Institut français du Proche-Orient, based in Beirut, Lebanon.

Mary Martin is Senior Research Fellow in the Department of International Development at the London School of Economics and Political Science, London, UK.

Michelle Pace is Honorary Professor in Politics and International Studies at the University of Birmingham, UK.

Oliver Schlumberger is Professor, and Director of the Institute of Political Science, at Eberhard-Karls Universität Tübingen, Germany.

Dorothée Schmid is a Research Fellow at the Institut français des relations internationales, Paris, France, focusing on the politics of the Mediterranean and the Middle East.

Eduard Soler i Lecha is Head Researcher at the Institut Barcelona d'Estudis Internacionals, and a Lecturer at the Universitat Autònoma de Barcelona, Spain.

Fabrizio Tassinari is Senior Researcher and Head of Unit for Foreign Policy Studies at the Danish Institute for International Studies, Copenhagen, Denmark.

NOTES ON CONTRIBUTORS

Frédéric Volpi is Senior Lecturer in the School of International Relations at the University of St Andrews, UK.

Richard Youngs is Professor of International Relations at Warwick University, UK, and Senior Associate at the Carnegie Endowment for International Peace.

Introduction: Twenty Years of Euro-Mediterranean Relations

RICHARD YOUNGS

Twenty years have passed since the creation of the Euro-Mediterranean Partnership (EMP). This span of a generation feels like a geopolitical lifetime. At its birth, the EMP was one of the EU's most comprehensive and forward-looking foreign policy initiatives. The hope this engendered was reflected in the very creation of the *Mediterranean Politics* journal. Two decades later, virtually none of the EMP's ambitions have been fulfilled. In 2009 the EMP was rechristened as the Union for the Mediterranean (UfM). Yet, despite many well-meaning policies and some islands of achievement in Euro-Mediterranean relations, on most vectors conditions in the southern Mediterranean have worsened since 1995. Relations between Europe and Arab states, Turkey and Israel have become more fractious.

The Middle East is today the source of acute strategic challenges. War rages in four Arab states: Libya, Syria, Iraq and Yemen. Sunni radicalization, especially in the form of Islamic State (IS) jihadis, is challenging national borders. More intense geopolitical rivalries are taking shape between the region's main powers. Sharper sectarian tensions exist between Sunni and Shia communities, amplified by regimes' power strategies. Egypt is rocked by instability and polarisation. The Arab-Israeli peace process is for now moribund, if not definitively dead; Gaza stands in ruins, having suffered a death toll in excess of a thousand in the summer of 2014. The region is suffering its worst-ever humanitarian crisis. Illicit trade, trafficking and smuggling are rife, providing financial sources for jihadist groups and undermining the regional rule of law and economic order. Far from representing a benign link between cultures, the Mediterranean Sea is in the headlines today as the site of frequent and tragically large numbers of migrant deaths. The growing influence of non-Western rising powers in the Middle East compounds competition for strategic alliances, geo-economic gain and access to energy supplies. Regional cooperation initiatives have run aground.

The EMP's twentieth birthday is hardly an anniversary to celebrate, then. Yet it is certainly a moment at which lessons need to be drawn from the past – not least to help understand where the initial promise of Euro-Mediterranean relations went so wrong, and how positive gains from the EMP might still be salvaged. In such retrospective vein, this volume collects together some of the key *Mediterranean Politics*

1

articles published on the EMP/UfM during the last twenty years. The aim is to give a flavor of how debates over the partnership have evolved since 1995.

It is pertinent to undertake this retrospective now as so many of the EMP's initial concerns have returned to the forefront of debate – indeed, in the case of some issues, with greater vengeance than at any time during the last two decades. In 2015, the EU has committed itself to a fundamental revamping of its southern (and eastern) neighbourhood policy. As geopolitical conditions have led many to call for a new EU policy towards the Middle East and North Africa, today's writings often read like epitaphs for the original EMP design – such is the gravity of this twenty-year turning point.

There are policy and academic lessons to be learned from the flurry of initial debates that took place over the EMP. It is striking just how many articles were published on the EMP in the early years of the *Mediterranean Politics* journal. It is equally notable how concerns have more recently turned to other issues, as Euro-Mediterranean relations appear to have calcified. If the EU and southern Mediterranean partners are to retain the aspirations they enshrined in the EMP in 1995, they could do worse than draw from the changing analyses of the last twenty years.

I have selected here a range of articles designed to give a flavour of the way in which the focus of analytical debates has evolved since 1995. The journal has published many more worthy pieces on the EMP and UfM than those presented in the following chapters. Indeed, it has been at the forefront of setting the terms of academic debate on a wide range of Mediterranean issues during the last twenty years. It was impossible to include all relevant articles here; in this selection I have tried to offer examples of writing that I see as representative of analytical approaches prevalent at particular moments in time. In this way, I hope to present a record of the way in which the geopolitical context has reshaped the EMP/UfM and of how leading thinkers have responded to these changing parameters. In essence, I try to recreate the fluctuating story of the EMP/UfM as leading writers saw the process at pivotal moments in its evolution.

The Early Years

In the years following the EMP's inception, expectations were high. This collection begins with an article written by Esther Barbé for the very first edition of the journal, which explains how the EMP represented an ambitious new multilateral approach to Euro-Mediterranean relations. This article highlights the symbolic political importance of the EMP's creation. The new Barcelona Process indicated that the EU would not neglect the southern Mediterranean as the Union immersed itself in preparing central and eastern European candidate states for accession. And its guiding philosophy was notable in rejecting realpolitik strategies – ostensibly basing itself on a progressive notion of cooperative security, joint decision-making, region-building, political reform and social integration. The very fact that the EU chose to focus on deepening a 'Mediterranean' rather than 'broader Middle East' policy suggested a preference for inclusive cooperation with the Union's neighbours. The EMP was not only an important policy milestone; it also nourished distinctive theoretical conceptualizations of EU foreign policy.

At a moment, in the mid-1990s, when the distorted spectre of a 'clash of civilizations' framed much analytical discourse, the EMP ostensibly enshrined a firm rejection of exclusionary and defensive geo-strategy. It was at this stage one of the most significant examples of the EU's commitment to a distinctive type of liberal-cooperative foreign policy. The EMP appeared to correct some of the ad hoc bilateralism that had previously dominated European-Arab relations. As Barbé's article reminds us, member states still held different perspectives on the southern Mediterranean, yet compromised sufficiently to agree an apparently common approach to the region – even if many details of how the EMP commitments would be implemented remained sketchy.

While hopes were high at this point, not all reactions were positive. The volume's second contribution is a 1997 article by George Joffé that recalls how southern Mediterranean states were unhappy at what they saw as the euro-centric assumptions sitting at the heart of the EMP. Both Joffé and Eberhard Kienle – in his 1998 article on the EMP's 'destabilizing' elements, reproduced below as our third essay – warned in these early days that the long-term consequences of the EMP template could be counterproductive. In particular, early concerns were raised that the EU was relying far too heavily on an assumption that support for economic liberalization and integration would deliver security benefits, inter-regional harmony and political modernization.

Several southern Mediterranean governments signed up to the EMP without enthusiasm and largely because in the mid-1990s they saw few other strategic alternatives. Critical voices at this stage bemoaned the extent to which the EMP enshrined European hegemony over Arab states – illuminating to recall, given that today there is far more concern over the absence of EU influence in the region. Critics did not believe the EMP's security elements were strong, inclusive or distinctive enough to off-set US primacy. Arab regimes disliked the focus on human rights and democracy. In contrast, civil society groups complained that the focus on democracy was not strong enough and feared that the EMP's economic dimension could worsen the prospects for political liberalization. Many observers felt the EU's understanding of political Islam was simplistic in the rather instrumental way the EMP treated this question. The then-raging Algerian civil war was one of the policy challenges that motivated the EMP's creation; but the EU appeared to have neither the will nor tactics to ensure that Algeria's Islamists were brought into inclusive, mainstream politics. Crucially, many of the points raised by Joffé and Kienle regarding the EMP's original design flaws have become more prominent and more debilitating as the years have gone by.

Paralysis in the Middle East peace process soon undermined the EMP. Debates by the late 1990s and early 2000 were heavily concerned with this 'infection' between the Arab-Israeli conflict and broader Euro-Mediterranean relations. The EMP was conceived on the back of the 1994 Oslo peace accords and in essence offered the social, economic and political means of locking-in the regional benefits of Arab-Israeli reconciliation. Without that reconciliation, the EMP's forums for low-politics cooperation became paralyzingly politicized. The faltering peace process encouraged a spate of analytical work on the EMP's shortcomings as a pan-regional framework that included Arab states, Israel and Turkey.

9/11 and Beyond

If initial enthusiasm in the EMP had begun to drain away, the political context was about to get even more complicated. While concerns over radicalization informed the EMP's comprehensive approach to security, they were not paramount. This changed on 11 September 2001. The terrorist attacks in New York and Washington DC, and then later in Madrid and London, opened a new phase in debates over Europe's Middle Eastern policies. For several subsequent years, analytical work focused on the dynamics of securitization in Euro-Mediterranean relations.

I include here as a fourth piece one of Richard Gillespie's articles from this period, which admirably captures the post-2001 turn within EMP deliberations. This article explains how the EMP's security basket had remained largely empty and notes how the EU sought to inject life into the social, cultural and human affairs basket as a route to addressing strategic concerns. This reflected the heightened importance of justice and home affairs matters, as well as incipient de-radicalization initiatives. These were corollaries to the more intense counter-terrorist cooperation that took shape across the Mediterranean Sea after 2001. Gillespie recalls here that this policy shift sharpened tensions between soft-power and direct security approaches – even as these two components were supposed to be mutually reinforcing within the EMP. This was because the justice and home affairs strand seemed to cut across the EMP's narrative of inclusion, its positive approaches to soft security and the primordial importance supposedly attached to rights-protection. It seemed to drag the EMP away from long-term community building to short-term threat-containment. While this policy shift may have been an understandable response to terrorist attacks, it was pursued in a way that compromised the EMP's geostrategic comparative advantage.

These tensions set the terms of debate for most of the decade that followed the 9/11 attacks – in many senses, of course, we are still living with their consequences. In the next article, Frédéric Volpi attempts an analytical conceptualization of how the EU was responding to security concerns. He neatly categorizes the EMP's constructivist tone of joint cultural shaping between European and southern Mediterranean states, and distinguishes this from realist recipes for the post-2001 geostrategic context. He observes how far short the EU had fallen in actually following through on its own liberal-cooperative ideals of shared identity building – and the consequent limits to the constructivist framework.

This article echoes other writings of the time: after the shock of 9/11 EU leaders rhetorically recommitted themselves to the founding principles of the EMP. The EMP seemed to have been ahead of its time in speaking of cultural understanding, regional integration, economic development and political reform being essential to reducing the risks of radicalization. The reaffirmed commitment after 9/11 raised the policy stakes and meant that by the mid-2000s much analytical work centred on the EU's failure to adhere to its own rhetoric.

The EU introduced a number of new democracy and human rights initiatives. Leaders spoke frequently about the need finally to 'get serious' about political reform: giving citizens a genuine voice to hold their governments accountable was the best way to address the social discontent that drove radicalization. They admitted the EMP had made limited progress in this area. The European Neighbourhood Policy was conceived, to add more tailored action plans in each partner state. Yet, after a flurry of post-2001 activity, any new momentum behind EU support for democratic reforms in the southern Mediterranean soon dissipated. The collection's sixth article by Dorothée Schmid reveals how cautious the EU remained on pressing for political reform, lest this hinder short-term counter-terrorist cooperation.

In a 2005 article included in this volume, Michelle Pace unpacks the obstacles to embedding an ethos of multi-level and co-shaped dialogue between European and southern Mediterranean partners. As security concerns intensified so did the challenges facing EU and Mediterranean states in developing mutually beneficial relations through a culture of dialogue. A plethora of links now existed between the northern and southern sides of the Mediterranean below the level of the state. The EMP was almost uniquely rich in this domain. It had facilitated dialogue between NGOs, municipalities, youth groups, journalists, unions, business actors, parliamentarians and artists. Yet the results of all this activity were disappointing and dialogue was increasingly imbalanced. In part this was because many cultural and social partners operated under regimes' restrictive tutelage. In part it was because the scale of such initiatives was not sufficient to make a decisive difference. And in part it was because many partners in the south complained that the nature of cooperation was being framed on European terms.

From a similar perspective, in their 2006 article on the shift in security discourses, Federica Bicchi and Mary Martin point out that the 9/11, London and Madrid attacks encouraged some European actors to engage more systematically with political Islam across the southern Mediterranean, invariably to the chagrin of regimes. Yet this engagement was less than whole-hearted. Sceptics thought that most European governments were not at all genuine in their claim to have realized the importance of reaching out to Islamist parties. Some states' securitization of Islam sat uneasily with the EMP's founding tenets.

In brief, by the mid-2000s, now ten years on from the EMP's creation, analysts were concerned that EU governments seemed to be reducing their commitment to the southern Mediterranean and reverting to some of their pre-EMP policy approaches. I am personally taken back to 2005 when Haizam Amirah Fernandez and I got together a group of experts to assess the EMP's first ten years.[1] Our resulting book recorded analysts' very downbeat evaluations of the EMP's responsiveness to a deteriorating security, economic, social and political environment. Another ten years on from that, I find it sobering that even in that fairly critical review we all generally failed to see just how dramatically events might proceed during the EMP's second decade – or just how amorphously insipid would be the EU's response to the impending turmoil.

Distracted Debates

In the late 2000s, the EU seemed increasingly introverted. It was immersed in drawn-out internal, institutional reforms. As the threat of radicalism and international terrorism appeared to have plateaued, EU-Mediterranean relations lost some of their drive. As its own economic crisis hit hard, the EU needed buoyant export markets. It began to accord greater priority to rising economies, especially in Asia. The Middle East slipped down its list of priorities. In hindsight, the period that preceded the Arab spring now seems notable for the EU's failure to foresee and prepare for the social upheavals that were just over the horizon. And such distractedness was also reflected in academic work from this period.

In 2010, the journal published a special edition on 'region-building dynamics' in Euro-Mediterranean relations. The subject of this volume suggested that some academics still approached the EMP very much through the lens of its supposedly unique and distinctive commitment to building a shared community and polity across the Mediterranean. At the same time, some contributors to this volume began to stress the contextual shifts that seemed to render this kind of approach increasingly questionable. They talked about more 'flexible' approaches to region-building and in some sectors flagged up the danger of fragmentation.

I have included an article by Eduard Soler i Lecha from this special edition, as it gives an excellent flavour of the very gradually shifting analytical lens through which Euro-Mediterranean relations were assessed. The piece unpacks the mix of convergence and divergence on security questions across the Mediterranean. It notes that policy dynamics depended on specific goals in relation to different issues and did not reflect any broader, all-encompassing regional security culture. Where the EU and Arab states could reach agreement it was for very pragmatic reasons, not as part of any deeply embedded ideational security community.

In line with this focus on very practical areas of cooperation, the French government proposed the creation of a new Union for the Mediterranean. After a number of diplomatic confrontations and a process of re-modelling, the UfM was effectively folded into the exiting EMP (although in policy debates both terms are still used). A new UfM secretariat was set up in Barcelona dedicated to funding joint development projects in the southern Mediterranean. With the benefit of hindsight, it seems puzzling today that so much hope was placed in this re-launch. The UfM started to focus on low-key, technocratic, development projects – apparently blind to the turbulent storm clouds that were evidently gathering over the Middle East.

Indeed, in this period, the EU often appeared immersed in arcane institutional questions, to the detriment of broad, geopolitical deliberation. To demonstrate this, I have selected here Oliver Schlumberger's article from a special edition published in early 2011 specifically dedicated to the Union for the Mediterranean. I could have chosen any number of articles from this edition, if more space were available: it is a collection that reflects well the focus of debates at that moment, as the Union for the Mediterranean added another layer of institutional complexity to EU initiatives in the region. It reflected what would soon be revealed to be a disastrous myopia at the heart of Euro-Mediterranean relations: the new initiative was designed to focus on uncontroversial areas of cooperation and to take politics out of the policy equation – the kind of politics that were just about to erupt in spectacular fashion in Tunisia, Egypt and then elsewhere.

Looking back at this volume, it is remarkable how focused EU debates were on institutional structures, internal processes and rivalries – at a moment when, we now know, social pressures were building up to burst forth in what would be labeled the Arab spring. Many articles were still concerned with very detailed EMP/UfM institutional questions. In hindsight, it is striking that virtually no articles linked the predictions of imminent social explosion in Arab countries with the need for EMP/ UfM policies to move up several political gears. Even less did work in the journal foresee the kind of geopolitical shockwaves created by the now-raging conflicts in Syria, Iraq and Libya. The precursors of Islamic State crept up the agenda without forewarning from analysts writing on the UfM's future challenges.

Impacts of the Arab Spring

Self-evidently, the Arab spring marked the beginning of another phase in analytical debate. I have selected just one illustrative article from the many published since 2011 on the Arab spring. Rasmus Boserup and Fabrizio Tassinari's short essay is a good example of the articles that appeared from 2011 criticizing the UfM for being insufficiently 'politicized' to react appropriately to the Arab spring. In this phase of the debate, the inadequacies of the UfM were front and centre of the analysis. The 'return of Arab politics' – if indeed they had ever gone away – more explicitly changed the terms of academic research. It brought fully to the surface many of the concerns that had been lingering over the EMP/UfM. As did many others in 2011, Boserup and Tassinari lambast the EU for a lame response that was based on a rather bland logic of 'continuity and upgrading'.

Beyond what most analysts saw as the EU's lacklustre response to the Arab revolts, this new phase has also had a profound impact on the analytical narrative of the EMP/UfM. An eclectic mix of policy dynamics characterized the EU's response to the Arab spring.[2] In some ways the EMP/UfM appeared to have become so firmly embedded and institutionalized that it struggled to react positively, strategically and in full measure to the emerging potential for political change. The relative weight of member states' policies became more significant. Governments' strategic calculations produced greater variation in policies towards different southern Mediterranean states, as these took divergent political paths. European governments sought to regain their sway in overall EU policies towards the Middle East.

Looking back at previous analytical work, one notes the longstanding and common view that democracy support is strongly internalized within EU identities and self-images, and pursued in a somewhat un-reflexive manner independent of geostrategic calculation. However, this was not sufficient as an explanation of EU foreign policy in the southern Mediterranean after 2011. The Arab awakening did not open the door to entirely harmonious cooperation and community building across the Mediterranean. Indeed, many of the architects of Arab change insisted that they sought more autonomy from such deep Western entanglement. And differences widened between member states as they read the potential of Arab reform in different ways. This divergence militated against the prospect of a common Europeanized cooperative security framework being fully realised in the post-2011 southern Mediterranean.

The UfM's tools of external governance were certainly relevant in accounting for the way in which some more technical areas of EU rules were adopted by Arab states from 2011. There was a certain unblocking of regulatory harmonization in the wake of the Arab revolts. But overall, there remained much resistance to the concept of importing EU governance across the Middle East. Indeed, popular control over decision-making in many areas tipped the scales against this technocratic vision of cooperation with Europe. A number of EU initiatives aimed to deepen civil society and people-to-people linkages. Yet government-controlled power politics also became more prominent.

While some areas of deeper cooperation were pursued within the rubric of the UfM, in some parts of the Middle East the Arab spring encouraged European governments to give greater priority to bilateral, national foreign policy action. Some member states celebrated and contributed to the Arab spring more than others. Geopolitical calculation became a more prominent strand of the EU policy-making mix. This was particularly so as the process of reform stumbled in many states and instability erupted. The new context challenged the analytical centrality of the 'EMP ethos' that was so extensively dissected in the early years of *Mediterranean Politics*. A different kind of research agenda was called for. A pattern of governance centred on national governments' strategic calculations and actions was at least as relevant as Europeanized models of governance in structuring relations with the new Middle East. European responses were as much about national governments' high diplomacy as they were predicated on Brussels-centred policy instruments.

While some elements of decentred, co-owned and non-state forms of governance certainly have advanced since 2011, these have been accompanied by some very traditional elements of realpolitik. European governments genuinely saw the fashioning of a new Middle East as a positive opportunity, but also sought to deploy national diplomatic means to protect against its risks and uncertainties. In some policy areas the balance between national foreign policies and common EU efforts shifted towards the former. This was seen particularly in Libya, where the divergence between member states was as fundamental as anything witnessed since the inception of the common foreign and security policy.

After 2011 a variation in European policies was driven by a combination of contrasting domestic political structures within different Arab states, on the one hand, and European governments' contrasting security-related calculations in different parts of the region, on the other hand. Both these variables sit uneasily with explanations of EU foreign policy that attribute sole importance to common, socialized EU identities and Europeanized policy instruments. As is evident in the selected articles from the last twenty years of *Mediterranean Politics*, writers have commonly criticized EU policies for being too uniform – and they have argued that this is because they proceed from entrenched institutional templates and elaborately designed external policy instruments. Some elements of the EU's response to the Arab revolts did indeed fit this institutionalist template. However, such inside-out explanations of EU foreign policy decisions look harder to sustain in the awake of the Arab revolts.

This has become even more evident as the momentum of the Arab spring has ebbed and the UfM, as well as member states' national diplomacy, has struggled to adapt to the complex political specificities of southern Mediterranean states. The faltering path of the Arab spring has posed serious questions for standard models of political transition – models upon which the EMP was heavily predicated.

In a sense, European foreign policy has become a dependent as much as independent variable – effected by, not just effecting domestic constellations in southern Mediterranean states. The EU has responded in flexible and even expedient fashion to the fluidity and specificity of domestic developments within different parts of the Middle East. As is apparent from the articles included in this volume, this represents a notable change from the EMP's early days. The EU has supported different types and degrees of political reform in Arab states. It has pursued different mixes of bottom-up civil society support and top-down security cooperation. It is not fully convincing today to accuse the EU of seeking to foist a 'one-size-fits-all' model across the whole region. The EU's reform-oriented strategy in Tunisia looks radically different from its more defensive strategy in Egypt, and both in turn diverge from the humanitarian-security turn to policy in beleaguered Jordan. Moreover, the disconnect between the EMP and the broader Middle East has become more incongruous and more of a handicap to coherent, region-wide geo-strategy.

In sum, the Arab revolts and region-wide geopolitical changes have given birth to a more pluralist set of European approaches in the southern Mediterranean. European policies today reflect less a singular identity and more a calibrated moulding to varied trends in different parts of the MENA region. The revolts and the 'new geopolitics' have contributed to making the EU a more eclectic foreign policy actor, both in terms of substantive output and the institutional-governance dynamics it employs. It is difficult today to describe EU foreign policy parsimoniously or convincingly to show that it unequivocally accords to only one dominant conceptual dynamic. This volume's twenty-year retrospective reminds us just how much this change contrasts with the foregoing EMP narrative – and helps emphasize just how much of an analytical shift this entails.

The Past's Path to the Future

In conclusion, I have tried to select articles that recreate the story of Euro-Mediterranean relations during the last twenty years. In sum, we can observe that debates have passed through several phases, shifting in turn from a focus on the EMP's institutional configuration, to reactions to 9/11 and the emergence of concerns over international terrorism, through to the Arab spring. The crucial question is what we should learn from this trajectory. How can the articles of the last twenty years inform current debates – when the consensual view is that the Middle East now stands on the precipice of pervasive instability?

The articles that follow are offered in the spirit of better delineating the terms of current debates. Some conclude in these essays that the EMP enshrined an enlightened, long-term strategic vision – of admirable foresight compared to today's lack of leadership and long-term thinking – that was simply not followed through. Others find in the selected articles evidence that the EU always had it wrong – and that its particular, euro-centric vision of international relations never had a chance of putting down roots in the southern Mediterranean.

Today it seems that the next phase of debate will have to include questions related to conflict, violence, instability, humanitarian tragedy and the pushback against democratic reform that dominate today's Middle East. The EU's focus is likely to be on protecting itself against such turbulence – this is implied in documents released as part of the ENP review process. The emerging, geopolitical policy dilemmas bring with them a conceptual dilemma. During the last twenty years, the way the EMP/UfM was designed fitted into a particular analytical-theoretical model of EU foreign policy. A crucial academic question is whether the same kinds of analytical, governance models will be so prominent in *Mediterranean Politics* articles during the next one or two decades – or whether analysts will have to re-adjust for the failures of the last twenty years just as much as EU policy-makers. One wonders what kind of work published now will stand the test of time, when the 30th or 40th anniversary of the EMP comes around – if indeed, the EMP or any comparable policy still exists then.

In terms of what should happen, my view is that the EU's 'geopolitical turn' should not divert the UfM from trying to tackle the most deep-rooted causes of today's strategic tensions. Taking geopolitics seriously means thinking what strategies are necessary to oxygenate EU efforts to foster structural reforms – it should not mean suffocating such approaches. The times indeed warrant a more hard-headed approach to security. But a wholesale switch from inclusive, cooperative policies to exclusionary realpolitik is not the answer. The adoption of a more geopolitical policy should not serve as a pretext for arguing that opening European markets or offering freer movement to Arab workers is no longer necessary. Nor should it become shorthand for a policy of keeping the region at a distance instead of working to deepen inclusive cooperation. And it should not point the EU towards using its funds to prop up regimes guilty of atrocious rights abuses. The EU would be equally ill advised to give up entirely on encouraging regional cooperation. With many medium sized powers competing for influence, and no clear hegemon in the region, efforts to build regional norms and rules are more, not less, necessary. While a focus on security is understandable and indeed necessary, exclusionary containment is unlikely to preserve the EU's long-term strategic interests in the Mediterranean.

Notes

[1] R. Youngs and H. Amirah Fernandez (eds.), *Ten years of the Barcelona Process*. Madrid: Instituto Elcano/Fride, 2005.
[2] This argument draws from R. Youngs, *Europe and the New Middle East: opportunity or exclusion?* Oxford University Press, 2014.

The Barcelona Conference: Launching Pad of a Process

ESTHER BARBÉ

The Euro-Mediterranean Partnership Initiative marks a shift in EU Mediterranean policy from bilateral economic agreements to a multilateral approach. The Barcelona Conference was above all a political gesture, an act of political recognition of the Euro-Mediterranean dimensions of socio-economic realities and security concerns. For Spain, the conference was also an opportunity to revive the government's domestic political fortunes and to repay Catalan nationalists for parliamentary support. The EU is now allocating more resources to its Mediterranean neighbours, and the conference itself created a propitious atmosphere for greater agreement. However, important differences were expressed over political and security questions, and the section of the Barcelona-approved Work Programme relating to such matters is the shortest and least precise. Official Spanish satisfaction over the conference must be set against more sceptical 'alternative' responses that point to a persisting European proclivity to impose its cultural values and economic interests on the South.

Towards the end of 1995, the Euro-Mediterranean Conference, organized by the Spanish presidency of the European Union, was held in Barcelona. The conference, held on 27–28 November, was described as a 'historic encounter' since it was the first time that the 15 members of the EU had met at ministerial level with their 12 Mediterranean partners (the countries that had signed agreements with the Union: Algeria, Cyprus, Egypt, Israel, Jordan, Lebanon, Malta, Morocco, Syria, Tunisia, Turkey and the Palestinian Authority). The historic nature of the event was due to the nature of the participants – a 'genuinely European' exercise, in the words of a Spanish diplomat (Moratinos 1995) – more than to the conference as such. In fact, a characteristic of the Mediterranean region in the 1990s has been a proliferation of fora for meetings and negotiations.

In this regard, mention should be made, first, of the co-operation schemes that have not gone beyond the planning stage (the case of the Conference on Security and Co-operation in the Mediterranean – CSCM), those such as the '5 + 5 Group' that by the mid-1990s were in a state of paralysis (Blanc Altemir 1995; Khader 1994), and the Mediterranean dimension of the Conference on Security and Co-operation in Europe – CSCE (Sainz 1995). Second, there is a series of negotiation frameworks that, as Aliboni (1995) points out, compete and complement each other: the Forum for Dialogue and Co-operation in the Mediterranean (also referred to as the Mediterranean Forum);[1] the multilateral dimension of the Middle East peace process in which the Working Group on Arms Control and Regional Security and the Regional Economic Development Working Group (REDWG) are prominent; the North Africa and Middle East Economic Summit, known as the Casablanca process; and the Euro-Mediterranean Partnership, whose launching pad has been the afore-mentioned Barcelona Conference.

The Euro-Mediterranean Partnership Initiative constitutes an updating of the EU's Mediterranean policy. The former policy of bilateral economic agreements has been replaced by an initiative with a multilateral design, which seeks to combine social, economic, and political and security objectives.[2] Up to a point, it can be stated that this Initiative emerged from failed projects. Concretely, the idea of combining the three areas and generating a process (conference and follow-up) is based on the CSCE methodology. In other words, the Euro-Mediterranean Partnership copies the CSCE/CSCM method, but has a narrower scope. This is patent with respect to the participants: the significant absence of the United States and reduction of the Mediterranean region to those countries that have signed agreements with the EU. All of this gives the EU a central role.

At the same time, this Partnership embraces the principal ideas of the Euro-Maghreb Partnership that were endorsed by the European Council held in Lisbon in June 1992, but which proved impossible to carry out because of the sanctions against Libya[3] and the civil war in Algeria. The main idea behind the Euro-Maghreb Partnership was to create a free trade area between the EC/EU and the countries of the Maghreb.[4] In this sense, the Euro-Mediterranean Partnership broadens the initial scope of the free trade area, going beyond the countries of the Maghreb to the 12 Mediterranean partners. In short, one can talk of a merging of former projects: the CSCM which (like the CSCE in its time) made its mark as a declaration of principles and a code of conduct, and the Euro-Maghreb Partnership, which sought to materi-alize in a multilateral economic framework (a free trade area).

During the preparation of the conference, the Council assumed that 'the fact of participating in the Barcelona Conference would only signify adhesion to the princi-ples embodying the Euro-Mediterranean Partnership' (EU Council 1995b: 17). Thus, the conference had as a preeminent objective the solemn adoption of a decla-ration of principles. This, in diplomatic terms, likens the Barcelona process to the earlier Helsinki process.

This article analyses the Barcelona Conference (its preparation, development and results),[5] emphasizing the significance of the event as a *political gesture*. Jacques Delors expressed this aspect when he spoke of the need to transmit a 'powerful message' to Europe's neighbours on the southern shores of the Mediterranean (Barbé 1995: 19). The event was a manifestation of a will to politically recognize the existence of a Euro-Mediterranean space based on socio-economic realities (commercial flows, energy dependence, migration) which, as things stand today, link the EU more to the Mediterranean countries than to the countries of eastern Europe (Khader 1995).

Preparing the Conference

As analysts and politicians have pointed out, interdependence between the EU and its Mediterranean partners in the 1990s is a reality. For the analysts, the Mediterranean forms a global space. Alongside the more traditional subjects of security, such as strategic matters and armed conflicts, they point to a multidimensional agenda which includes environmental, socio-economic and cultural issues (Buzan 1991).

This view of the Mediterranean as a globalized space – a multidimensional link between European security and Mediterranean security – has become commonplace in Spanish political discourse since the end of the Cold War. A good example was provided by Felipe González in his closing speech at the Euro-Mediterranean Conference, when he said:

> We are deeply interdependent in agriculture, migratory flows, trade patterns and industrial production, as well as in the resolution of problems of environmental deterioration, water shortages, pockets of poverty, drugs or ethnic tensions. It is not by chance that the countries of the southern seaboard of the Mediterranean are the European Union's third trading partner and supply 27 per cent of its energy. Trade between us amounts to eighty thousand million ECU per annum and represents two-thirds of the overall external trade for the Maghreb and the Mashraq countries. Furthermore, some five million people from those countries live within the frontiers of the Union (González 1995: 34).

This Euro-Mediterranean interdependence has made the Mediterranean a priority area for Spanish diplomacy. Thus, between 1989 and 1994, Spain played a relevant role as a promoter (together with France and Italy) of several diplomatic initiatives for the Mediterranean region. However, it was not until 1994 that the EU became involved in a global approach to the region in geographical and multidimensional terms. The concerns of the Mediterranean lobby, led by Spain and France, were registered in the final communiqué of the European Council of Corfu in June. From then on, a rapid process was initiated,[6] beginning with a communiqué issued by the Commission in October, in which the creation of the Euro-Mediterranean Partnership was proposed, with special mention being made of a free trade area and a zone of political stability and security.

The European Council of Essen in December 1994 endorsed the idea of the Partnership on the basis of '. . . the Mediterranean constituting a priority zone of strategic importance for the European Union' (EU 1994). It accepted Spain's offer to organize, during the forthcoming Spanish presidency in the second half of 1995, a Euro-Mediterranean Conference at ministerial level as the launching pad of the Partnership. Spanish diplomacy was busy with the preparation of this conference throughout 1995. Fortuitously, the main members of the preparatory group were drawn from the so-called Mediterranean lobby. Spain was a member of the so-called troika (the EU coordinating group consisting of the country that presides over the Union, plus its immediate predecessor and the country next in line), first with Germany and France and later with France and Italy. Thus, the troika that, together with the Commission, negotiated the details of the conference over several months with the Mediterranean partners was predominantly Mediterranean. The work of the Commission, focusing on the creation of a free trade area, was presided over by the Spaniard, Manuel Marín, who politically and personally is very close to González.

The political aspects of the Euro-Mediterranean Conference were prepared within the framework of the EU's Common Foreign and Security Policy (CFSP). To this end, during the French presidency the troika of the Council named three coordinators (the German, Bernard Zepter, the Frenchman, Bernard Prague and the Spaniard, Gabriel Busquets) who were entrusted with most of the consultations with the Mediterranean partners. An essential part of the work consisted of elaborating the texts to be adopted at Barcelona. The EU created a specialist group to work on the drafts. As we shall see further on, the text of the Barcelona Declaration was the focal point of attention through the long preparatory months as well as during the conference itself.

The work of the Spanish diplomats, crucial for the success of the conference, was not always facilitated by the attitude of the French government. On the one hand, the French presidency during the first half of 1995 was barely active because the term coincided with an electoral period in the country, and, on the other hand, France's traditional protagonism in the Mediterranean (or at least in relation to the Maghreb) was not conducive to its collaboration in projects not led by France. In this sense, Spain's greater protagonism in the process initiated by the EU in Corfu led France to favour alternative diplomatic fora, such as the Mediterranean Forum.[7]

Over and above international priorities, the interest of Spain in the organization of the Euro-Mediterranean Conference can also be explained in terms of internal politics. In contrast to the Italian case, where internal problems have directed attention away from the Mediterranean, the internal problems of the Spanish government have been externalized in the guise of an active diplomacy. That is to say, the only way identified by the Socialists to counteract their internal loss of prestige, which threatened to produce a victory for the opposition in the following general election in March 1996, was by means of the diplomatic successes of Felipe González. This is why the Spanish presidency of the EU, with the Euro-Mediterranean Conference occupying a prominent position in its agenda, was seen as a trump card to be played in internal politics, as a source of prestige for González and his PSOE. Moreover, the selection of the city of Barcelona as the meeting place, and the scheduling of a 'Fòrum Civil Euromed', organized by the government of Catalonia,[8] immediately after the conference itself, were decisions linked largely to internal politics. The parliamentary backing that Felipe González had received from the Catalan nationalists in order to govern was thus rewarded. Catalan president Jordi Pujol, forever active in European politics, was given great protagonism in the Euro-Mediterranean proceedings.

In addition to the Fòrum Civil Euromed, which enjoyed the direct support of the Spanish government and the European Commission, Barcelona became for several days the venue for various Euro-Mediterranean encounters, the most important being: an 'alternative' meeting of NGOs (24–28 November) and the Cities' Conference organized by the Permanent Secretariat of the Mediterranean Cities, presided over by the mayor of Barcelona. The scarce interest that the Euro-Mediterranean Conference devoted to matters of migration was criticized at both meetings. Thus, in an open criticism of EU laws regarding foreigners, one resolution at the Cities' Conference stated:

> The cities stress that the initiative of constructing a 'common space' of trade, cultural and human exchanges (one of the prime objectives of the Euro-Conference) seems incompatible with maintaining a rigid migratory framework that hampers the mobility of persons, and recommends harmonization and flexibility of the migratory policies that facilitate this mobility (Sierra 1995: 7).

Besides these two meetings, other encounters of a more monographic nature were held (on migration, the Olympic tradition and the Mediterranean, etc.). The total number of meetings held in Spain during 1995 on Euro-Mediterranean relations of various kinds (seminars, technical sessions, exhibitions, etc.) and at different levels (regional governments, universities, NGOs, etc.) has been put at more than a hundred.

The Mediterranean versus Central and Eastern Europe

From the guidelines laid down at the European Council of Essen on the Euro-Mediterranean Partnership, the European Commission drew up a new communiqué – COM (95) 72 – which was unanimously adopted on 8 March 1995. Manuel Marín presented this communiqué (together with a 'work programme' produced in collaboration with the French presidency) to the press, indicating that in the view of the Commission, the time had come to come together with the non-member Mediterranean countries and commence the same type of process that had been entered upon with the countries of central and eastern Europe. Two concepts justified it: interdependence and security. However, from the very start, it was made clear that the objective of the Euro-Med policy, in contrast to policy on central and eastern Europe, was not to eventually incorporate the partners into the EU.

The underlying philosophy behind the Commission's communiqué – the symmetrical nature of the South with respect to the East – had already been defended by some countries. From the second half of 1994, this idea had influenced information issuing from Brussels. Thus, 'France and Spain agree on the need for the European Union to maintain a sense of proportion in their aid to countries of Central and Eastern Europe, on the one hand, and to the Mediterranean countries (particularly the Maghreb), on the other. According to diplomatic sources, Spain would be in favour of a kind of Mediterranean Phare Programme' (*Europe*, 30 Sept. 1994: 10). A series of formulas were considered to create the said symmetry: European Economic Space, EBDR, Phare Plan and the Stability Pact.

The communiqué drew its inspiration from the EU's *Ostpolitik*, the proposed Meda Plan being inspired by the Phare Plan. With respect to budgetary resources, the Commission presented a proposal (Ecu 5.5bn) with a precise objective. In the words of Marín (*Europe*, 9 March 1995: 6), it was a matter of reestablishing the credibility of the EU's strategy for the Mediterranean countries as compared to the treatment reserved for the eastern European countries. The idea of treating the

Mediterranean partners and the countries of central and eastern Europe on an equal footing was thus insisted upon.

The Commission's orientations, together with the work done within the framework of the CFSP, formed the basis of the Synthesis Report adopted by the Council on 10 April 1995. On the basis of this report, the troika initiated contacts with the Mediterranean partners. The text of the report set in motion a long process of negotiations which did not end until the Barcelona Conference itself.

The Synthesis Report was based on the idea already referred to: the will of the EU to complement its policy towards the East with a policy for the South in the interests of geopolitical coherence (EU Council 1995a: 2). The report was divided into three sections dealing with political and security, economic and financial and, finally, social and human issues. It was thus similar in structure to the Helsinki Declaration of 1975 which initiated the CSCE process.

The preamble to the report made a clear distinction between the Euro-Mediterranean Partnership to be established at the Barcelona Conference and the Middle East peace process. Here the EU clarified its project by explaining that it was not a forum for resolving conflicts, nor was it a framework within which to broach the Middle East issue. Rather the Partnership was seen as complementary to 'other actions and initiatives in favour of peace, stability and development of the region' (EU Council 1995a: 4). The document went on to say that the project was based on a global approach (both multidimensional and regional) which differentiated it from other projects. However, in no way did it seek to be exclusive. On the contrary, in diplomatic terms, the Mediterranean was recognized as a space of variable geometries. The report emphasized this in relation to the Middle East, where the 15 play a role of financial-technical accompaniment in the peace process (presiding over the REDWG, the organization of elections in the occupied territories, economic co-operation) alongside the diplomatic actor *par excellence*, the United States.

The methodology of the Synthesis Report, based on a thematic division into three 'baskets' or sections, deserves some comment at the outset. The first section was formed by a declaration of principles that were essential, according to the report, to stability in the region. However, it was recognized that several internationally accepted principles, such as respect for territorial integrity, the fight against terrorism and curbing the arms race, posed real problems of interpretation in the region. It was in this section of the report that the Stability Pact applied to the countries of central and eastern Europe was cited as a model for future EU joint action in the Mediterranean, aimed at transforming it into 'a space of peace and stability' (EU Council 1995a: 6).

The second section, on the economic and financial partnership, was the most developed and detailed part of the report. A quick look at the text, reinforced by some basic familiarity with the work preceding the conference (including the agreements negotiated with Tunisia, Morocco and Israel during 1995), is enough to show that this aspect is at the heart of the evolving partnership. The third section, focusing on the social and human dimensions, posed some problematic issues: references to demographic policies, terrorism and drug trafficking, migration, and so on. The

Synthesis Report ended by mentioning the possibility of a follow-up after Barcelona, without being very specific. However, it underlined the idea of the participation of civil society over and above that of governmental institutions.

The credibility of the process initiated by the EU ran the gauntlet during the European Council of Cannes in June 1995. The French-Spanish desire to reallocate resources between the East and the South – as proposed by the Commission and translated into aid proposals for the period 1995–99 of Ecu 5,500m for the Mediterranean, compared to Ecu 7,000m for eastern Europe – clashed headlong with the views of the North (the United Kingdom, Denmark and Holland). In effect, the latter countries, opposed to a new distribution of resources, showed that they were not keen to change substantially the 5:1 ratio of aid distribution for the period 1992–96, favouring the East over the South. The European Council of Cannes was the scene of a clash between Kohl and González over the distribution of aid. The final result, a shift in ratio from 1:5 to 3.5:5 for the following period, can be considered a success for the Mediterranean Europeans, especially in view of the decision to entrust the organization of the Euro-Mediterranean Conference to the Spanish presidency. In effect, the resources for the Mediterranean (Ecu 4,685m) were increased by 22 per cent while those for central and eastern Europe rose by 8 per cent.

A Problematic Agenda

The European Council of Cannes was the scene of EU disagreements regarding the policy to be developed on the Mediterranean. Behind these was a deep cleavage of interest with the northern Europeans wanting to offer further trade concessions to the non-member Mediterranean countries, and the southern European countries defending their own agricultural interests and wanting future Mediterranean policy to be based instead on increased financial aid. This clash of interests, reconciled by the time of the Barcelona Conference, could reappear in the future.

Spain adopted tough negotiating tactics at Cannes and made the issue of increased resources for the non-member Mediterranean countries its top priority. This toughness can be explained in terms of European considerations: Cannes was the last opportunity to obtain sizeable resources for the South. For Spain, the Barcelona Conference was seen as offering 'an optimum opportunity for opening a window of hope in the region' (Moratinos 1995). However, it soon became apparent that it would be difficult for the EU to arrive at a consensus on a series of subjects related to the organization of the conference. There were disagreements over the text of the declaration, the composition of the participants, the envisaged follow-up mechanisms, and so on.

The troika, accompanied by members of the Commission, travelled to several Mediterranean countries (the Middle Eastern countries as well as Morocco, Tunisia, Algeria, Cyprus, Malta, Turkey and Egypt) between February and May. The first major stumbling block that it came up against was the mistrusting attitude of Syria and Lebanon who were not very willing to participate in a ministerial meeting together with Israel. Since the Madrid Conference (1991) there had been no meeting at this level and the two countries were afraid that the Barcelona Conference might become a 'Trojan Horse' of the Middle East peace process. The eventual presence of these two countries in Barcelona thus took on an important symbolic significance. Although their presence in Barcelona was essential for the success of the project, it in no way signified that arriving at a consensus on the final declaration, which Syria, Lebanon and Israel would sign, would be at all easy.

Another country that, to a lesser degree and for different reasons, raised doubts about attending the conference was Morocco. Rabat's attitude was based on a wish to maintain privileged relations with the EU (negotiations for the Association Agreement being underway) and a reluctance to lose protagonism in a multilateral framework. It was in this mood that Hassan II, during Chirac's visit to Morocco in July 1995, expressed his desire to once again apply for Morocco's admission into the EU. Mindful of such aspirations, throughout 1995 the Spanish authorities expressed their wish that the follow-up of the Barcelona process should favour Morocco (as the location for permanent bodies, the organizer of the second ministerial meeting, etc.) in order to offer it greater protagonism. Morocco's attitude was a clear sign of the failure of the idea of regional integration in the Maghreb.

Morocco's fears could provide the explanation for the only change that was made to the Synthesis Report. In the version adopted by the Council on 29 May, to be presented as the European position at the European Council of Cannes, the following paragraph was added: 'the existing bilateral agreements and negotiations in progress to conclude a new generation of agreements will make it possible to safeguard, and even emphasize the specificity of each one of the bilateral relations in the new multi-lateral framework' (EU Council 1995b: 2). In this way, the value of 'bilateralness' was stressed within the new global framework.

Clearly the absence of Syria, Lebanon or Morocco could have spelt failure for the organizers of the Barcelona encounter. What was not so clear was the identity of the EU's counterparts for Mediterranean matters. Although the European Council of Essen identified the Mediterranean partners as being the 11 countries (plus the Palestinian Authority) that have agreements with the EU, the preparations for the conference soon ran into difficulties with respect to the participants. The United States, Russia and the Gulf countries, among others, showed an interest in the event. The USA wanted to participate fully, whereas Russia requested observer status (*Europe*, 24 May 1995: 8). The idea of a Libyan presence at the conference was the most controversial. In June 1995 the Arab Maghreb Union (UMA) had adopted a common position, indicating that it would like Libya to be associated with the process. However, the majority of the European countries, particularly France and the UK, vetoed the idea. Eventually, at the end of October, Libya withdrew its request to participate in the conference, describing the attitude of the organizers as 'high treason' and a 'conspiracy' (*Europe*, 26 Oct. 1995: 9).

The various participation requests led to several formulas being considered regarding the status of participants (as guests or observers, or possibly of allowing certain Arab organizations to be represented by a Libyan, etc.). Spain's more amenable attitude clashed with the French position, which wished to include only Mauritania in the process besides the uncontested participants. The issue was finally resolved by following the Essen orientations and making the Barcelona Conference a limited and 'genuinely European' project, with the participation of the 15 plus the 12 Mediterranean partners. This decision, adopted by the General Affairs Council on 31 October, on the basis of a proposal put forward by the Spanish presidency, limited the Barcelona process to 27 countries, plus the EU as a body. Beyond the core participants, only Mauritania, the UMA and the Arab League played a role through their presence in the public sessions, and there was also a diplomatic tribune for countries that wished to follow the debates (such as the central and eastern European countries, the USA, Russia and others).

Drafting the Declaration

After the European Council of Cannes, the Spanish presidency replaced the visits by the troika with regular meetings of the 15 plus troika and their 12 Mediterranean partners. Successive meetings in Brussels enabled the southern Mediterranean countries to participate, as they had requested during the first meeting on 24 July, in the drafting of the Barcelona Declaration. The composition work was based on a European draft of the Declaration, adopted by the Council shortly before the second Euro-Mediterranean meeting (5–6 October), at which socio-political aspects of the Declaration were broached. At this meeting, the European draft was criticized by the southern partners, both generally and specifically: the Europeans were imposing their values on the Arab countries; they were treating subjects of a social nature (terrorism, drugs, immigration) as 'security' isues; some countries feared that the Partnership might distort other regional processes, such as the Casablanca Process led by the United States, or sub-regional ones like the Black Sea Economic Cooperation grouping headed by Turkey; there were suspicions that the Barcelona process was in some way linked to the Middle East process; and then there were specific questions, such as Egypt's desire to see a clear reference to the Non-Proliferation Treaty (NPT), the Palestinians' wish to mention the right to self-determination, and the Syrian-Lebanese insistence upon a distinction between terrorism and the fight to defend one's own territory.

As a result of this meeting, some changes were made to the principles outlined in the European draft of the Declaration. A couple of examples deserve mention. In one case, the sentence was shortened (the deleted phrase is underlined): 'develop the rule of law and democracy in their political systems, recognising at the same time the right of each one of them to freely elect and articulate their political, socio-cultural and economic system; as long as it is in keeping with commonly accepted international norms' ('Projet . . .' 1995: 2). In the other case, the text was lengthened in the light of comments on the European draft (the new text is underlined): 'give favourable consideration, through dialogue between the parties, to exchanges of information on matters relating to human rights, fundamental freedoms, racism and xenophobia' ('Barcelona . . .' 1995: 4).

In the third preparatory meeting for the conference (Brussels, 24–25 October), which focused on the Work Programme to be appended to the Declaration, the troika proposed a new Declaration. Although the changes were mostly of a cosmetic nature, they involved more emphasis on equality in relation to the obligations mentioned, and they led to more precise references to the norms of international law (Syria and the Palestinians having criticized timid references to the right to self-determination in the earlier draft) (*Europe*, 23–24 Oct. 1995: 9). With respect to the Work Programme, an attempt was made to outline the specific economic and financial objectives of the Partnership, such as the creation of a free trade area, regional planning, and aims relating to energy, fisheries, water resources, and so on.

The lack of consensus on some issues, particularly in the political sphere (Syria's wish, for example, to distinguish between terrorism and the legitimate right to defence against occupiers), and the desire to define more clearly the Work Programme, led to a final meeting being held on 13–15 November, before the conference. At this meeting, the Mediterranean Arab countries specified that they wished to develop, simultaneously with the free trade area, sector by sector dialogues on, among other subjects, foreign debt, accompanied by adequate financing by the EU. In the social sphere, the southern countries called for the free movement of people within the Euro-Mediterranean framework in order to give real content to the European proposal for dialogue between the 'civil societies' along the two shores. Thus greater financial aid, inclusion of the subject of debt and the elimination of visas became objectives pursued by the South.

This last meeting served to reach almost total agreement on the two texts to be approved in Barcelona, the Final Declaration and the Work Programme. But just one week before the conference, a series of matters were still not settled: 'formulating the right of peoples to self-determination, the problem of non-proliferation, the dialogue on debt, formulating the progressive elimination of tariff and non-tariff obstacles (specially for agricultural products and "physical persons needed for providing services"); the readmission clause for illegal immigrants, designating the Committee to be entrusted with ensuring the continuity of the Declaration' (*Europe*, 18 Nov. 1995: 5).

The conference thus began with a series of problems still to be resolved. The hours before the official inauguration were used for meetings between senior officials. In the political domain, the problems of the Middle East were very much in the air: there were the questions of disarmament and the NPT, on the one hand, and the controversy about terrorism and the fight for self-determination, on the other. It must be remarked that the latter question, raised by the Palestinians and the Lebanese, was also of concern to Turkey because of the problem of the Kurds. In the economic sphere, greater financial commitments made by the EU to the Mediterranean were hoped for, in addition to the creation of a space for agricultural products in the proposed free trade area. In the social sphere, the most divisive issue was the EU proposal to oblige signatories to readmit illegal immigrants. With respect to the future, there were other matters of a lesser order, such as the name of the follow-up committee, over which Spanish and French protagonism clashed, and the choice of country to host the following meeting.

The 'Spirit' of Barcelona

Javier Solana, the Spanish minister for foreign affairs, delivered the inaugural speech as President of the Council of the EU. His brief address covered the basic objectives of the Barcelona process, whose future was symbolically linked to the adoption of the Barcelona Declaration (followed by the Work Programme). In the words of Solana:

> The documents which we will be adopting express the solemn political commitment of all of us to the Euro-Mediterranean Partnership. The Barcelona Declaration must be the backbone of the system. It is based on a balanced and comprehensive vision which throws into relief the interdependence of the political, economic and cultural dimension of the association, all of these being equally necessary (Solana 1995: 3).

Solana also referred to two more issues of considerable interest. In the first place, he emphasized the complementarity between the Partnership and other relations with the EU. He pointed out that 'the comprehensiveness of the approach is perfectly compatible with the prospect of enlargement of the European Union towards the South and the development of its bilateral relations with each of its Mediterranean partners. We have concluded Association Agreements with Tunisia, Israel and Morocco. We expect to do the same with the other countries of the region' (Solana 1995: 2–3). In the second place, an attempt was made to create a spirit of mutual trust in the region, along the lines of Geneva or Helsinki. As the Spanish minister put it:

> This meeting, which is the culmination of a lengthy maturing process, is also the beginning of a new stage. Above all, we must look resolutely ahead. I therefore appeal to all of us to face the future of Euro-Mediterranean relations in a spirit of openness and generosity enabling a climate of trust to be created in the region. This must be the spirit inspiring the Conference. Allow me to dub it the 'spirit of Barcelona' (Solana 1995: 6).

Thus, the adoption of the Barcelona Declaration was to have a symbolic significance: it was to mark the beginning of a new stage in Euro-Mediterranean relations.

The general structure of the text – twelve pages long in the English version, followed by the 16-page Work Programme – is well known: three main sections, followed by some final considerations on the follow-up to the conference. In short, it attempted to establish a code of conduct, to create a free trade area and to institutionalize political dialogue.

It was not until the last minute that the contacts made before the conference and those developed among ministers in the hotel in which the meeting was held finally led to agreement on the final text of the Declaration. Indeed, the closing ceremony was delayed by more than two hours because of the difficulties encountered in reaching a consensus on the political and security section of the document.

The section dealing with the economic and financial partnership to create an area of shared prosperity did not pose any difficulties, once an amendment relating to agricultural products had been included (under pressure from Egypt) in the references to the creation of a free trade area for industrial products: 'trade in agricultural products will be progressively liberalized through reciprocal preferential access among the parties' ('Barcelona . . .' 1995: 7). The part of the Work Programme relating to this section of the Declaration was the longest and most detailed. The question of finance (the financial package approved at Cannes) and instruments (the Meda Programme) were to provide the subject matter for the early meetings. Issues such as water, energy, desertification and the environment were put down on the agenda for sectorial meetings to be held during 1996.

The third section, on the creation of a partnership in social, cultural and human affairs by developing human resources, promoting understanding between cultures and encouraging exchanges between civil societies, had to overcome the misgivings of the Arab countries regarding the Europeans' perception of social problems in the South as security issues. After several drafts, the final obstacle to an agreement on illegal immigration centred on the EU's wish that the countries of origin should readmit their nationals involved in this. Disagreements were settled by resorting to a formula drawn from previous bilateral agreements. Thus, it was agreed 'to adopt the relevant provisions and measures, by means of bilateral agreements or arrangements, in order to readmit their nationals who are in an illegal situation' ('Barcelona . . .', 1995: 11). With respect to both illegal immigration, terrorism and drug trafficking, the Work Programme established that there would be regular meetings of officials and that there was a need to take account of the diverse situations existing in the different countries.

It was the first section of the Declaration (on political and security partnership: establishing a common area of peace and stability) that became, as expected, the major stumbling block at the conference. The most eagerly awaited speeches of the inaugural session were those by the foreign ministers of Israel and Syria. The public offer of peace made by the Israeli minister was responded to by his Syrian counterpart with a reference to total Israeli withdrawal from the Golan Heights. Attempts by Solana to bring the two representatives together were rebuffed with a clear response: the peace process was being dealt with in another forum and the mediator was a different one (the United States). 'Only the United States can bring Israel and Syria together', were the words of the Israeli minister. Despite the often repeated desire to differentiate between the Barcelona process and the Middle East peace process, the success of the Euro-Mediterranean Conference was certainly jeopardized by Israel's tense relations with Syria and Lebanon. The Middle East question contaminated Barcelona – a situation that the Arab countries themselves criticized, particularly the Algerian foreign minister, speaking on behalf of the Arab countries present at the conference.

Even after the conference sessions had ended, and despite the numerous nocturnal negotiations that had taken place between senior officials, agreement still had not been reached on the text of the first section of the Declaration. There were three points of discord: (1) the formulation of a reference to the right of peoples to self-determination; (2) the non-proliferation of nuclear arms; and (3) the fight against terrorism. The three issues confronted Israel with the Arab countries, generically with respect to the issue of nuclear arms, and with Lebanon and Syria over the other two issues linked to territorial integrity. In the end, the subject of self-determination was included in the declaration of principles in the following terms: 'Respect the equal rights of peoples and their right to self-determination, acting at all times in conformity with the purposes and principles of the Charter of the United Nations and with the relevant norms of international law, including those relating to territorial integrity of States, as reflected in agreements between relevant parties' ('Barcelona . . .' 1995: 4). To Israel's displeasure, the subject of territory appeared in the introductory part of the Declaration, where the principle of land for peace was included as it appeared in the letter of invitation to the Madrid Middle East Peace Conference. Syria insisted, with little success, on linking the right to self-determination to the legitimate right to fight against territorial occupiers. Israel, for its part, did not agree with the references to self-determination and territorial integrity because of their significance for southern Lebanon and the Palestinians.

On the fight against terrorism, Syria's wish to make a distinction regarding the struggle against the occupiers of a territory was not included. Turkey, among other countries, defended the wording of the text as it stood. Thus, the final Declaration stated that the signatories would '. . .strengthen their co-operation in preventing and combating terrorism, in particular by ratifying and applying the international instruments they have signed, by acceding to such instruments and by taking any other appropriate measure' ('Barcelona . . .' 1995: 5).

The subject of non-proliferation led to the elaboration of a lengthy text in which several ideas were combined, without any firm commitments being made: (1) adhesion to the NPT, applicable to Israel and promoted by Egypt; (2) the mention of other arms-control agreements (covering chemical and biological weapons) that would affect some Arab countries; and (3) the objective of establishing a 'mutually and effectively verifiable Middle East zone free of weapons of mass destruction, nuclear, chemical and biological, and their delivery systems' ('Barcelona . . .' 1995: 5). In this way, both Iraq and Iran were to be involved in the process, an Israeli condition for acceding to a process of denuclearization.

The differences over these issues persisted until the end of the conference, despite the multiple negotiations. Finally, the Spanish presidency decided to be firm. With the backing of all the EU partners, the Spanish foreign minister presented, in the form of an ultimatum, the text that was adopted finally. Any country that would not accept it would bear the responsibility for the failure of the conference. Both Israel and Syria, which disagreed on some points, thus ended up by accepting the text. Solana, together with his Algerian counterpart and the Vice-President of the Commission, Manuel Marín, made the text public two hours later than expected, insisting that it had been adopted without signatures and unanimously, with no reservations. Despite this initial information, both Israel and Lebanon later presented, both orally and in writing, their own interpretations of the text adopted by the Spanish presidency.

Having seen the difficulties experienced over political and security questions, it is little wonder that the section of the Work Programme relating to this section is the shortest. It contains generic references, with no precise statements whatsoever, to political dialogue to examine the most appropriate means and methods of implementing the principles adopted in the Barcelona Declaration. Therefore, it is paradoxical that the text of the Declaration includes a reference to the possibility of establishing a Euro-Mediterranean Pact within the framework of creating an area of peace and stability. The pact proposal, made by the French, was not clear. Initially, during the first few months of 1995, there had been talk of an exercise similar to the Stability Pact. However, the French foreign minister himself, Hervé de Charette, categorically denied such an idea in Barcelona. This, undoubtedly, is one of the 'loose ends' of the Declaration.

The last section, relating to the follow-up to the conference, was a compromise between those who wanted to institutionalize the arrangements and those who were less keen to do so. No more than very 'light' follow-up structures had ever been proposed for the process. Finally, regular meetings of foreign ministers (the next to be held in 1997) and thematic meetings at different levels (ministerial, senior officials, civil society, etc.) were agreed to. A 'Euro-Mediterranean Committee for the Barcelona Process'[9] was created at senior official level, formed by the troika and the 12 Mediterranean partners to oversee the implementation of the Work Programme. The ground work for the agreed meetings was to be done by the Commission. Only one subject remained to be agreed upon: the venue for the following conference. No agreement was reached regarding the three candidate countries: Morocco, Tunisia and Malta. However, the Moroccan representatives felt certain that their country would be chosen.

Despite the last minute difficulties, the Barcelona Conference left behind it a feeling of diplomatic success. The work still remained to be done, yet a propitious atmosphere had been created by the event, which has to be seen above all as a political gesture. In the words of Felipe González (1995a: 10): 'Barcelona is the launching pad of an ambitious process which will rely on follow-up mechanisms and incentives to institutionalize our dialogue and move forward'. The success of Spain's diplomats was quickly translated into the appointment of Javier Solana as secretary general of NATO. All the same, a long time will elapse before it will be seen whether the Barcelona Declaration has laid the basis for the creation of really effective instruments to transform the Mediterranean, in its own words, into 'an area of dialogue, exchange and cooperation guaranteeing peace, stability and prosperity' ('Barcelona . . .' 1995: 3).

In the very same city of Barcelona, at the alternative conference organized by NGOs, far more sceptical conclusions were reached regarding the outcome of the EU-sponsored conference, the balance sheet being more negative than positive. The Final Document from the alternative conference concluded that 900 years after the first crusades began, one could still talk of 'an obstinacy in imposing cultural values and economic interests without understanding or treating the Other on an equal footing' (Conferencia Mediterránea Alternativa 1995: 7). The debate on the Euro-Mediterranean policy and the Barcelona process has only just begun.

Notes

[1] The Mediterranean Forum included a limited group of north African and southern European countries: Algeria, Egypt, France, Greece, Italy, Malta, Morocco, Portugal, Spain, Tunisia and Turkey. It was created in Alexandria in July 1994, upon the initiative of Egypt which was absent from other fora such as the '5 + 5 Group' (Khader 1995: 4). The initiative was welcomed by France. An outstanding objective of the Forum was the creation of a mechanism for Mediterranean political co-operation.

[2] The Process was initiated with the presentation by the European Commission to the Council and the Parliament of a communiqué – COM (94) 427 – of 19 Oct. 1994, drawn up at the request of the European Council (Corfu, July 1994). After the European Council meeting in Essen in Dec. 1994, the Commission issued a communiqué on 8 March 1995 – COM (95) 72 – on which the Synthesis Report approved by the Council (10 April 1995) was based.

[3] The EU adopted a common position in relation to the reduction of economic relations with Libya (Decision 93/614 of the Council, 22 Nov. 1993).

[4] See the 'Report to the European Council of Lisbon on the possible development of the Common Foreign and Security Policy (CFSP) with a view to determining the spheres in which common actions can be developed between countries or groups of specific countries', *Bulletin of the European Communities* (1992) pp.6, 19–22.

[5] On other aspects of the Euro-Mediterranean Partnership Initiative, see the article by Jon Marks, this issue, pp. 1–24.

[6] See note 2.

[7] See note 1.

[8] The Forum Civil Euromed was held in Barcelona on 29 Nov.–1 Dec. with more than a thousand participants from different walks of life (business, the universities, the cultural world, etc.). Eleven parallel working fora were organized: trade without frontiers, investment, tourism, technology and co-operation, transport and territory, universities and research, cultural dialogue, media co-operation, the role of women, migration, and environmental and energy challenges.

[9] Initially, this committee was to be called the Barcelona Committee, but France refused to accept this name.

References

Aliboni, Roberto (1995): 'Institutionalizing Mediterranean Relations: Complementarity and Competition', paper presented at the second session of the Mediterranean Study Commission, Alexandria, 30–31 March.

Barbé, Esther (1995): 'Reinventar el Mare Nostrum: el Mediterráneo como espacio de cooperación y seguridad' *Papers* 46, pp.9–23.

'Barcelona Declaration adopted at the Euro-Mediterranean Conference' (27 and 28 Nov. 1995).

Blanc Altemir, Antonio (1995): 'Estabilidad y codesarrollo en el Mediterráneo: de una Conferencia de Seguridad y Cooperación para el Mediterráneo (CSCM) a la Conferencia Euromediterránea (CEM)' *Anuario de Derecho Internacional* 11, pp.63–128.

Buzan, Barry (1991): *People, States and Fear. An Agenda for International Security Studies in the Post-Cold War Era,* 2nd ed. New York: Harvester Wheatsheaf.

Conferencia Mediterránea Alternativa (1995): 'Documento de valoración de las propuestas y textos de la Conferencia Intergubernamental Mediterránea, 28 Nov.

EU (1994): 'Conseil Européen. Réunion des 9 et 10 décembre 1994 à Essen. Conclusions de la présidence' *Europe* 6376 (11 Dec).

EU Council (1995a): 'Conférence Euro-Méditerranéenne de Barcelone. Rapport de Synthèse', 6532/95 (10 April).

—— (1995b): 'Conférence Euro-Méditerranéenne de Barcelone. Position de l'Union Européenne', 7906/95 (29 May).

Europe (Agence International d'Information pour la Presse, Brussels), 1994–95.

González, Felipe (1995): Text of the closing speech, Euro-Mediterranean Conference, Barcelona, 28 Nov. Madrid, Ministerio de la Presidencia, Secretaría General del portavoz del Gobierno.

Khader, Bichara (ed.) (1994) *L'Europe et la Mediterranée. Geopolitique de la proximité.* Paris: l'Harmattan.

—— (1995): *Le partenariat euro-méditerranéen.* Louvain-Ia-Neuve: CERMAC.

Moratinos, Miguel Angel (1995): 'Una ventana de esperanza' *El País* (Madrid), 23 Nov.

'Projet de déclaration à adopter lors de la Conférence Euro-Méditerranéenne de Barcelone' (1995), texte résultant de la réunion entre la Troika et les partenaires méditerrabéens du 5 et 6 octobre 1995. Unpublished working document.

Sainz, Nora (1995): 'La dimensión mediterránea de la Conferencia sobre la Seguridad y la Cooperación en Europa (CSCE): de región limítrofe a campo de aplicación' *Papers* 46, pp. 139–53.

Sierra, Lluís (1995): 'Las ciudades piden menos trabas a las migraciones' *La Vanguardia* (Barcelona), 28 Nov.

Solana, Javier (1995): 'Inaugural speech by the Minister of Foreign Affairs at the Euro-Mediterranean Conference in Barcelona'.

Southern Attitudes towards an Integrated Mediterranean Region

GEORGE JOFFÉ

The Euro-Mediterranean Partnership reflects the hegemony that Europe has established over the Mediterranean region. Southern Mediterranean countries have participated for lack of an alternative, but they remain highly sceptical. The project's security aims are flawed by EU disunity over a common foreign and security policy and the fact that a third party – the USA – remains the region's key security player. Southern Mediterraneans feel that Europeans have misunderstood the significance of Islamism and in fact may be unwittingly helping illiberal political forces by imposing a neo-liberal economic agenda. Southern Mediterraneans complaints relate to controls on population mobility, rigid EU prescriptions for economic reform, and the reliance of the project on increases in foreign investment which will not necessarily materialize. The Partnership is paternalistic, full of contradictions and offers little hope of resolving the social, economic and political problems of the region.

The advent of the European Union's Euro-Mediterranean Partnership policy, inaugurated at the Barcelona Conference, has created a completely new, albeit still unclear, set of relationships inside the Mediterranean region. This is particularly true for the southern participants in this new process who feel ambivalent over a project which they believe they could not resist. Underlying the details of the European Union's new policy are implications that will profoundly alter the structure of the Mediterranean region in the years to come.

The Euro-Mediterranean Partnership

The new Mediterranean policy of the European Union has been through a long and unpredictable process of gestation. Its origins lie in the colonial past of the Maghreb, for it was in response to France's continuing links with its former colonies there that the southern Mediterranean shore became a specific arena for Commission policy [Marks, 1996: 7].

The Background

That policy evolved through a series of bilateral co-operation and association agreements from 1969 onwards, towards a system of preferential access for Moroccan and

Tunisian agricultural goods and an attempt to create a more global policy based on financial aid to the whole Mediterranean region, with specific attention being paid to the Palestinian issue. By the end of the 1980s, however, Europe had become aware that, not least because of demographic pressure [Lesser 1996: 4], most southern Mediterranean economies were failing, and that Europe itself faced the possibility of increased labour migration (see Table 1) unless something were done to convert economic failure into success.

It was under this more global pressure and in the context of profound changes created in the Middle East and North Africa by the end of the cold war, the collapse of the Soviet Union and the war against Iraq in 1991 that European Union policy towards the southern Mediterranean had to be designed anew. In effect, European economic influence was such that both the Middle East and North Africa could no longer avoid the fact that, as with eastern Europe, the European Union was not only their major trade partner by far but would become increasingly important in their economic horizons for the foreseeable future. Europe is not only the dominant source of imports but also represents a major market for the southern Mediterranean region, whose influence extends beyond the Mediterranean littoral into the Persian Gulf.

This is particularly well demonstrated by the role of energy, for both the Middle East and North Africa are major energy suppliers to Europe. In 1995, the Middle East supplied 28 per cent of the European Union's crude requirements of 12.79 million barrels per day (b/d), whilst North Africa supplied a further 15.8 per cent. In addition, Algeria supplied 11.2 per cent of European requirements in natural gas, either through the TransMed pipeline via Tunisia or as Liquefied Natural Gas (LNG). Libya supplied an additional 0.5 per cent as LNG. In all, some 26.8 per cent of the European Union's imports of natural gas came from North Africa, compared with 20.9 per cent from Norway and 52.3 per cent from the former Soviet Union [British Petroleum, 1996: 10, 18, 23, 26, 28]. In addition, North Africa's importance in terms of gas supply will rise by a further 8–10 billion cubic metres per annum now that the Algeria–Maghreb–Spain (Trans-Maghreb) gas pipeline project is complete. In fact, as Table 2 demonstrates, the European Union is by far the largest trade partner for the Middle East and North Africa, easily outpacing its nearest rivals, the United States and Japan.

Table 1   Middle East and North Africa, Population 1970–2010 (Population in millions; annual growth rate in %)

	1970	gr 70–90	1990	1995	gr 90–10	2010
Maghreb	36.2	2.8	62.7	70.3	2.0	95.0
Mashreq	43.3	2.5	71.5	80.4	2.0	107.6
GCC	7.7	5.4	22.1	25.0	3.0	39.4
Other*	44.1	3.3	85.1	100.0	3.0	152.0
Israel	3.0	2.2	4.6	5.6	2.0	6.8
Total	134.2	3.0	246.0	282.0	2.5	400.0

Source: World Bank, *Economic Research Forum, B6.*
Note: * Turkey, Cyprus, Malta, Iran.

Table 2   Middle East and North Africa, Market Shares 1992 (%)

	Imports	Exports
North America	17.3	13.3
European Union (12)	47.1	38.3
Japan	10.6	21.4
East Europe & former USSR	1.2	1.7
Newly industrialized count.	8.3	12.7
East Asia developing count.	3.5	3.2
Other developing countries	2.8	4.2
Other developed countries	9.2	5.3

Source: World Bank, *Economic Research Forum*, A16.

This might suggest that the true arena for European concerns should include the Gulf as well as the southern Mediterranean. In fact, Gulf trade patterns, in addition to Europe, emphasize a Far East connection and, in any case, the European Commission has, since 1988, been trying to negotiate a separate free trade area agreement with the Gulf Co-operation Council. In the short-to-medium term, therefore, the Mediterranean basin itself is the appropriate arena for co-operation, although, after 2010, when the bilateral North–South economic relations of the Euro-Mediterranean Partnership Initiative are supposed to be complete, economic integration in the southern region between states in the Maghreb and the Mashreq might well extend to include the Gulf.

Although the Middle East has a more diversified export picture (Table 3), with oil exports to the United States and the Far East forming an important part of the whole, Europe is still the dominant partner, particularly in terms of imports. This pattern is even more striking in the case of the Maghreb (Table 4).

Not surprisingly, therefore, the aftermath of the end of the cold war and the growth in hegemonic stability within the Mediterranean region, under American aegis, has led to the recognition amongst regional and national leaders that Europe has established an economic hegemony over the region, even if its political clout is far weaker. Even Israel, which has an economy unlike those of its neighbours in the southern Mediterranean region and which has traditionally sought privileged links with the United States, has had to come to terms with this realization. The European Union and the United States together control around 60 per cent of Israel's foreign trade, with the Union being responsible for 65 per cent of this figure. Israel had a $7.8 billion trade deficit with Europe in 1993, compared with a $4 billion deficit with the United States. The Union generated 50.2 and 60.9 per cent of Israel's imports in 1992 and 1993 respectively and absorbed 34.5 and 29.6 per cent of Israel's exports in the same years. The comparable figures for trade with the United States are 31.5 and 30.9 per cent for Israel's imports and 17.2 and 17.7 per cent for Israel's exports respectively [Diwan *et al.,* 1995: 48].

Table 3   Middle East-European (Eu) Trade, 1989–93 (% of total trade)

	1989	1990	1991	1992	1993
Exports	27.7	27.6	27.2	25.8	24.4
Imports	37.1	39.1	37.8	38.7	38.6
Total Middle East trade ($bn)					
Exports	118	150	135	145	145
Imports	101	110	123	139	145

Source: IMF, *Direction of Trade Statistics Yearbook 1994*, Washington, DC, pp.50–52.

Table 4   The Role of the EU in UMA Country Trade, 1990 (% of total trade)

	Imports	Exports
Algeria	55.6	37.0
Libya	83.2	22.3
Mauritania	35.4	44.6
Morocco	33.7	57.1
Tunisia	34.8	56.6
Total	53.5	31.8

Source: World Bank, Washington, DC, 1992.

The Partnership Policy: Economics

Essentially, the Euro-Mediterranean Partnership is an attempt to come to terms with this economic reality; on the one hand to reduce the threat of migration flows northwards and, on the other, to stimulate economic development in the southern Mediterranean region under the aegis of the regional economic hegemon, the European Union. The core of the partnership policy is, therefore, economic in nature and is based on the concept of a bilateral industrial and services free trade zone between the Union and its southern Mediterranean partners, together with transi-tional aid – grants valued at Ecu4.68 billion together with additional loan aid of the same amount through the European Investment Bank for a period of five years, with further sums to follow in future financial protocols – directed primarily at the private sector. These bilateral arrangements with individual southern Mediterranean states – Israel has a somewhat different free trade agreement and Turkey has its own customs union agreement – are, however, only the first stage, for, once they are in place 'horizontal integration' is due to begin after 2010 so that, eventually, the equiv-alent of a single market structure will be created in the southern Mediterranean, to partner the one that already exists to the north inside the Union itself.

Restrictions will still remain between the two halves of the Mediterranean, however, notably in the field of agricultural trade where the demands of the Common Agricultural Policy inhibit any introduction of a free trade area in such commodities. Although promises have been made that such restrictions will be the subject of future negotiations, the likely advent of the Visegrad countries in eastern Europe to European Union membership by the end of the century or within the first decade of the next century makes any positive change here seem highly unlikely. And since one of the major – if undeclared – objectives of the new partnership policy was to prevent migration flows into Europe, restrictions on the free movement of people as part of any future extended free trade area encompassing both sides of the Mediterranean seem almost certain to remain in place.

Of course, the partnership policy is not the only economic plan open to the states of the southern Mediterranean to encourage economic reform. There are at least two other proposals that run alongside it: the Regional Economic Development Working Group, which is part of the multilateral track of the US-inspired Middle East Peace Process (REDWG) and the Middle East and North Africa (MENA) Economic Conference proposal – also part of the peace process which is designed to end conflict between Israel and the Arab world. The conference secretariat organizes conferences that occur annually and are designed to bring private sector interests into Middle East economic development processes, particularly for the 'quadrilateral' countries of Israel, Palestine, Jordan and Egypt. The REDWG forum is also primarily directed towards providing economic support for the Middle East peace process and thus neither initiative really addresses the global issue of regional economic development and growth. In short, the European Union is the primary economic player in the region and the partnership policy is, therefore, the only realistic option through which economic development can be achieved.

The Partnership Policy: Security and Related Issues

At the same time, the Barcelona Conference approved a partnership policy that went far beyond the economic issues. These, in fact, only formed one of the three 'baskets' of measures that were discussed and agreed, albeit the most important one. The economic basket, incidentally, has acquired such importance because, on the one hand, it is a topic on which European Union member states find it easiest to agree – unlike security, political, social and cultural issues where national foreign policy concerns tend to produce more acute divergence – and, on the other, there is a generalized perception in Europe that economic failure in the region has become a major European security concern because of its implications for Mediterranean security. The actual structure of the economic basket is dictated both by a consensus that a neo-liberal approach based on free trade is the most appropriate pattern for future economic development, and by the perception that European aid programmes now must meet the Edinburgh budgetary limits which have provided the financial restraints on the Union that are required for eventual monetary union. This has meant that, compared with eastern Europe, the funding package offered under the Partnership Initiative's MEDA funding programme is not generous: it represents only a 25 per cent increase on previous financial protocols, together with a loan package from the European Investment Bank of similar magnitude. Meanwhile, the European Union's new financial arrangements for the Africa–Caribbean–Pacific (ACP) region have been far more severely constrained.

The other two baskets dealt with political and security issues, and with social and cultural development [Marks, 1996: 19–21]. Of the two, the political and security basket was the more important and, in it, security concerns dominated over political ones. The security issues stem from the crucial role that the Middle East and North Africa play in European trade access to the wider world and in energy provision for Europe itself. They also reflect the internal tensions within the southern Mediterranean region – supposedly now eased by the Middle East peace process – and form part of a long-term European concern over regional security which has been addressed in various fora in the recent past.

Indeed, the partnership policy itself stems in part from the Italian and Spanish proposal for a 'Conference on Security and Co-operation in the Mediterranean' (CSCM), itself inspired by the success of the 'Conference on Security and Co-operation in Europe' (CSCE) which was initiated by the Helsinki Conference in 1975. The CSCM was a security proposal that took a far wider view of security than had been usual, bringing in economic, social, cultural and political issues over a geographic area that stretched far beyond the Mediterranean itself, reaching down into the Persian Gulf. Although it was abandoned in the early 1990s as being too ambitious, the proposal remains on the table and may yet be integrated into the Barcelona process [Lesser, 1995: 18]. Indeed, the partnership policy could also be seen as a potential harbour for the other security vessels that have emerged, particularly in the western Mediterranean, in recent years. They include the 'five-plus-five' proposal, ranging France, Italy, Spain, Portugal and Malta against the five member states of the Arab Maghreb Union (Libya, Tunisia, Algeria, Morocco and Mauritania) and the Mediterranean Forum proposal, sponsored by Egypt in 1994.

There are also the more informal arenas of the NATO Mediterranean Dialogue – which is still very tentative, partly because NATO needs to reformulate its 'southern flank' policy in the context of the 'Partnership for Peace' initiative and partly because of atavistic regional suspicions about NATO's real purpose [Moya, 1996: 1–2] – and the Western European Union (WEU) dialogue initiative. The WEU initiative forms part of the third pillar of Maastricht and is limited by all the hesitancies that characterize the European Union's 'common foreign and security policy'. It is also compromised, in the eyes of its Maghrebi counterparts, by the creation in 1996 of EUROFOR and EUROMARFOR as rapid reaction ground and naval forces respectively, ostensibly for humanitarian and collective security purposes – the southern Mediterraneans wonder against whom the reaction would be directed!

Southern Mediterranean governments also suspect western motives over the regional arms race which they see as caused by western indifference to genuine regional security problems but which western statesmen all too often blame on regional (non-member country) irresponsibility and aggressiveness [Lesser and Tellis, 1996: 25–30] The real problem with these initiatives is that they lack credibility as far as southern Mediterranean states are concerned because there is another security player in the region. This is the United States which, after all, controls the Middle East peace process and has refused to consider genuine partnership in this respect with Europe. For southern Mediterranean states, the combination of the hesitancies of the European 'common security and foreign policy' with the reality of

American military power means that regional security issues within the partnership policy carry little weight compared to their dominant economic concerns.

Quite apart from the issues of 'hard security', Mediterranean security has acquired other dimensions as well. The Barcelona process has a specific objective of combating both international terrorism and crime, particularly drug smuggling. Although southern Mediterranean governments agree with these objectives in principle, they also argue that there is a financial implication in which Europe has obligations. Eradication of either problem is going to be costly, both in terms of the measures actually taken and in terms of the implied lost revenues to the economies concerned. Even though these revenues accrue to the informal economy, they have effects on the formal economy as well. Morocco, for example, is estimated to receive up to $1.8 billion annually from illicit exports of cannabis and, although these revenues are outside formal governmental control, their investment within Morocco – in real estate, for example – has a direct effect on government revenues. To some extent, European states individually and the European Commission recognize the justice of these arguments and Morocco, for example, has received considerable aid (around $400 million in the first instance) in order to eradicate cannabis cultivation in the Rif region of northern Morocco.

Southern Mediterranean governments also object that they are excluded from European deliberations on these topics which are usually carried on in the cloistered confines of the informal Trevi group, created originally in the 1970s to deal with the implications of the Red Brigades and the *Rote Armee Faktion* for Europe. Informal networks between interior ministers from both sides of the Mediterranean do not compensate for this sense of exclusion because such networks have no executive authority – unlike the Trevi group and its associated, albeit clandestine, committees.

More important, perhaps, is a more basic European anxiety which lies behind the partnership policy and forms part of the generalized security agenda. This relates to the security implications of the growth of Islamism throughout the Middle Eastern region. Western views of this problem have been increasingly dominated by assumptions such as those behind the 'clash of civilizations' thesis put forward by Samuel Huntington at the start of the 1990s [Huntington, 1993], although there is little objective evidence to support such a thesis [Halliday, 1995: 2, 161]. In fact, this growing ideological tendency in the region, with all its political and security implications, is far more effectively explained in terms of the contemporary history of the Middle East and North Africa, as well as by its economic failures. The failure or lack of 'good governance' amongst southern Mediterranean states has also had a significant role to play, but the evolution of regional affairs and economic decline provide more immediate explanations for this chiliastic, millenarian and universalist phenomenon.

Southern Mediterraneans are acutely aware of this and often blame Europe for its apparent myopia over the consequences of the policies it imposes, particularly in the economic arena. Their resentment of European demands for democratic, legitimate government and the rule of law are far less justified, however, and arguments based on the alleged specificity of Islamic concepts of human rights, as opposed to Western values, carry little weight [Halliday, 1995: 133–59]. Similarly, it is a little difficult to accept complaints from governments which are arbitrary and repressive, objecting to European criticism of their behaviour, for the criticisms are usually completely justified and would be supported by the populations of the states concerned, had they the opportunity to voice them! None the less, there is a legitimate field for complaint when the types of political regime to be imposed are considered, for political cultures differ and assumptions about European democratic structures do not necessarily apply throughout the region [Joffé, 1994]. What is important for southern Mediterranean populations – if the undesired political consequences from EU policy impositions are to be avoided – is that governments should be seen to be legitimate, accountable and willing to maintain the rule of law.

To some extent, the European Union is more willing to be flexible over these political issues than is the United States [Lesser, 1996: 12]. Although each of the new bilateral free trade area agreements has requirements for democratic government and respect for human rights, these are usually treated as formalities by both parties to the agreement. Pressure is certainly applied, but usually outside the framework of the agreements and on a state-to-state basis. In recent years, this has produced significant change in Morocco, for example, although the same has not been true of Tunisia. Indeed, it could be argued that the whole issue is one of some embarrassment to the European Union and that it has tended to shy away from its implicit and explicit responsibilities for political change within the Barcelona process. It remains to be seen whether this will continue to be the case as more bilateral free trade area agreements are signed. It is far more likely that change will be forced on southern Mediterranean governments by the activities of non-governmental organizations, particularly those concerned with human rights and political change, in Europe and, perhaps, more by the European Parliament than by the European Commission. The political basket is, however, likely to be an arena of continued irritation as the new relationship unfolds.

The cultural and social basket of the partnership policy is of even less significance than is the political and security basket. In part this is because it is a new initiative, in which the European Union is seeking to construct cultural ties that did not exist before through its Med-Media and Med-Campus programmes – now redesignated under the new MEDA funding programme. Over time, these programmes might well produce significant cultural and social links. However, they run counter to the prevailing trends within the southern Mediterranean region which tend to emphasize separation, rather than integration. Indeed, it could be argued that, until the economic and political issues have been resolved, little genuine cultural development between the northern and southern Mediterranean regions can be expected. Fundamentally, southern Mediterranean populations and their governments accuse Europe of a basic paternalism in the political and cultural spheres. They feel that little effort is expended on trying to understand the region and its problems in its own terms and that, instead, a European perspective is applied to analysis which fundamentally distorts both the prescription and the prognosis.

The Economic Conundrum

It is precisely such criticisms that are increasingly directed towards the major plank of the partnership policy, the new economic relationship enshrined in the proposed free trade area which will eventually encompass not just the Mediterranean but the Gulf as well. To date, two countries have signed the new agreements – Tunisia in July 1995 and Morocco in November 1995 – while Israel has signed a more complex free trade area agreement and Turkey has signed a customs union agreement with Europe. There is, in addition, an agreement under negotiation between the European Union and the Gulf states of the Gulf Co-operation Council (GCC) which primarily regulates petrochemical exports to Europe, although it, too, is eventually to lead to a free trade area agreement. Finally, Egypt is currently negotiating its own bilateral agreement with the European Union and Algeria is seeking to do the same. Other states, such as Jordan, are expected to join in soon and, in theory, any state may do this, including Syria and Lebanon, although the problems of the Middle East peace process are likely to delay any such decision in the near-to-medium term. The one state that is currently banned from any approach of this kind is Libya, because of the continuing United Nations sanctions against it as a result of the Lockerbie crisis [Waller, 1996].

Given such apparent enthusiasm to join the new European initiative, it may seem surprising that there should be any objection from southern Mediterranean states about the policy itself. This feeling is reinforced by the fact that, without European help, the southern Mediterranean region is likely to lose heavily from the trade liber-alization expected from the Uruguay Round of the GATT negotiations, completed only three years ago. Although the liberalization process is expected to yield an increase in world trade conservatively estimated at $572 billion annually, North African states face a $600 million annual decline in their overall trade and the southern Mediterranean region as a whole could see trade losses of up to $5.5 billion a year without integration into the wider European economic arena. Only the oil-rich Gulf states could expect an increase in trade equivalent to $1.2 billion, as a result of the proposed liberalization. If integration into this arena does occur, however, the net gains in trade terms have been estimated at $32 billion annually – a very attractive alternative [Diwan *et al.*, 1995: 48]!

The complaints exist, however, and they centre around three objections: the issue of free movement of populations; the implications of the Washington Consensus and the cost of transition; and the issue of adequate investment. Beyond these expressed objections there are other, more ideological issues as well, which reflect southern Mediterranean concerns over cultural infiltration from Europe and America as well as anxieties over western intolerance of indigenous political and cultural paradigms.

Migration and Free Population Movement

As Table 1 indicates, population growth in the southern Mediterranean region is considerable and populations there will outstrip their northern Mediterranean coun-terparts by the end of the century. Since these populations are youthful, they make a very heavy demand on state-provided services – social security, education and housing – which most states in the region cannot meet. Nor can they provide the employment that these populations, with over 50 per cent under the age of 30 years old, will require. Even though population growth rates are falling – dramatically in some cases, such as Iran or Tunisia – they are still considerable and the heavy demand on state support will continue into the next century.

Without outside support, southern Mediterranean states are unlikely to be able to satisfy the demands placed upon them. Yet European official development assistance has fallen in recent years and, as will be shown below, private sector and multilateral investment has not made up the shortfall. Thus social conditions will worsen and this, in turn, will intensify the alienation of indigenous populations from existing modes of government and their search for an alternative in terms of political Islam.

In addition, there is an inherent illogicality in European attitudes towards labour migration which, in the wake of European xenophobia, have virtually ensured that all inward migration should stop, with 4.6 million foreign workers inside Europe, 2.3 million of whom come from North Africa [Marks, 1995b: Appendix 3]. The illogicality resides in the facts that there is still a demand for cheap migrant labour, which now arrives illegally and therefore cannot be controlled, and that in any case there will be a growing semi-skilled and unskilled labour demand in Europe, expected to reach 56 million by the year 2100 [Weidenfeld and Hillenbrand, 1994: 26]. This will almost certainly have to be satisfied by migrant labour and southern Mediterranean states feel that freedom of movement of people must, in the end, form part of the overall Barcelona package to allow for this.

The Washington Consensus and the Cost of Transition

The economic assumptions behind many of the economic aspects of the Barcelona process reflect the principles of the Washington Consensus. This is the general action plan developed by the International Monetary Fund (IMF) and the World Bank during the 1980s to cope with the increasing number of countries in the developing world that experienced serious problems with their external payments balances as a result of the accrual of foreign debt. In essence, the solution to this problem was to argue that such states had misappropriated their resources as a result of unrealistic pricing policies. When this had occurred in the external trade arena, it had often been dealt with by a short-term palliative: the acquisition of foreign debt, which had been enlarged by recourse to large-scale borrowing to fund domestic capital development. The cure, essentially, was to liberalize trade and currency regimes, encourage export-oriented industry and abandon import substitution policies, and reduce the role of the state in the domestic economy by eliminating official subsidies and allowing the logic of the market to satisfy demand.

The IMF/World Bank prescription proved to be extremely difficult for states to apply, largely because it caused significant increases in domestic disadvantage in the countries to which it was applied. The 1980s and early 1990s were marked in the Middle East and North Africa by periodic bouts of large-scale rioting to which governments responded with repression – in Morocco in 1981, in Morocco and Tunisia in 1984, in Algeria in 1986 and 1988, in Egypt in 1986, in Morocco again in 1990 and in Jordan in the following year, not to speak of the widespread disturbances that have wracked Egypt for the past five years and Algeria ever since January 1992. In both the last two cases, other factors were also involved, but the role of economic reform should not be underestimated, nor should the implications of foreign debt (Table 5).

These principles have been imported into the partnership policy as well, for it requires that economies participating in the bilateral free trade areas should undergo economic reform to enable them to cope with European competition. In fact, even the requirements of the Washington Consensus are insufficient for effective participation and prolonged and expensive additional economic adjustment will be required. Both Morocco and Tunisia have been granted 12-year transition periods in which major industrial and services restructuring will have to take place at considerable cost – $2 billion in the case of Tunisia, of which 80 per cent will have to come from external sources, and $5.5 billion in the case of Morocco. Without this aid, 60 per cent of Moroccoo's industrial base will be destroyed and 2,000 Tunisian companies will be forced into bankruptcy with a further 2,000 having 'questionable' futures [Marks, 1995a: 3–4]. The additional finances made available as part of the Barcelona process will be insufficient to meet these demands and both countries will see their total debt stock rise as a result. Not surprisingly, this is a source of considerable resentment, even if businessmen in both countries anticipate a major opportunity once the transitional period is complete.

Table 5   Foreign Debt, 1992 ($ bn)

Country	Total debt			Long-term debt	
	1992	*1993*	*1994*	*1992*	*1993*
Maghreb					
Algeria	26.813	25.757	29.898	25.225	24.587
Mauritania	2.138	2.203	2.326	1.867	1.960
Morocco	21.305	21.430	22.517	20.536	20.659
Tunisia	8.475	8.701	9.254	7.644	7.627
Mashreq					
Egypt	40.517	40.626	33.358	36.712	37.204
Iran	12.866	20.550	22.712	1.716	11.666
Jordan	7.183	6.972	7.051	6.914	6.825
Lebanon	1.812	1.358	–	0.304	0.375
Oman	2.855	2.661	3.084	2.340	2.319
Sudan	16.085	16.560	–	9.480	9.490
Syria	19.016	19.975	–	15.912	16.234
Turkey	55.605	67.861	66.332	42.945	49.329
Yemen	6.571	5.923	5.959	5.253	5.341

Sources: World Bank, *Debt Tables 1994* (Washington), pp. 200–201; World Bank, *World Data 1995* (Washington, DC); World Bank, *World Development Report 1996* (Washington, DC), T. 17.
Note: Countries not listed have not reported; only Iraq has significant debt, estimated at around $80 billion. Saudi Arabia had a $5.4 billion loan which was paid off in 1995.

Foreign Investment

The major problem facing the states of the southern Mediterranean region is that, in the absence of adequate official development assistance and multilateral assistance, they must rely on direct private foreign investment and portfolio equity investment to fund economic reconstruction and economic development. As Table 6 shows, the region has been ineffective in both directions, compared with other developing regions of the world. It has been less successful than any other region except South Asia; even Sub-Saharan Africa has been more effective. The failure is due, no doubt, to the political turbulence of the region, but this is not the whole answer.

The fact is that foreign investors have little confidence in the region both because of the political risk involved and because labour costs are relatively high so that the return on investment is poor. The latter problem is compounded by corruption and high servicing and transactional costs. Yet, indigenous entrepreneurs argue that much of the disinterest in the region is based on incorrect assumptions and on a lack of adequate infrastructural investment in the past, in terms of both the physical and human resource base. Were this to be countered, the southern Mediterranean region could then exploit its closeness to the European market and offer a viable alternative to the Far East and Latin America as investment destinations.

The size of the problem is underlined by Table 7 which demonstrates that, apart from Turkey, Morocco and Tunisia, foreign investment has been declining in the region (the Saudi figures are an aberration caused by the war against Iraq). Even in these three countries, the total amount of investment has been only around half of what had been anticipated or required, despite modifications of law and regulation to encourage foreign investors. Indeed, it is difficult to see what these countries can do in addition to the measures they have already taken to persuade foreign investors to take up the opportunities they offer. Furthermore, as Table 8 demonstrates, without adequate investment, it is most unlikely that these states can begin to match the patterns of development experienced by the countries of the developed world or of

Table 6   Foreign Investment: Developing Countries by Region, 1993 ($ billion)

	FDI	(%)	PEI	(%)
East Asia/Pacific	36.5	54.8	18.1	38.3
Latin America/Caribbean	16.1	24.2	25.1	53.1
Europe/Central Asia	9.6	14.4	1.3	2.8
Sub-Saharan Africa	1.8	2.7	0.4	0.8
Middle East/North Africa	1.7	2.6	0.4*	0.8
South Asia	0.8	1.3	2.0	4.2
Total	66.6		47.3	

Source: *Comet*, 43 (May 1995), p.21.

* World Bank projection.

FDI = foreign direct investment; PEI = portfolio equity investment.

Table 7   Foreign Direct Investment ($ million)

	1989	1990	1991	1992
Turkey	663	684	810	844
Saudi Arabia	−20	572	659	1873
Morocco	167	165	320	424
Egypt	1250	734	253	459
Tunisia	79	75	150	379
Syria	74	71	71	330
Qatar	−1	16	43	−
Libya	1225	159	24	−
Iran	−19	−362	23	−170
Algeria	12	6	10	12
Oman	112	144	7	59
Lebanon	2	6	2	−
Iraq	3	−	−3	−
Bahrain	181	−4	−7	−
Jordan	−1	38	−12	41
UAE	39	−116	−69	−
Kuwait	4	−1	−	−
Yemen	5	−	−	0
Sudan	4	−	−	0
Mauritania	4	−	−	2

Sources: *Comet*, 41 (July 1994), p. 11; IBRD, *World Development Report 1994*, pp. 204–5.

Table 8   The Role of Direct Foreign Investment, 1986–91 (FDI/GDCF – %)

Middle East		Others – Europe	
Egypt	7.80	Belgium	16.00
Oman	6.90	United Kingdom	14.40
Tunisia	3.50	Netherlands	12.30
Morocco	2.60		
Jordan	1.70	*Others – Far East*	
Yemen	0.90		
Sudan	0.10	Singapore	29.40
Algeria	0.05	Hong Kong	12.10

Source: *Comet*, 41 (July 1994), p.12.

FDI = Foreign direct investment; GDCF = Gross domestic capital formation.

the rapidly developing world of the Far East. The European Union must, in short, provide far greater quantities of transitional aid if it really wishes to see genuine economic development. The alternative is that enclave economies will be created in southern Mediterranean states, designed to serve the European market, and that the national economies will become mere satellites of the European Union without experiencing genuine economic development and the prosperity that should accompany it.

The Underlying Anxieties

It is anxieties such as these that lie behind the groundswell of dissatisfaction manifest within the southern Mediterranean region. Behind them, however, are more basic fears. Even if, in macroeconomic terms, the development gamble succeeds on the terms proposed by the partnership policy, will this produce genuine prosperity? On the face of it, this seems unlikely, for there is little convincing evidence that wealth 'trickles down' the economic pyramid created by neo-classical economic development. And, if it does not, the political tensions already growing in the region will intensify. 'Good governance', in short, may be countered by the very process of economic development itself, unless genuine prosperity is one of the by-products.

Similarly, continued bars to migration, in a world in which information is ever more readily available, will both feed popular frustration and incite support for the indigenous Islamist alternative, although the commercial elite, by virtue of its participation in the globalized business culture that is emerging, will be able to participate. Thus cultural divides within states are likely to intensify as part of the consequence of the pattern of economic development proposed under the partnership policy – as large segments of the population are excluded from the developmental process – and this, in turn, will transform the European Union's political and security projects into additional sources of conflict.

Regimes also fear such cultural changes, although for different reasons. There are great anxieties in countries such as Tunisia and Algeria about the implications of the information flow now sweeping through the world, particularly through the Internet. Governments find it difficult to control and fear that it will presage a wave of disaffection and potential dissidence. This, in turn, leads them to be suspicious of the cultural and social basket of the Euro-Mediterranean Partnership Initiative, for this encourages direct contacts with independent groups and non-governmental organizations in the southern Mediterranean region and threatens government control, just like the new flood of information.

Governments also fear the consequences of economic transparency which is supposed to accompany the economic restructuring required by the Barcelona process. After all, much of the occult political and economic power in North Africa and the Middle East is controlled by elites that operate the patronage systems of the state. Transparency, whether economic or political, threatens this hegemony and regimes are bound to resist it – even as they protest their enthusiasm for the Partnership Initiative and the benefits it promises them. This is particularly true of the endemic problems of corruption and the repressive, arbitrary use of state power, neither of which will survive the changes now under way, provided they are fully implemented. That, as always, is the catch, for the European Union is only as effective as its least committed member state will permit, given its system of making collective decisions. And, since the Union is ultimately dominated by its northern members who are generally attracted far more by eastern Europe than by the

Mediterranean, it is not clear that the commitments made at Barcelona in November 1995 will actually be followed through. That air of northern insouciance adds to the anxieties felt by southern non-member countries now engaged in fulfilling their part of the Barcelona bargain.

In essence, therefore, the Euro-Mediterranean Partnership policy is ambitious but flawed. It may be the only opportunity available to the states of the southern Mediterranean rim, but it offers little guarantee of a solution to their social, political and economic problems. It contains inherent contradictions in the prohibition of the free movement of populations and in the limitations imposed on agricultural trade. It suffers from an intolerance and incomprehension of the political realities in which the North African and Middle Eastern worlds operate. It offers virtually nothing to resolve the problem of Middle Eastern peace, since it deliberately avoids engaging in moral issues and the EU would, in any case, be excluded by American and Israeli pressure from intervening. In short, the Euro-Mediterranean Partnership policy does not go far enough, and it remains to be seen whether European statesmen will have the vision and the authority to correct the errors they have made.

References

British Petroleum (1996): *World Energy Review 1996*, London.

Diwan, I. *et al.* (1995): 'The Arab Economy, the Uruguay Round Predicament and the European Union Wildcard', in World Bank, *Economic Research Forum*, Gammarth (Tunisia).

Halliday, F. (1995): *Islam and the Myth of Confrontation*, London: I.B. Taurus.

Huntington, S. (1993): 'The Clash of Civilizations?', *Foreign Affairs*, Summer.

Joffé, E.G.H. (1994): 'Relations between the Middle East and the West", *Middle East Journal* 48(2).

Lesser, I.O. (1995): 'Growth and Change in Southern Europe', in J. Holmes (ed.), *Maelstrom: The United States, Southern Europe and the Challenges of the Mediterranean*, Cambridge, MA: World Peace Foundation.

Lesser, I.O. (1996): *South Europe and the Maghreb: US Interests and Policy Perspectives*, Santa Monica, CA: Rand.

Lesser, I.O. and A.J. Tellis (1996): *Strategic Exposure: Proliferation around the Mediterranean*, Santa Monica, CA: Rand.

Marks, J. (1995a): *Maghreb Quarterly Review* 18 (June).

Marks, J. (1995b): *Maghreb Quarterly Review* 20 (Dec).

Marks, J. (1996): 'High Hopes and Low Motives: The New Euro-Mediterranean Partnership Initiative', *Mediterranean Politics* 1(1).

Moya, P. (1996): Draft Interim Report: Cooperation for Security in the Mediterranean: NATO and EU Contributions – Sub-committee on the Mediterranean Basin, North Atlantic Assembly (May).

Waller, R. (1996): 'The Lockerbie End-Game', *Journal of North African Studies*, 1(1).

Weidenfeld, W. and O. Hillenbrand (1994): 'Migration is a Necessity, Not a Choice', *European Brief* (Dec.).

World Bank (1995): *Economic Research Forum*, Gammarth (Tunisia).

Destablization through Partnership? Euro-Mediterranean Relations after the Barcelona Declaration

EBERHARD KIENLE

The new 'partnership' which the European Union offers its neighbours on the southern shores of the Mediterranean may well have more negative than positive consequences for the prosperity and stability of the countries concerned. Contrary to the expectations of their advocates, policies of internal and external economic liberalization are not likely to increase the economic performance of the southern Mediterranean countries. In terms of productivity, investment, job creation and overall prosperity, losses will have to be faced. On the political level, these losses, seen as imposed by the 'West', pose many threats to the stability of the southern countries. While increasing repression may guarantee the survival of their regimes, it will further erode the stability of these countries. However, even economic growth and an equitable distribution of wealth would not be sufficient to ensure transitions to more participatory forms of government and thus stability based on more than repression. A serious yet circumspect political dialogue is also needed as an essential contribution to the stability of the countries concerned and of the entire Mediterranean basin.

According to the wishes of its architects, the new Partnership between the European Union (EU) and the southern Mediterranean countries, as sketched out in the Barcelona Declaration of November 1995, is intended to transform the *Mare Nostrum* into an area of 'peace, stability and prosperity'. The measures envisaged in the three chapters of the declaration, devoted to political and strategic issues, to economic and financial co-operation, and to social, cultural and human affairs, are all supposed to contribute to the realization of these objectives, which a priori appear to be of equal importance. Apart from the need to find a new equilibrium within the EU, whose southern members fear that they will benefit less than their northern counterparts from closer relations with eastern Europe, it is however the search for stability that dominates this 'new Mediterranean policy'.[1]

The view that the EU privileges stability over prosperity and thus politics over economics is not always shared in the southern Mediterranean countries where the colonial and imperialist past of the European powers is part of the living memory. However, given the limited size of the Mediterranean market and its equally limited significance for Europe, EU trade interests there cannot possibly explain adequately such an important initiative as the Euro-Mediterranean Partnership. EU exports to the southern Mediterranean amount to only 11 per cent of total exports and imports from the region do not exceed 8 per cent [Eurostat, 1994]. To the extent to which the partnership is supposed to contribute to prosperity, it is aimed at the prosperity of the southern Mediterranean countries. Increasing their prosperity appears to the EU as a necessary, possibly even a sufficient, condition to guarantee their internal stability and thus the stability of the Mediterranean as a whole.

In order to avoid possible confusions, it is useful to distinguish here between the stability of a country in the sense of a political entity or polity, and the stability of its political regime which may be closely linked to that of the rulers. The stability of a polity does not necessarily entail the stability of the regime or its leadership. Similarly, the stability of a ruling group or a regime does not exclude the instability of the wider political entity, as the case of Algeria amply demonstrates.

With specific reference to the stability of the southern Mediterranean countries, the Barcelona Declaration abounds in references to 'human rights', 'fundamental freedoms', 'diversity and pluralism', the 'rule of law' and 'democracy', which are supposed to inform the 'political dialogue', the linchpin of the political chapter. However, at the same time, the declaration refers to principles and objectives that would enable the EU to support the existing regimes against unwelcome opponents, should the need arise.[2] These principles and objectives include respect for the 'sovereign equality of states', the 'right of each of them to choose and freely develop its own political, socio-cultural, economic and judicial system' and the fight against 'terrorism'. The ambiguity is all the more obvious as the declaration fails to envisage the possibility to link any form of co-operation to political liberalization, whose most important components are, of course, human rights and political participation. The idea of political conditionality is far less prominent than in the Lomé Convention (Lomé IV) or in the strategies proposed by the World Bank since the late 1980s.[3]

More importantly, the association agreements with Morocco and Tunisia only hint at democratic principles and human rights. In each document, they are evoked in a four-line article, which forms a preamble of sorts, and are thus separated from the provisions governing the political dialogue which, in turn, is reduced to a vague search for stability. The attention paid to political rights is indeed marginal if compared with the numerous provisions concerning trade and financial issues, which are further amplified by detailed annexes several times longer than the agreements themselves.[4]

The following pages are an attempt to determine the extent to which the partnership in its present form will be able to reinforce the stability not only of the regimes but also of the countries along the southern shores of the Mediterranean. In this context, we will examine the capacity of the partnership to contribute to economic growth and to an equitable distribution of wealth, on the one hand, and to the respect for human rights and participatory, or even democratic, procedures, on the other. In contradistinction to some interpretations of the Barcelona Declaration, we do consider such respect as an aim in itself, not only as a means to enhance stability.

Political Objectives, Economic Strategies

Although the EU is concerned primarily with political stability, it does not necessarily seek to achieve it through the political dialogue. The ambiguity over the principles that should guide the dialogue, as well as the absence of the notion of political conditionality, indicate this to be the case. The development of cultural, social and human relations and the consolidation of civil society in southern Mediterranean countries are also likely to be marginalized in the EU strategy. Like democratic principles and human rights, social and cultural issues are more prominent in the Barcelona Declaration than in the actual association agreements. Unlike the chapters on trade and financial co-operation, those on non-economic issues moreover lack any provisions concerning their implementation.[5]

Everything seems to indicate that political, social and cultural objectives, including political stability, are primarily sought through economic growth, which is itself supposed to flow from policies of free trade and internal economic liberalization.[6] Although it is subordinate to the political chapter in terms of objectives, the partnership's economic chapter dominates in terms of interactions and exchanges.

If we are to believe the arguments of its supporters, such an approach based on free trade and domestic economic liberalization would first affect productivity and investment, including direct foreign investment. Helped by low wages, growth in investment would increase export revenues and improve the trade balance. Export revenues would, in turn, contribute to the reduction of external debt, even though the instruments of the partnership fail to address this issue in detail. Investment would also lead to job creation and, more generally, to an increase in revenues and an improvement in the standard of living. On the political level, this new prosperity could only reinforce the stability of the countries concerned. In turn, this stability and prosperity would contribute automatically to the stability of the EU.

Those among the supporters of this policy who seek to promote political liberalization and democracy in the southern Mediterranean countries expect it to favour such outcomes through at least one of the following three mechanisms. According to a first argument, it is prosperity that leads to democratization. A second argument holds that stability enables political liberalization and the transition to democracy to take place, while according to a third argument there is a direct and inevitable link between economic and political liberalization as economic markets are supposed to favour the emergence of political markets. In all these cases, political liberalization is supposed to strengthen the stability of the countries concerned and indeed often is reduced to a means in the pursuit of the latter.

In all these cases, political liberalization is also considered as a long-term rather than a short-term objective. It would, and is meant to, follow economic liberalization and its allegedly positive welfare effects. Thus it would be possible to avoid a feared scenario in which political liberalization would first of all benefit Islamist forces which are considered as anti-European and as manifestations of material decline and poverty. More often than not, in fact, the parts of the Barcelona Declaration concerned with human rights and political participation seem to spell out general principles to be realized some time in the future and not to be entirely neglected in the meantime.

This approach is a retouched version of the theory of markets as a democratizing force. The superiority of the market economy is no longer questioned, now that the Soviet Union has collapsed. The emergence of semi-liberal democracies in the successor states to the USSR and in eastern Europe appears to confirm the link commonly established between economic and political liberalization. Although this argument is not surprising in a period in which economic liberalization is triumphant, it is none the less problematic in several respects. Firstly, it omits the fact that the establishment of new democratic regimes in eastern Europe and in the Community of Independent States preceded economic transformation except for partial measures of liberalization, for example in Hungary, which led to the mushrooming of small private enterprises. Secondly – as illustrated by the experience of eastern Europe – the argument comes down to a reductionist and distorted generalization of historical developments in some parts of western Europe.

Economic Liberalization and Economic Development

Doubts over the positive link between political and economic liberalization – which we will return to below – are compounded by uncertainties over the potential effects of the recommended economic policies on growth and distribution.[7] Indeed, there is no guarantee that free trade and the domestic liberalization recommended under the EU's new Mediterranean policy will have the anticipated effects. However, any failure in terms of growth and distribution would prevent liberalization from spilling over from the narrow confines of the economy into politics. Put differently, most of the economic transformations expected to favour political liberalization would simply not take place.

First, the liberalization of foreign trade such as it is envisaged may expose local producers to a degree of competition which they are unable to cope with. Thus gains in productivity would be replaced by the elimination of units of production. While foreign trade liberalization is to occur gradually over a transitional period of some 12 years, some sectors will be affected from the start.[8] Other sectors will have more time to adapt to new conditions, but their success is still not guaranteed. Even though the intention is, as is already the case in Tunisia, to begin with reduced tariffs on imports of capital goods which will provide some initial protection for producers of consumer goods [Hoekman and Djankov, 1996], this will be at the expense of industries that, potentially at least, are more capable of technological innovation. In parallel to this, the effects of the new GATT agreement on trade exchanges still governed by the multi-fibre agreement may endanger the southern Mediterranean textile producers' share of the European market [Yeats, 1994]. Foreign trade liberalization may be inevitable, but only if adequately regulated will it be the factor of growth that it is expected to be. Otherwise one may witness even the erosion of traditional comparative advantages which, however, already prevent southern Mediterranean countries from gaining from trade as much as their northern partners.

At the same time, the withdrawal of the state from the economy – which is avidly sought by the supporters of economic liberalization – can reduce private sector competitiveness rather than reinforce it. Like agricultural subsidies, infrastructural development and the granting of soft credit facilities belong to the arena of public intervention where the effects on competitiveness do not necessarily mean chronic price distortions [Mosley, 1995]. Especially during transitional periods, low interest rates, for example, can be used for investments which later ensure profitable returns. State intervention in these domains may as well be considered as a catalyst for the emergence of new industries. Many economically 'developed' countries resorted to such forms of aid in the past or still continue to do so, even though rhetorically they are ardent defenders of the market.

Moreover, non-economic factors will prevent southern Mediterranean enterprises from using the transitional period effectively to increase their competitiveness. These factors are organization and management structures in enterprises where seniority often prevails over competence, and patrimonial attitudes prevail over the systematic and effective allocation of responsibility. Nor is there much room for innovation and initiative amongst employers and employees trained in an educational system based on learning by rote and on obedience. In so far as these problems arise from socialization and education, they cannot be overcome rapidly. Entire age groups will be unaffected by the social and cultural changes that may occur within the framework of the partnership. Sceptical views of this kind are confirmed by the difficulties experienced by most east Germans over the age of 25 in adapting to the demands of the market economy. The period of adaptation may be much longer than the transitional period provided for by the partnership and this may easily lead to the disappearance of a large proportion of local production.

No smaller are the uncertainties surrounding investment. The capacity of the partnership to attract foreign investment to the southern Mediterranean countries and to retain local capital is much more doubtful than it seems to be on the surface. The association agreements provided for in the partnership framework will open up southern rather than northern markets, the latter being already largely open to southern manufactures. However, as many commentators have pointed out in the past, such favourable conditions have often failed to increase southern exports to Europe. In sectors subject to EU import quotas, the latter have often not been filled.[9]

The opening of southern markets to northern products may result therefore in disinvestment in the countries concerned. In some industries, low labour costs – the main asset of southern countries – seem to be more than compensated by potential economies of scale in European production units which, thanks to the association agreements, henceforth can produce for North Africa and western Asia as well.[10] Car manufacture in Egypt is one of the industries threatened [*Egypte/Monde Arabe*, 23: 234]. The obvious solution to this problem resides in a strategy that would seek to achieve economies of scale in southern countries by exporting to other markets with low purchasing power, particularly in North Africa and in the Middle East. However, the free trade agreements within the partnership framework only apply to trade between the EU and southern Mediterranean countries, not to trade among the latter themselves. This lack of 'strategic advantage' does not increase their attractiveness to investors [Page and Underwood, 1995; *al-Hayat*, 11 Oct. 1996].

The appeal of southern Mediterranean countries for investors also depends on factors relevant to the viability of existing production facilities. These include productivity, infrastructure, information and transaction costs, and the education and socialization of economic actors. In each of these domains the creation of conditions favourable to investment will depend on state action and therefore on the means available to underpin such action. However, governments are financially in dire straits, struggling with substantial public debt and, under conditions of economic liberalization, supposed to limit public spending anyway. The appeal by the EU and the World Bank to the private sector during the October 1996 Istanbul conference, urging it to invest in infrastructural projects in the Mediterranean,[11] reflected less the realism of the proposal than the current approach of both institutions. Funds released by the EU within the framework of the partnership will only amount to Ecu 4.685bn over five years, which will be the equivalent to less than $100 million per country per year, in addition to loans granted by the European Investment Bank and to bilateral aid. It is therefore obvious that European aid will not finance major structural transformations in the southern Mediterranean states [Dauderstaedt, 1996].

A favourable climate for investment also depends on the transparency, efficiency and independence of the judiciary and, finally, on political stability.[12] However, the administration of justice is a problem in most southern Mediterranean countries; the contradiction between laws, the length of litigation and official failures to implement court decisions are the most obvious examples. Political stability certainly exists at the level of regimes and their leaderships, but far less at the level of countries or political entities as a whole. Political stability could be increased by job-creating investment, but investors are likely to be discouraged by the obstacles they face. They may also fear that investment initiatives may not improve conditions in time to avoid political turmoil which therefore could threaten their investments themselves. In this context it is useful to remember that World Bank structural adjustment programmes, which in many ways are similar to policies recommended by the partnership, have generally proved disappointing in terms of investment.[13]

Without a substantial increase in investment, there is little hope that southern Mediterranean countries will be able to increase substantially their export revenues and thus repay their public debt. In any case, export revenues alone – which in a more liberal economy will be created by the private sector – cannot achieve this objective unless they are taxed, and this is something which current liberal doctrines do not encourage. Even if it manages to stimulate exports, economic liberalization will thus not necessarily facilitate the repayment of public debt.

Increased foreign competition for local producers – which forces them either to increase productivity or to close down – and the decline in investment will not contribute to the creation of new jobs. The effects of export-directed investment will not prove any more useful in this respect in view of the degree of mechanization and automation required. At the same time, the slimming down of the public sector and its privatization will increase pressures on the labour market.[14] Even international financial institutions which are generally favourable to economic liberalization policies do not believe that the partnership will have positive effects on employment. More pessimistic studies suggest that the partnership may entail the loss of up to 40 per cent of existing jobs.[15]

However, without the creation of new jobs, prosperity for all is an unattainable objective. The creation of low salary jobs will be just as futile in this respect. Indeed, the children employed in the textile industry in India can hardly be regarded as prosperous even though they receive a salary. Of course, lack of prosperity for all does not exclude prosperity for some. Thus, in Egypt internal and external economic liberalization within the framework of macroeconomic stabilization and structural adjustment has widened the income gap.[16] If the number of people living in extreme poverty has diminished, the so-called middle classes are facing steady impoverishment [Arab Republic of Egypt, 1996: 66–8]. Unemployment affects 20 per cent of the economically active population according to the World Bank, and is even higher among university graduates.[17] Salaries in the public sector and in government services are now less than half of their 1973 value [World Bank, 1991]. These trends towards unequal development will not be reversed by the partnership, at least not in the short term, even if structural adjustment and liberalization are no longer subject to the additional constraints of macroeconomic stabilization. Nor will the partnership stop the relative impoverishment of the southern Mediterranean countries in relation to the EU. Even if their GNPs double, which is one of the objectives of EU policies, this will not be sufficient to prevent the prosperity gap between them and the EU from doubling from 10:1 today to 20:1 by the year 2010.[18]

In summary, the economic policies advocated by the partnership are based on hypotheses that seem not only simplistic but also far too optimistic. Instead of increasing productivity, free trade could increase redundancy and output levels. At the same time, the effects of free trade on investment could turn out to be negative rather than positive. If such a scenario dashes the hopes for an increase in exports, such an increase in itself will not translate into revenues available to the treasury to pay back public debt. Furthermore, the proposed positive linkage between investment and job creation depends on additional factors, including the countervailing effects of productivity increases. The link between job creation and general prosperity in a low wage economy is just as uncertain.

Emphasizing the uncertainties and improbabilities of economic policies advocated within the framework of the partnership does not imply that policies that failed in the past should be revived. In economic terms, greater openness towards the outside world is inevitable for the countries concerned. However, the way in which this aim is to be achieved needs to be looked at critically, particularly if the ulterior motive is to contribute to political stability.

Economic Liberalization and Political Development

Although political stability does not depend solely on economic growth and fair income distribution, these two factors are essential, particularly in the case of southern Mediterranean countries. Lack of growth would prevent any 'soft' redistribution, however limited it might be, of resources and opportunities. On the other hand, respectable growth rates alone do not guarantee an equitable redistribution of wealth.

The social calm and popular demobilization which currently prevail in most southern Mediterranean countries do not indicate the consent of the unemployed, the

public sector employees and the other victims of current policies of economic liberalization to the sacrifices that have been imposed on them for years. The fact that
there has been no major or generalized social unrest can be explained by the universal
presence of 'security' forces and their informers. In Tunisia, the number of secret
police agents is said to have increased four- or fivefold since the introduction of
economic reforms. In some industrial cities in Egypt, trade union elections take
place under the watchful eye of riot police and, as in Morocco, parliamentary elections are stage-managed. In the best of cases, the heads of state are acclaimed in
pseudo-participatory proceedings; and of course, the Moroccan king is not subject to
any such semblance of election. The lack of agitation is also explained by mass
resignation. Discouraged and tired, people have abandoned not only social protest,
but often also any genuine form of economic or political participation. It is, of
course, true that such groups will not overthrow existing regimes, but they will not
defend them either and, what is more, they will not contribute to the economic dyna-
mism so avidly sought by the states in question. Often, this social malaise is
expressed through more diffuse movements of protest and demands for social justice.
The growing influence of various Islamist movements is partly the result of the
decline in living conditions and the marginalization of certain social groups [Fandy,
1994: 607–26; S.E. Ibrahim, 1995a: 4–9].

Of course, social quietude is often only a facade. The number and size of strikes
in Egypt are increasing, despite the official media blackout. The September 1994
strike in Kafr al-Dawwar and the subsequent police intervention which resulted in
four deaths and many serious casualties is just the tip of this iceberg.[19] Although it is
currently difficult to envisage the transformation of these essentially local events
into a coherent nationwide protest movement, an increase in them would undoubtedly affect economic performance and political stability. Whatever the truth of
claims about the spontaneity and the lack of organization of the 1977 bread riots in
Egypt or elsewhere, they do have wider consequences.

The long-term passivity of social groups whose living standards have declined
for many years and who are likely to face more sacrifices therefore cannot be taken
for granted. In this respect, the reduction in output by 50 per cent and the loss of 40
per cent of existing jobs which may result from the adjustment to the requirements
of the partnership do not augur well. Indeed, the decline in living standards seems
likely to increase conflict, both within Mediterranean Arab societies and in their
relations with Europe, since it appears to be closely linked to the consolidation of
unequal relations between North and South. These new economic difficulties,
whether they are only temporary in nature or even necessary for long-term development, will follow the association agreements with the EU and will be identified with
them. They will recall the relationship that characterized the colonial past and thus
will be viewed as a new stage of neo-colonial relations characterized by unilateral
exploitation. Whether inspired by nationalism or Third Worldism, protests will
assume a significant religious dimension since the adjustment efforts will be required
of Muslims by non-Muslims. Thus, reforms imposed by foreign powers could bring
us closer to a clash of civilizations, though not for the reasons imagined by Huntington
[1993: 22–49]. The hope that some shared Mediterranean identity might soften the

blow is vain, precisely because this sense of common identity is not shared by the inhabitants of southern Mediterranean shores.

Of course, the stability of regimes can always be ensured, as the example of Algeria has shown in recent years. Hovever, even more than in the past it will be ensured by means of restrictions on human rights and political participation and by coercion and constraint. Thus, stability based on legitimacy, authority and consensus will become ever more remote. While this may ensure the survival of a regime, it is not necessarily true of economic growth which may tolerate authoritarianism, but not the conflicts it engenders and exacerbates.

Even if economic adjustments required by the partnership do not result in additional material losses or imbalances, there is little hope that they will favour political liberalization according to any of the three scenarios referred to above. The positivist hypothesis according to which a transition to liberal democracy might be facilitated by prosperity is the easiest one to reject. According to one representative of this extreme version of modernization theory, the threshold to achieve this corresponds to a per capita national income of US$4000, in 1988 prices [Wade, 1990]. Thus, although the situation in Egypt requires no explanation, the separation of powers in India is an absurdity and repression in Saudi Arabia can be explained only as an unfortunate accident of history.[20] Though frequent, the coincidence of prosperity with political liberalism of sorts does not in itself prove a causal relation. More generally, the hypothesis that links democratization to economic development is not convincing either [Lipset, 1959; Cutright and Wiley, 1969]. Once more, the examples of India and Saudi Arabia, as well as fascism in Europe, cast doubts over such a simplistic explanation. Emphasizing the emergence of a strong and self-aware bourgeoisie, of which economic development would be just a reflection, does not explain why this class should be more democratic than others. In the last analysis, the frequent chronological coincidence between economic development and political liberalism cannot be understood without taking into account the democratizing role of conflicts between classes, forces and actors whom the evolution of capitalism is pitting against each other in changing balances of power [Rueschemeyer, Stephens and Stephens, 1992].

It is not only from this point of view that the argument that political stability contributes to political liberalization is unsustainable. For the rulers it is certainly easier to relinquish power partially, or rather to refrain from using it, if the country is calm and their position secure. In times of internal social conflict, even some of the ruled may prefer a strong leader to political participation and respect for human rights. The real problem with this argument is that it implies that liberalization occurs from above.

Historically, genuine processes of political liberalization were imposed on the rulers from below. The French Revolution was no more the work of Louis XVI than was the first German Republic the creation of Wilhelm II. The same is true of England, from the Magna Carta to the achievement of universal suffrage. Moreover, changes due to pressures from below or from counter-elites have proved more lasting and profound than the come-and-go of democracy *à la jordanienne* or *à la marocaine*. In Amman, the king opens and closes the doors of political expression and representation according to circumstance; in its formal and parliamentary form, such representation does not imply any participation in the major decisions concerning the kingdom. Finally, from a purely logical point of view, it is not surprising that processes of political liberalization are initiated by their beneficiaries rather than by their victims.

In order for intra-societal conflict to lead to political liberalization and eventually to democracy, it is essential that the contenders for power be willing, able and sufficiently confident to enter into a political pact of sorts [O'Donnell, Schmitter and Whitehead, 1986: 37; Leca, 1994]. Such a pact may be defined as the founding act of a democracy without democrats which however in the course of time and thanks to negotiations and compromises may produce its democrats [Salamé, 1994]. As illustrated by the Glorious Revolution in England, the French Revolution or the uncertainties of the Third Republic in France, such pacts are not always easily or rapidly agreed upon. From this point of view, Algeria may still have a chance. There is no certainty, however, that contemporary rulers in southern Mediterranean countries and their opponents are willing, or able, to conclude such pacts. The struggles and conflicts that characterize political instability could easily be exacerbated or even prolonged should the protagonists prefer to exhaust themselves in a struggle for victory rather than compromise over a share in power. In this case, the end of an old regime does not necessarily herald the beginning of a more representative or less authoritarian successor. The return to the Hobbesian state of nature or the advent of another authoritarian regime are just as likely.

Finally, the hypothesis that economic liberalization, through its stress on market relations, leads necessarily to political liberalization, or at least that it facilitates such a development, is no more convincing than the argument about the role of prosperity or stability. First, this hypothesis as well crumbles once it is confronted with history. Present-day mainland China, Indonesia under Suharto and Singapore are powerful counter-examples. In the past, the imperial and Nazi regimes in Germany maintained cordial relations with the private sector which, moreover, was more important in terms of size than the public sector.

As argued above, and quite apart from what history may teach us or not, there is no reason why private sector growth or the rise of the bourgeoisie *ipso facto* should lead to political liberalization. There is no reason either why the generalization of market relations in the economic sphere should be sufficient to produce such an outcome in the political sphere. Even the most orthodox economics text books explain without ambiguity that markets can be deficient and thus encourage the emergence of monopolies [Samuelson and Nordhaus, 1995: Ch.2]; if the evolution of the 'political market' were linked to that of the economic market, the growth of economic monopolies should lead to the growth of political monopolies and thus to undemocratic developments. Although the growth of the economic market still would have contributed to the growth of the political market, the latter would be as deficient as the former.[21]

This is obviously not yet the case in the southern Mediterranean. Economic liberalization – and therefore the introduction of market principles – remains partial. The role of the state as a producer and regulator remains far more important than in most western European states. Despite European and international pressure, it is still not certain that economic liberalization will lead to a genuine liberal transformation of the economies in question (which of course is not necessarily desirable if one accepts the argument developed above). This other deficiency of the market, if there really is a link between economic and political liberalization, would only allow for partial political liberalization in any case.

The impact of economic liberalization moreover is limited by the creation of enterprises by the rulers and their relatives, who thus transform their political capital into economic capital. Economic liberalization stops where it affects captive markets or elite profits. This truncated economic liberalization even reinforces – or at least consolidates – the dominant position of the rulers which it is sometimes supposed to weaken. The influence and the power that they lose through the contraction of the public sector comes back to them through their own private enterprises.

Furthermore, economic liberalization conventionally tends to strengthen the position of owners of capital and to weaken that of wage earners. In terms of distribution, revenues from capital increase more rapidly than salaries – which might even stagnate or decrease, as figures given above for Egypt demonstrate. At the same time, chambers of commerce and industry and business or producers' associations tend to be consulted more often by the rulers than trade unions.[22] Through their growing economic power and by virtue of their neo-Saint Simonian reputation as modernizers, entrepreneurs and other owners of capital extend their political influence and increase their opportunities for political participation at the expense of labour. Depending on the circumstances, owners of capital either become junior partners of the rulers, who themselves become increasingly involved in business,[23] or they become even more powerful – either directly, like Rafik Hariri in Lebanon (or Silvio Berlusconi and Michael Heseltine in Europe), or indirectly, as pressure groups or as the financiers of political parties.

Combined with the decline in the position of labour, this reinforcement of the position of the rulers and of owners of capital could provoke the kind of struggles and conflicts that contributed to democratization in Europe. The omnipresence of the state, the survival of corporatism and the lack of organization of the losers, however, seem to point away from this scenario. To the extent to which there will be conflicts, their consequences will be restricted to the further weakening of political stability.

The emergence of a number of powerful economic actors, such as private banks that control credit and even production, does not constitute a guarantee for political liberalization either. Such a polyarchic concentration of private property can create parallel powers capable of defying each other or the state and its leaders, something that would be impossible for even a large number of small owners [Henry, 1996]. Hence it may also provoke the type of conflicts that are liable to favour democratization. However, there is no guarantee that the evidence of parallel powers will entail a separation of powers of sorts and that they would not, on the contrary, form a new oligopoly, either together with the regime or without it.

Economic liberalization thus tends to influence the possibilities of political participation selectively, favouring some constituencies while marginalizing others [Ayubi, 1994; Kienle (ed.), 1994]. The beneficiaries will certainly not seek the formalization of mechanisms of participation, for example through strengthening legislative power or ensuring fair elections. In an age in which it is no longer acceptable to link electoral suffrage to property, the formalization of political participation would entail the risk of reducing the advantages of the propertied classes or sectors of society [Bahout, 1994; Perthes, 1994; Kienle, 1994].

Political liberalization and the additional stability it would provide to political entities are, therefore, difficult objectives to achieve solely through economic liberalization.[24] Neither general prosperity, nor the relative political stability that in the best of cases could result from economic reforms, leads *ipso facto* to a widening of political participation or increased respect for human rights. The pursuit of political liberalization through economic liberalization as a force favouring the generalization of market relations appears all the more hazardous if one examines the political development of countries that have initiated or undergone economic reforms of that sort. In particular, the policies of macroeconomic stabilization and structural adjustment advocated by the Bretton Woods institutions involve a considerable degree of internal and external economic liberalization. Policies implemented within this framework by Morocco from 1983, Tunisia from 1986 and Egypt from 1991 are no exception to this rule. However, neither in Morocco nor in Tunisia or in Egypt has this type of economic reform been followed by the extension of possibilities of political participation or by an improvement in the human rights situation. Neither the occasional release of political prisoners in Egypt nor the latest parliamentary elections in Morocco, as usual stage-managed by the king, prove the contrary [Kienle, 1998; Bennani-Chraibi and Leveau, 1998].

These political developments, which run counter to the aspirations of the partnership, do not challenge the principle on which the latter is based. Just as with the potentially negative economic effects of a strategy based solely on free trade and the market, they require a closer examination of the means that are supposed to serve the ends of the partnership.

The Indispensable Rehabilitation of the Political Dialogue

Furthering political liberalization in the southern Mediterranean necessarily implies stressing the political dialogue and the development of the social, cultural and human side of the partnership. The political dialogue will not be effective, however, without an element of political conditionality. The signatories of the Barcelona Declaration and the association agreements are bound by their commitment to respect human rights and to 'develop the rule of law and democracy'. By insisting on the unity rather than on the independence and separability of the three chapters of the partnership, the EU would have no difficulty in linking commercial and financial provisions to the application of political reforms. These, of course, would have to be more than superficial reforms that avoid questions of substance. With a view to equality among the partners, such reforms in southern Mediterranean countries could provide their future governments with additional legitimacy to insist on the respect of their own citizens' rights in Europe.

A European policy that insists on respect for human rights and political participation in the southern Mediterranean would be helped by the emergence of a genuine civil society there.[25] Consequently, European policy should seek to expand and rein-force such a civil society. However, this concept, which is referred to in the Barcelona Declaration, is absent from the association agreements with Tunisia and Morocco. An increase in the number and weight of well-organized associations, which operate democratically and are entirely independent from the state and from those who control it, would undoubtedly relativize the powers of the latter. These associations would have to be different from the chambers of commerce, trade unions and the many associations that exist presently in the southern Mediterranean. They should be freed from the shackles that currently tie them, to a greater or lesser extent, to the state. The concept of civil society is, for example, incompatible with the *de facto* and *de jure* powers held by the Egyptian government in relation to private voluntary associations [al-Sayyid, 1995: 284]. Decisions on financial matters, general policy and personnel need to be taken democratically and voting itself should be considered a serious process in its own right, free from constraints. In other words, the privi-leges often enjoyed by the founders of these associations or by other prominent members need to be abolished and political culture needs to become more egali-tarian and participatory.[26]

It is by no means certain, however, that even a genuine civil society would be able to substantially limit the powers of the state.[27] Such capacities have never been tested outside political systems based on the separation of powers. The efficacy of civil society seems mostly based on its capacity to mobilize one part of the state against another: thus, actors from civil society may lobby the judiciary or parliamen-tarians in order to influence decisions made by the executive. What is important here is not necessarily the classical separation of powers as described by Montesquieu, but the principle of such a separation of powers itself. In other words, the growth of civil society will only contribute effectively to a substantial liberalization of politics when it is accompanied by a reform – or a partial dislocation of the structures – of the centralized states of the southern Mediterranean.[28] Civil society will not be able to replace the effects of multiple centres of power or of political pacts.

Largely dependent on foreign pressure and on significant domestic change modelled on the experience of European countries, political liberalization in southern Mediterranean states poses, however, two important questions. The first concerns the impact of these changes and pressures on the political survival of incumbent rulers. These may not be willing to play the game; if they do, they may not regain their position under the new rules since political liberalization implies the possibility of an alternation in power. With a change of leadership, policies may change too, perhaps even at the expense of those who had originally called for political liberalization.

The second question concerns the nature of the structural and normative changes implied by political liberalization as well as the legitimacy and advisability of the use of external pressure to achieve them. The necessary changes may seem contrary to the customs, values and traditions of the countries in question, even in the eyes of those who are their most direct beneficiaries. This incompatibility, which of course is subjective in nature, may seem all the more substantial because the changes are imposed or proposed from the outside, by parties often considered hostile and compromised by their colonial past. The question is no less sensitive than that of economic reforms initiated from the outside. The question is first and foremost one of ethics, but it also takes on an important pragmatic dimension. While political liberalization is indispensable for the consensus-based stability of southern Mediterranean countries, the 'technical' impossibility of achieving it without adverse reactions in the societies concerned could erase the potential gains in terms of stability.

This dilemma cannot be solved here. It will have to be solved by politicians, whether they like it or not. The aim here is only to clearly identify two political choices. The first one gives priority to free trade and economic liberalization in general; it will not make political liberalization easier and, because of its uncertain economic results, it will only lead to a contingent and uncertain stability based largely on coercion. The second choice takes into consideration not only the partnership's economic components but also its political and social aspects; it can only succeed if it is applied with caution as well as respect and understanding for those who will have to make the adjustment effort. *Tertium non datur* – not even the abandonment of the very idea of the partnership or its functional equivalents of a more multilateral nature.

Translated from French by Valerie Day-Viaud
Translation revised by the editor

Notes

[1] On the origins and development of the 'reformed Mediterranean policy' or the EU's new Mediterranean policy since 1990, see Khader [1994].

[2] Barcelona Declaration [European Commission, 1996], chapter on political partnership.

[3] On the concept of political conditionality and its application, see Sørensen [1993], Tomasevski [1993] and World Bank (International Bank for Reconstruction and Development) [1989].

[4] Article 2 of the accords signed with Tunisia and Morocco in 1995, whose texts may be found in the European Commission documents COM(95)235final of 31 May 1995 and COM(95)740 final of 20 Dec. 1995.

[5] See the association agreements, articles 64–74.

[6] Without establishing any link with the partnership's political objectives, the economic chapter of the Barcelona Declaration is based on free trade and structural adjustment principles.

[7] On the importance of distribution and its relative independence of economic growth, see the critical examination of the present state of research on the subject in Rodrik [1996: 9–41].

[8] The association agreement between the EU and Tunisia allows for variable lengths and starting dates for transitional periods from product to product: see Hoekman and Djankov [1996].

[9] This is the case with thread and textile exports to the EU. See Kheir el-Din and el-Sayed [1996].

[10] On this subject, see the IMF fears reported in *al-Hayat*, 11 Oct. 1996.

[11] *al-Hayat*, 17 Oct. 1996.

[12] For an argument on institutional economics, see Handoussa [1994] and World Bank [1996: 87–97].

[13] See the proceedings of the colloquium organized by the World Bank and published in Corbo, Fischer and Webb [1992], in particular section 7.

[14] The short-term negative effects of privatization programmes on employment are accepted by the representatives of institutions advocating privatization. See, for example, the interview with the IMF representative in Egypt, A. Subramanian, in *al-Ahram*, 11 Oct. 1996.

[15] On this scenario, see Koehler [1995]. For a less pessimistic but cautious assessment, see Diwan [1996].

[16] See Korayem [1994; 1996: for income distribution, see Table 4].

[17] Noshi [1995: 151]. *Egypte/Monde Arabe*, 25 (1996), p.216, gives the most recent official figures.

[18] Koehler [1995: 3]; the studies by Rutherford, Rustrom and Tarr [1993; 1995] are somewhat less pessimistic.

[19] On the Kafr al-Dawwar strike, see Markaz Ibn Khaldun [1995: 56] and Clement [1996: 241–6]. On workers' protest movements in general, see 'Adli Ruman [1996: 156–88] and Pripstein Posusney [1995].

[20] According to the World Bank, the 1993 per capita gross domestic product (GDP) reached US$660 in Egypt and US$300 in India (World Bank [1995], Table 1). The figures are much lower than the threshold postulated by Wade, even if calculated in 1988 prices or in purchasing power parity (PPP). In terms of PPP, the per capita GDP in Egypt in 1991 amounted to US$620 which is equivalent to US$2440. See F. Ibrahim [1995: 12–18].

[21] For a critical assessment of the link between the economic and political markets, see Leca [1990].

[22] For example, the complaints made by the Egyptian labour unions over the drafting of a new labour law. According to the trade unions (and despite their close links to the regime), they are consulted far less than the employers. Another example is the Egyptian-American 'presidential council' which, besides the two presidents, essentially includes businessmen.

[23] Economic liberalization in Syria provides a good illustration of this kind of development. See Bahout, Perthes and Kienle, in Kienle (ed.) [1994].

[24] On this subject, see the study on Morocco by Ben Ali [1995].

[25] As in the definition given by Norton [1995: 7]: 'If democracy as it is known in the West has a home, it is civil society, where a mélange of associations, clubs, guilds, syndicats, federations, unions, parties and groups come together to provide a buffer between state and citizen'. See also Turner [1984]. These definitions of course exclude family structures and those concerned mainly with the production or the sale of goods and services.

[26] A 'civic mind' must therefore complete the trend for independence from the government and the state. See Norton [1995: 11].

[27] Thus, the existence of civil society is not sufficient in itself for the establishment of democracy, although the linkage between the two is obvious [S.E. Ibrahim, 1995b: 29].

[28] These are the only conditions in which civil society can function as a safety-valve for the emergence of a representative regime and for the political enfranchisement of workers in the sense used by Bromley [1994].

References

'Adli Rinnan, H. (1996): 'Al-musharika al-siyassiyya li al-'ummal al-misriyyun', in M. Kamil al Sayyid (ed.), *Hariqat al-ta'addudiyya al-siyasiyya fi Misr: Dirasat fi al-tahawwul alra'smali wa al-musharika al-siyasiyya*, Cairo: Madbuli.

al-Sayyid, M.K. (1995), 'A Civil Society in Egypt', in Norton [1995].

Arab Republic of Egypt (1996): *Egypt: Human Development Report 1996*, Cairo: Institute of National Planning.

Ayubi, N. (1994): *The State and Public Policies in Egypt since Sadat*, Reading: Ithaca Press.

Bahout, J. (1994), 'The Syrian Business Community, its Politics and Prospects', in Kienle (ed.) [1994].

Ben Ali, D. (1995): 'Economic Adjustment and Political Liberalisation', *ERF Working Paper 9509*, Cairo: Economic Research Forum.

Bennani-Chraibi, M. and R. Leveau (1998): 'Maroc 1997: Des élections pour quoi faire?', paper presented at a conference on 'Election Year in the Middle East and North Africa' organized by the Bertelsmann Foundation, Brussels, 18–20 Jan.

Bromley, S. (1994): *Rethinking Middle East Politics*, Cambridge: Polity Press.

Burgat, F. (1988): *L'islamisme au Maghreb: la voix du Sud*, Paris: Karthala.

Clement, F. (1996): 'Libéralisme, restructuration du secteur public et réforme du code du travail', in CEDEJ, *Age Libéral et néo-libéralisme: VIe rencontres franco-égyptiennes de science politique*, Cairo: CEDEJ.

Corbo, V., Fischer, S. and S.B. Webb (eds.) (1992): *Adjustment Lending Revisited: Policies to Restore Growth*, Washington, DC: World Bank.

Cutright, P. and J.A. Wiley (1969): 'Modernization and Political Representation 1927–1966', *Studies in Comparative International Development.*

Dauderstaedt, M. (1996): 'Europa und Nordafrika: Mehr Paranoia als Partnerschaf', *Reihe Eurokolleg*, 36, Bonn: Friedrich-Ebert-Stiftung.

Diwan, I. (1996): 'Globalisation, EU Partnership and Income Distribution in Egypt', paper presented at the colloquium on 'How can Egypt Benefit from its Partnership Agreement with the EU?', Al-Markez al-Masri li la-Dirasat al-Iqtisadiyya, Cairo, 26–27 June.

Egypte/Monde Arabe (1995): 'Round Table on Egyptian Economy and the Prospects for Peace in the Middle East', No.21.

European Commission (1996): *Barcelona Declaration*, Brussels: Direction Générate IB.

Eurostat (1994): *Commerce extérieur: Annuaire statistique, Rétrospective 1958–1993*, Luxembourg: Office des publications officielles des Communauté européennes.

Fandy, M. (1994): 'Egypt's Islamic Group: Regional Revenge?', *Middle East Journal*, 48/4.

Handoussa, H. (1994): 'The Role of the State: The Case of Egypt', *ERF Working Paper 9404*, Cairo: Economic Research Forum.

Henry, C.M. (1996): *The Mediterranean Debt Crescent: Money and Power in Algeria, Egypt, Morocco, Tunisia and Turkey*, Gainesville, FL: University Press of Florida.

Hoekman, B. and S. Djankov (1996), 'Towards a Free Trade Agreement with the European Union: Issues and Policy Options for Egypt', paper presented at the colloquium on 'How can Egypt Benefit from its Partnership Agreement with the EU?', Al-Markez al-Masri li a Dirasat al-Iqtisadiyya, Cairo, 26–27 June.

Huntington, S.P. (1993): 'The Clash of Civilisations?', *Foreign Affairs*, 72/3.

Ibrahim, F. (1995): 'Quelques caractéristiques de l'évolution économique de l'Egypte depuis 1991', *Egypte/Monde Arabe*, 21.

Ibrahim, S.E. (1995a): 'The Changing Face of Islamic Activism', *Civil Society*, 4/41.

Ibrahim, S.E. (1995b): 'Civil Society and the Prospects of Democratisation in the Arab World', in Norton [1995].

Khader, B. (1994): *L'Europe et la Méditerranée: Géopolitique de la proximité*, Paris: L'Harmattan.

Kheir el-Din, H. and H. el-Sayed (1996): 'Potential Impact of Free Trade Agreement with the EU on Egyptian Textile Industry', paper presented at the colloquium on 'How Can Egypt Benefit from its Partnership Agreement with the EU?', Al-Markez al-Masri li la-Dirasat al-Iqtisadiyya, Cairo, 26–27 June.

Kienle, E. (1994): 'The Return of Politics? Scenarios for Syria's *infitah*', in Kienle (ed.) [1994].

Kienle, E. (ed.) (1994): *Contemporary Syria: Liberalization between Cold War and Cold Peace*, London: British Academic Press.

Kienle, E. (1998): 'More than a Response to Islamism: The Political Deliberalisation of Egypt in the 1990s', *Middle East Journal*, 52/2, pp.219–35.

Koehler, M. (1995): 'Die neue Mittelmeerpolitik der Europaeischen Union: Herausforderung fuer die Gemeinsame Aussenund Sicherheitspolitik', Friedrich-Ebert-Stiftung, Bonn, June.

Korayem, K. (1994): *Poverty and Income Distribution in Egypt*, Cairo: Third World Forum.

Korayem, K. (1996): 'Structural Adjustment Policies and the Poor in Egypt', *Papers in Social Science*, 18 (4), Cairo: American University of Cairo Press.

Leca, J. (1990): 'Social Structure and Political Stability: Comparative Evidence from the Algerian, Syrian and Iraqi Cases', in G. Luciani (ed.), *The Arab State*, London: Routledge.

Leca, J. (1994): 'La rationalité de la violence politique', in B. Dupret (ed.), *Le phénomène de la violence politique: Perspectives comparatistes et paradigme égyptien*, Dossiers du CEDEJ, Cairo: Editions du CEDEJ.

Lipset, S.M (1959): 'Some Social Requisites of Democracy: Economic Development and Political Legitimacy', *American Political Science Review*, 53.

Markaz Ibn Khaldun (1995): *Al-Mujtama' al-madani*, al-taqrir al-sanawi 1994, Cairo.

Mosley, P. (1995): 'Analyse des effets de l'ajustement structurel en Afrique sub-saharienne', in R. van der Hoeven and F. van der Kraij (eds.), *L'ajustement structurel et au-delà en Afrique sub-saharienne*, Paris: Presses Universitaires Françaises.

Norton, A.R. (ed.) (1995): *Civil Society in the Middle East*, Leiden: E.J. Brill.

Noshi, A. (1995): 'Principaux résultats des trois premières années du programme de stabilisation et d'ajustement structurel', *Egypte/Monde Arabe*, 21.

O'Donnell, G., Schmitter, P.C. and L. Whitehead (1986): 'Tentative Conclusions about Uncertain Democracies', in O'Donnell, Schmitter and Whitehead (eds.), *Transitions from Authoritarian Rule: Prospects for Democracy*, Baltimore, MD: Johns Hopkins University Press.

Page, J. and J. Underwood (1995): 'Growth, the Maghreb and the European Union: Assessing the Impact of the Free Trade Agreement on Tunisia and Morocco', paper presented at the International Economic Association, Eleventh World Congress, 18–22 Dec, Tunis.

Perthes, V. (1994): 'Stages of Economic and Political Liberalization', in Kienle (ed.) [1994].

Pripstein Posusney, M. (1995): 'The Political Environment of Economic Reform in Egypt vs. Privatisation Revisited', *Amsterdam Middle East Papers, 2*.

Rodrik, D. (1996): 'Understanding Economic Policy Reform', *Journal of Economic Literature*, 34.

Rueschemeyer, D., Stephens, E.H. and J.D. Stephens (1992): *Capitalist Development and Democracy*, Chicago, IL: University of Chicago Press.

Rutherford, T., Rustrom, E. and D. Tarr (1993): 'Morocco's Free Trade Agreement with the European Community: A Quantitative Assessment', *Policy Research Working Paper 1173*, Washington, DC: World Bank.

Rutherford, T., Rustrom, E. and D. Tarr (1995): *The Free Trade Agreement between Tunisia and the European Union*, Washington, DC: World Bank, Policy Research Department.

Salamé, G. (1994): *Democracy without Democrats: The Renewal of Politics in the Muslim World*, London: I.B. Tauris.

Samuelson, P.A. and W.D. Nordhaus (1995): *Economics*, 15th edn., New York: McGraw Hill.

Sørensen, G. (ed.) (1993), *Political Conditionality*, London: Frank Cass.

Tomasevski, K. (1993), *Development Aid and Human Rights Revisited*, London.

Turner, B.S. (1984): 'Orientalism and the Problem of Civil Society in Islam', in A. Hussain, R. Olson and J. Qureishi (eds.), *Orientalism, Islam and Islamists*, Brattleboro: Amana Books.

Wade, R. (1990): *Governing the Market*, Princeton, NJ: Princeton University Press.

World Bank (International Bank for Reconstruction and Development) (1989), *Sub-Saharan Africa: From Crisis to Sustainable Growth, A Long-term Perspective*, Washington, DC.

World Bank (1991): *Egypt: Alleviating Poverty during Structural Adjustment*, Washington, DC.

World Bank (1995): *World Development Report 1995*, Oxford: Oxford University Press.

World Bank (1996): *World Development Report 1996: From Plan to Market*, Washington, DC.

Yeats, A. (1994): *Export Prospects of Middle Eastern Countries: A Post-Uruguay Round Analysis*, Washington, DC: World Bank.

Reshaping the Agenda? The Internal Politics of the Barcelona Process in the Aftermath of September 11

RICHARD GILLESPIE

The Euro-Mediterranean Partnership (EMP) was criticized during its early years, among other things, for an uneven development of the three baskets of the Barcelona Declaration of 1995. While the second basket, outlining plans to develop an economic and financial partnership, was pursued with the greatest vigour, and the first basket, concerning a political and security partnership, became the subject of regular meetings between senior foreign ministry officials, the third basket – devoted to a partnership in social, cultural and human affairs – was pursued only half-heartedly. Why this was so is not firmly established, but probable reasons that led to this relative neglect of the third basket include: the assumption that economic liberalization was the key to the success of the whole Barcelona Process (thus prioritizing the second basket); the top-down approach taken to partnership-building, which lent itself much more easily to the development of the first two baskets; and the EU's relative lack of practical experience with the cultural dimension of partnership envisaged in the third basket. Nevertheless, the third basket did feature in the Barcelona Declaration, both as a result of the genesis of EU approaches to partnership-building across the Mediterranean, which in terms of methodology can be traced back to the Conference on Security and Co-operation in Europe (CSCE), and because of the importance acquired by human rights in the Community's ideological baggage by the 1990s.

In the new millennium, however, the third basket of the EMP agenda has begun to acquire a more substantial script. While there is still a lack of consideration among policy-makers of how the different baskets should interact in order to serve the Barcelona objectives, there is now a more serious attitude to the idea of a partnership in social, cultural and human affairs. This began to emerge well before September 11, as a reflection of the expansion of the EU's own justice and home affairs (JHA) agenda, but it has been reinforced since then as part of general efforts to 'reinvigorate' the EMP and more specific attempts to develop inter-cultural dialogue and co-operation in the wake of the September 11 attacks and the challenge they represent.

This study looks at how the third basket has developed and with what significance for the EMP. It examines a process that is still unfolding and about which only provisional observations may be made at the present time. Nevertheless, some useful indications have been provided by the Action Plan approved at the conference of Euro-Mediterranean foreign ministers in Valencia in April 2002 [Gillespie, 2002] and more generally by the evolution of policy initiatives within the EU during the period of the Spanish Presidency of the European Council (from January to June of 2002).

In the analysis that follows, the first section is devoted to the changing international context within which the agenda of the Barcelona Process has developed, and how this has served as pressure on EMP policy-makers to upgrade the third basket. Subsequent sections focus on the two major policy dimensions that now feature in the third basket of the EMP, namely JHA and cultural dialogue (although the former not so neatly as the latter, given that JHA references are present in both the first and the third baskets whereas cultural dialogue is fully accommodated in the third one). Finally, some tentative conclusions are offered as to the significance of the recent policy initiatives for the Barcelona Process.

The Changing International Context

For the EU in general, changes in the external environment and in relations between Europe and the outside world have been crucial in convincing policy actors of the need to take the third basket more seriously, their earlier ambivalence having been demonstrated by the chequered existence of the EMP's Civil Forum [Jünemann, 2003]. The upgrading of the third basket can be seen as the fruit of three separate processes.

First, since the early 1990s, and especially since the Tampere Council of the European Council in October 1999, with immigration concerns foremost, the EU had been developing its own JHA agenda [Monar, 2001; Huysmans, 2000]. So far as migrants were concerned, the European Union began to differentiate more categorically between immigrants who were legally present in Europe, in whose case the policy objectives aimed at fostering social inclusion, and immigrants who were present without authorization, who in future were to be the subject of a combination of preventive and exclusionary police measures. Although this agenda was pushed largely in the name of new 'security' concerns (and thus bore relation to the first basket of the EMP), the EU's desire to engage Mediterranean Partner countries (MPCs) in collaborative efforts to regulate migratory flows tended to lead the EU to locate the new JHA element primarily in the third basket of the Barcelona Process. Hitherto, whenever the Europeans had raised the question of migration for debate within the EMP, southern partners had responded by expressing grievances over the xenophobia and racism encountered by migrants in the EU, while calling for greater human mobility across frontiers to be achieved through the Partnership. In other words, the response had involved linkage by MPCs of ostensible first basket issues with third basket issues.

Seeking to facilitate a more positive southern response, to 'legitimize' the very idea of security co-operation and to overcome the total blockage of progress on security issues caused by southern objections to the proposed Charter for Peace and Stability (see below), the Europeans eventually came out in favour of locating the emerging migration agenda in the third basket of the EMP. That this was not altogether a coherent strategic decision is perhaps best indicated by the fact that in the Commission communication adopted in February 2002, in preparation for the Valencia Conference, JHA matters were given their own section, separate from the sections of the document devoted to the three traditional baskets of the EMP. Commission officials were aware of North–South divergence on several JHA issues and the highly sensitive nature of this policy domain [Mira Salama, 2002: 16–17].

While the preparations for Valencia were being made (chiefly by the Commission and by a working group based in the Spanish Ministry of Foreign Affairs), the perception of linkages between migration policy, cultural tensions and electoral competition was becoming more prevalent within the EU. By the time of the Valencia Conference, public controversy in Europe over asylum seekers and economic migrants had grown, and had found reflection in a shift to the right in various western European elections. Indeed, the atmosphere of the Valencian ministerial conference was charged by the particularly dramatic success of Jean-Marie Le Pen the previous day, in the first round of the French presidential elections (*Financial Times*, 23 April 2002).

Second, the diversion of activity away from the first basket, as efforts to build a security and political partnership became bogged down against a background of protracted collapse of the Middle East peace process (MEPP), was a factor in itself. The aspiration to build up from modest confidence-building measures to the establishment of collective security arrangements fell victim to a combination of structural and conjunctural impediments: the former constituted by the contrasting national security concerns of the EMP-27 [Attinà, 2002], the latter by the deteriorating situation in the Near East. These obstacles had brought the EMP to a moment of real crisis at the time of the Euro-Mediterranean foreign ministers conference in Marseilles in November 2000 [Spencer, 2001]. Boycotted by the Syrians and Lebanese, earlier hopes of adopting a Charter for Peace and Stability at this meeting were dashed, notwithstanding considerable efforts in Paris to drive the Barcelona Process forward during the French Presidency.

None the less, with the Middle East conflict looming large, the need for confidence- and partnership-building now seemed clearer than ever. Increasing numbers of European policy practitioners came to see the third basket as a context within which to broach security issues that could not, for the moment, be addressed in the first basket, and/or to undertake a more sustained cross-cultural dialogue, involving greater contact and co-operation at the level of civil society. Moreover, a new emphasis on the third basket was seen as a means of maintaining or regaining some momentum within the Process at a time when the overall project was threatened by delays and blockages affecting not only the proposed Charter but also some crucial negotiations on certain EMP association agreements.

Third, there was the increased pressure for the EMP to respond to new security challenges around the Mediterranean, initially in the form of the resurgence of Israeli–Palestinian political violence and then with the advent of a more global yet decentralized and diffuse form of terrorism heralded by the attacks on 11 September 2001 (followed since by alleged Al-Qaeda activity in countries such as Morocco and Tunisia). In terms of policy responses, an unprecedented urgency began to surround European and other efforts to engage in direct forms of collaboration against imme-diate existential threats from terrorism. In addition to new forms of international and European security collaboration, EU policy actors saw the third basket of the EMP as a ready-made framework within which to develop new cultural initiatives in response to the deep alienation and burning sense of injustice, focused on the Middle East, that was seen to lie behind much of the Islamist radicalism and violence. The new interest in the EU undertaking such initiatives was heightened by European concerns at the militaristic fashion in which the Bush Administration had announced its 'war on terrorism' and was beginning to target an 'axis of evil'.

European officials had broadly rejected Huntington's 'clash of civilizations' thesis when it was first articulated. Following September 11, however, it appeared to some to be a rather more plausible scenario, although not an inevitable one – indeed one that could be averted partly by making conscious efforts through the EMP, both in the form of reinforced security co-operation and of enhanced dialogue and cultural co-operation, aimed at challenging cultural stereotypes and gradually constructing a security community in the Mediterranean [Adler and Crawford, 2002]. Whereas, prior to September 11, Spanish thinking on the development of the third basket had revolved around the idea of giving it a JHA content, with an emphasis on migration, after this date there was a considerable shift towards developing the cultural agenda, chiefly through proposals to establish a Euro-Mediterranean Foundation.

Thus there are a number of factors that have influenced European policy practi-tioners in recent years, prompting them to rethink their objectives within the EMP. It was by no means certain, however, that their responses to new challenges would be sufficiently similar to permit a consensus to emerge, substantial enough to reshape the EMP policy agenda in a particular direction. After all, officialdom in the coun-tries involved in the Partnership already possessed nationally differentiated profiles in relation to various aspects of the Barcelona policy agenda (democracy promotion, human rights, agricultural export access for the South). Although the immediate impact of September 11 was to suppress national differences and sensitivities in the search for effective forms of international co-operation against terrorism, there was none the less the possibility that fresh controversies would arise as the third basket was given content, with disagreements arising within the EU as well as between member states and MPCs, or between MPCs themselves.

Nevertheless, the Valencia Conference was able to take new programmatic initia-tives, not simply as a response to impersonal contextual influences but also as a result of the activity of certain policy actors, the constraints inhibiting others and the existence of a spirit of compromise. The Spanish hosts deserve credit in the first place for the very fact that the conference took place, despite some expectations that it would have to be postponed as a result of escalating violence in the Middle East. The event was only one of several activities envisaged by the Spanish Presidency [2002b] as a contribution to the EU's development as a global actor, yet was perceived in Madrid as one of relatively *few* items on the EU policy agenda over which member states were likely to entertain Spanish initiatives. Besides enjoying the prestige derived from having provided the birthplace of the Barcelona Process, Spain was in a rare position to exert influence within the EU: on the one hand, the Aznar–Blair relationship had reached unprecedented heights; on the other hand, the traditionally influential Germany and France were behaving cautiously owing to electoral competition at home.

In relation to the EMP agenda, Spain had also found at least one new European ally for its purposes through converging with the Swedes on the importance of cultural dialogue. Sweden is the only EU member state to have seen the third basket of the EMP as a priority from the very start of the Barcelona Process. It organized joint conferences with Jordan and Egypt on third basket themes in the late 1990s, both held in Stockholm, before establishing the Swedish Institute in Alexandria in October 2000 as a centre for cultural dialogue [Schumacher, 2001]. Although the possibility of an EMP policy initiative during the Swedish Presidency of the EU (during the first six months of 2001) was knocked sideways by the fallout from the Al-Aqsa Intifada, the Swedes eventually found a southern European interlocutor and collaborator in Spain. The two countries worked together on ideas to develop a 'dialogue between cultures and civilizations', which eventually would be adopted as part of the Action Plan during the Spanish Presidency.

An important novelty of the Spanish Presidency lay in its determination to establish a broad North–South consensus around new EMP initiatives. Here, the Spaniards departed from the traditional EU practice of negotiating a European consensus first and then seeking MPC endorsement. Even before the Valencia Action Plan existed in draft form, Spanish diplomats (during the latter months of 2001) made visits to the capitals of the MPCs in an attempt to reconcile the various aims and aspirations of each country. The Spanish claim is that the Valencia Action Plan represents the first EMP document adopted by consensus among all its members [Montobbio, 2002: 17].[1]

The Action Plan eventually presented to the foreign ministers in Valencia was thus one that had already been approved by the EMP at senior official level. The Spaniards themselves contributed to the compromise package by finally back-peddling on one of their own major proposals, that of creating a Euro-Mediterranean Bank, despite the fact that originally this had been envisaged by *Partido Popular* leaders in Madrid (with their characteristic emphasis on the economic aspects of external relations) as their 'big idea' for progress at Valencia. Spain had to be satisfied with an assurance that this proposal would be reconsidered in a year's time. Though the idea was popular among MPCs, some northern member states saw the proposal as ill-conceived and unnecessary. Several European countries sought to establish 'red lines' in advance of Valencia, ruling out – in different cases – approval of any new resources or new institutions, or any policy innovation relating to agriculture, aid or debt. Nevertheless, a degree of compromise emerged with, for example, certain northern member states and Commission officials acceding to Spanish desires to play down the democracy promotion agenda of the Barcelona Process. Consensus at Valencia was assisted too, in a paradoxical way, by the absence of Syria and Lebanon, and by skilful management of discussion on the Middle East conflict [Gillespie, 2002].

The result was sufficient consensus and compromise to secure the adoption of a new framework for co-operation in the third basket, but with very little definition of the specific ways in which either JHA or cultural co-operation might be enhanced. While opening the door to the discussion of enhanced co-operation, the conference provided no guarantee that such co-operation would ensue.

Transferring or Adapting the JHA Agenda?

Developments in the EMP policy agenda must be understood in the first instance in the context of European integration advances, most directly the rapid growth of JHA co-operation from 1999 in response to diverse 'soft' security concerns in Europe. The migration and other JHA concerns registered at the Tampere meeting of the European Council in Autumn 1999 found reflection in the Common Strategy on the Mediterranean adopted by the EU in Santa Maria da Feira in June 2000, a whole section of which was devoted to issues that had received only passing mention in the Barcelona Declaration [European Council, 2000] (*Euromed Report* 10, 20 June 2000). The same document committed the EU to a review of the Barcelona Process, 'with the aim of reinvigorating the Process and making it more action-oriented and results-driven' (*Euromed Report* 10, p.3). Responding to this mandate, in September the Commission produced proposals for 'Reinvigorating the Barcelona Process', aimed at the approaching conference of Euro-Mediterranean foreign ministers in Marseilles. Among these proposals was the idea of developing a regional JHA programme embracing issues such as asylum and refugees, illegal immigration, social inclusion, judicial co-operation and organized crime [European Commission, 2000]. The Marseilles Conference itself called on senior officials to expand their work on both migration and terrorism, but it achieved desperately little in concrete terms owing to the impact of the sharp deterioration in the Middle East conflict (which affected Arab participation) and the preoccupation of the French EU Presidency with the adoption of the – for the moment 'unadoptable' – Charter for Peace and Stability.

From spring 2001, JHA went on to become 'one of the main domains' of EMP activity, seen most clearly in the establishment of regular meetings of JHA senior officials, parallel to the meetings of senior officials on political and security matters [Bicchi, 2002]. The first such meeting was held in Montpelier in June 2001 and began a dialogue in preparation for a regional JHA programme (*Euromed Synopsis* 144, 8 June 2001). The focus on terrorism was sharpened considerably by the events of September 11, yet was to be accompanied, at the EMP foreign ministers' meeting in Brussels early in November, by an emphasis on 'dialogue between cultures and civilizations' and the need to combat racism and xenophobia. Commission information bulletins reporting the event referred to the 'high significance' of the third basket 'in the present international situation' (*Euromed Report* 31, 31 Oct. 2001). Whereas enhanced anti-terrorist co-operation had been the dominant chord in EU-focused post-September 11 deliberations (immediate approval of the European arrest warrant, enhanced intelligence sharing, the listing of terrorist organizations whose assets might be frozen), in the EMP context – with work on the Charter stalled – the emphasis was much more on third basket reinforcement. In practice this meant that existing JHA themes would be imported from the EU and placed alongside the idea of a cultural dialogue, where the immediate priorities were programmes relating to youth, education and the media.

This strategic approach was endorsed in April 2002 at the Valencia Conference, whose agenda was shaped by largely convergent proposals emanating from the European Commission and the Spanish Presidency [European Commission, 2002; Spanish Presidency, 2002a]. A framework document was endorsed at the Conference, anticipating a 'regional cooperation programme in the field of Justice, in combating drugs, organised crime and terrorism as well as cooperation in the treatment of issues relating to the social integration of migrants, migration and movements of persons' ('Presidency Conclusions', *Euromed Report* 42 W, 26 April 2002; *Euromed Report* 44, 29 April 2002). The title itself (which hardly rolls off the tongue) is clearly a product of bargaining between the EU and the MPCs. It implies that the introduction of this new policy dimension may not represent an instance of effective policy transfer by the EU, as originally intended by the Europeans [Bicchi, 2002]; indeed, the title suggests more a process of policy *adaptation* within the asymmetrical multi-lateral context of the EMP. Of course, considerable scepticism is in order here, given the way in which EMP policy content was shaped almost exclusively by the Europeans during the early years of the Barcelona Process, and the relatively modest results of Arab attempts to co-ordinate their input into the policy process. The prac-tical consequences of this programme are not yet clear.

It would seem from the contents of Commission information bulletins that initially there was a greater MPC readiness to expand third basket co-operation in the social and cultural fields than in relation to terrorism. Of course, there has been *ad hoc* anti-terrorist collaboration between EU and MPC interior ministries since the late 1990s, with some suggestion of greater co-ordination since September 11 (notably the *ad hoc* meeting of senior officials and experts on terrorism held in Brussels in late March 2002). But as was seen at the Valencia Conference itself, structured co-operation in this field is prevented by the lack of a common definition of terrorism among the partners with, for instance, the Arab states unwilling to include the activities of militant Palestinian organizations under this heading. A clear sign of the basic lack of consensus in this area was the way in which the Conference, rather lamely, looked primarily to the UN – rather than regional initiatives – for a response to global terrorism (*El País*, 24 April 2002).

Even over migration, where prima facie the foundations exist for North–South co-operation (improved treatment of MPC citizens legally present in the EU in return for MPC collaboration with the EU in combating irregular migration), the outlook is not entirely positive. Despite the much larger resources that the EU now seems ready to invest in a Common Migration Policy (significantly overshadowing its modest investment in CFSP), it remains far from certain that the prerequisites for effective North–South co-operation are present. In recent years, there have been considerable benefits (reduced pressure from unemployment, financial remittances) as well as losses (in human capital) for the MPCs from emigration, and thus few incentives for them to invest their scarce resources in the policing of approach routes to Europe.

Moreover, as one saw shortly before the European Council meeting in Seville in June 2002, the readiness of certain EU member states (Spain, Britain, Germany) to contemplate sanctions against any Third Countries refusing to enter into readmission agreements with the Union (*Financial Times*, 21 June 2002) provokes real concern in countries such as Morocco, which has been in dispute with Spain partly because of this very issue. Even in the domain of migration, where the Barcelona rhetoric about a partnership in 'social, cultural and human affairs' could conceivably be approached through genuine partnership-building efforts, there still appears to be a knee-jerk tendency within the EU to rely upon its economic muscle in order to impose its own agenda on others.

Towards a Cultural Partnership?

Besides heralding future innovations in the field of JHA, the Valencia Conference has done more than any previous conference of EMP foreign ministers to establish a political basis for development of the cultural component of the Barcelona Process. Although there were some steps taken in the first basket (the introduction of defence matters into a reinforced political dialogue; support for the creation of a Euro-Mediterranean Parliamentary Assembly) and in the second (an enhanced European Investment Bank facility for the MPCs; strong support for the Agadir initiative in horizontal sub-regional integration), the dominant theme was provided by the moves to give content to the third basket. The shift of agenda focus between Barcelona IV (Marseilles) and Barcelona V (Valencia) which this represented sought to minimize the negative fallout from the Middle East conflict, despite the further deterioration of the same. It was calculated to bring progress notwithstanding the continuing absence of the Syrian and Lebanese partners from the ministerial gathering – neither of which, in any case, had questioned the document to be approved at Valencia [Montobbio, 2002: 14].

In fact the Valencia Action Plan contains a 'plan within a plan'. All new initiatives approved at Valencia are outlined in the Plan, and within the section devoted to the third basket there is a specific 'Action Plan on Dialogue between Cultures and Civilizations', with particular focuses on youth, education and the media. In this context, the extension of the Tempus programme to the MPCs promises to significantly multiply contacts among EMP universities from 2003. At the same time, the decision to establish a Euro-Mediterranean Foundation could be important in several respects: as an instance of EMP institution-building; through the decision to adopt the principle of 'co-ownership' (between North and South); and through implying a more continuous programme of intellectual, cultural and 'people to people' exchanges than in the past.

However, it is one thing to establish new institutions and programmes and another to make them function in the manner and spirit intended or required. At the time of the Valencia meeting, no consensus had emerged as to how the new Foundation would be structured. This left wide open the question of how or whether 'co-ownership' was to be introduced into the new project in practice, and the issue of the respective roles to be played in the Foundation by states and by civil society.

The degree of commitment of the EU to this project has been called into question by member state responses to a Commission proposal that the Foundation be funded by a €1 million contribution from each of the member states and the Commission, while MPCs would be invited to make voluntary contributions. This was agreed upon in principle at Valencia but, as Chris Patten revealed in a speech shortly afterwards, there was 'some reluctance among the Member States to make the 1m Euro contribution as requested from each of them' (*Euromed Report* 43, 26 April 2002). In fact, it was not simply northern European parsimony and reservations about EMP institutionalization that prevented a rapid implementation of the Foundation project:[2] some countries, including Spain, protested that it was impossible to establish an appropriate budget for the Foundation without clarifying first the structure it would have. While the Spaniards advocated the creation of a substantial new foundation, the Italians preferred a model according to which the new body would be just the centrepiece of a network of foundations, based in Italy.

Thus, while the idea of cultural dialogue was given fresh impetus by the Valencia Conference, its development is surrounded by a number of questions and the innovations introduced at the programmatic level could prove just as contentious as previous initiatives in the first basket. Though one of the reasons for increasing the emphasis on the cultural component has been the belief that there are less obstacles to co-operation in this field than elsewhere, the cultural domain has not been immune to political controversy: witness the campaign by some academics to persuade the EU to suspend funding for Israeli universities in protest over military actions by the Sharon government in Palestinian-controlled areas (*The Guardian*, 27 May 2002); or the way in which cultural dialogue within the EMP thus far has been circumscribed severely by an official exclusion of Islamist currents [Youngs, 2002: 50–51].

Moreover, by introducing JHA as a theme in the third basket, there is the potential for disputes over migration or responses to terrorism to 'spill over' and thwart the attempt to reinforce the cultural dialogue, especially if the European approach to migrants from MPCs continues to emphasize policing rather than welfare and mutual economic interests. The third basket could become an incoherent hotchpotch, and one can imagine circumstances in which southern partners might decide to block constructive projects in the field of cultural dialogue in order to demonstrate dissatisfaction over northern immigration policies.

Consequences for the EMP

What does the mild refashioning of the EMP agenda outlined above signify for the Barcelona Process? If the plans are implemented and the new policy frameworks acquire real content, policy will extend into relatively virgin territory, reflecting new priorities that have emerged or have been reinforced since September 11. It could even be that the emergent JHA agenda may lead to more sophisticated strategic thinking about the EMP as a whole, given the linkage that it implies between the first and third baskets [Bicchi, 2002]. However, experience thus far has demonstrated the difficulty of developing cross-pillar approaches to security issues within the EU context and the inadequacy of existing inter-ministerial co-ordination mechanisms at the national level [Gillespie, 2001]. Moreover, for the moment at least there are few signs of movement around first basket co-operation (as opposed to dialogue). While promising to introduce new forms of co-operation in the field of JHA along with a more sustained and extensive cultural dialogue, the initiatives approved at the Valencia Conference are largely confined to one basket of the Barcelona Process and seem unlikely to do much to 'reinvigorate' the first basket (at least in the short term) or the second.

The significance of several of the plans approved at Valencia will depend on how they are implemented in practice and on the degree of real resonance they prove to have in the South. The degree of commitment of the MCPs to these plans will be a test of the generalized, essentially bilateral,[3] Euro-Med consultations that took place in preparation for the Valencia Conference, through visits conducted by the Presidency, Commission and Council General Secretariat to MPC capitals. Will the apparent consensus around the new initiatives hold up as policy actors get down to the detail of implementation? It is worth noting here that, in the short distance between Valencia (the EMP Conference) and Seville (the European Council meeting held in June 2002), at least one crucial element in European migration policy objectives – readmission agreements – almost came unstuck, when Spain and the UK started to speak of the possibility of sanctions being used against Third Countries that refused to co-operate with EU measures in this area.

Equally, there is scope for the narrow consensus achieved at Valencia to be overwhelmed by the discordant notes that were simply written out of the script of the Conference – that is, the areas of disagreement within the EMP that led to various proposals being dropped before the final version of the Action Plan was produced. Even the limited consensus that existed at the time of Valencia may prove fragile following the US-led war against Iraq, as governments in the Arab world come under pressure from below to distance themselves from the military occupation and the countries involved in it.

Another concern about the development of the third basket must be that it will tend to reinforce the elitist nature of the Barcelona Process. Hitherto, the partnership in social, cultural and human affairs has been seen as the component most amenable to decentralized co-operation and the involvement of civil society. Yet large parts of this basket are now susceptible to being developed in the same top-down manner as the other two, not least because cultural co-operation is mixed in with JHA issues in which security perspectives seem likely to privilege an elitist approach. The fact that the Observatory on Employment and Migration, approved at Valencia as part of the social dimension, is to be established in authoritarian Tunisia, a country where genuine NGOs are simply not tolerated, is hardly very reassuring in this regard. Equally, it may be significant that the Conference on Migration and Social Integration of Emigrants, approved for 2003, is to be based at ministerial level.

In principle, there is still considerable potential in the decision to create the Euro-Mediterranean Foundation (a decentralized body), but it remains unclear whether in practice this entity will be dominated by government institutions or permitted to develop a certain autonomy and become a focus of opportunity and initiative for civil society bodies. While the pre-Valencia Commission document placed emphasis on the Foundation's purpose being to promote intellectual, cultural and 'people to people' exchanges, the final declaration of the IV Meeting of the Euro-Mediterranean Parliamentary Forum, which took place in Bari in June, contended that the main players in the Foundation should be governmental and parliamentary institutions of the 27, plus public and private bodies. Of course, it is important that governments do commit themselves to developing this initiative, but it will surely fail if they are too *dirigiste*.

Even if the new initiatives approved at Valencia prosper, it is worth recalling that a number of other 'reinvigoration' proposals were blocked, rejected or ignored at Valencia. Above all, the ideas that had been floated for political reform and institutional innovation in the Barcelona Process were paid little more than lip-service and then left for future consideration. The far from revolutionary idea of establishing a Euro-Mediterranean Parliamentary Assembly was supported by the foreign ministers, and left for examination by senior officials in conjunction with the parliamentary bodies of the 27 and the European Parliament. Similarly, European Commission ideas to promote 'co-ownership' of the Barcelona Process, such as joint preparation of the Euro-Mediterranean Committee (EMC) agenda [European Commission, 2002: 17], were left by the foreign ministers for further consideration in the future. The outcome was simply a decision to examine ways and means of restructuring the EMC. Of course a huge practical constraint remains in the asymmetrical nature of the EMP and the continuing lack of political integration among southern partners, notwithstanding the existence of the Agadir Process at the economic level.

The modesty of the Valencia innovations is seen when one considers some of the proposals that failed to make it into the Action Plan. The EMP continues to lack a dynamic co-ordinator, Spanish ideas for the introduction of a 'Mr Med', funded by the EU but representing the 27, having been blocked by Chris Patten in the run-up to the conference. Moreover, while the European Parliament welcomed the Commission proposals shortly before the Valencia Conference, it also mentioned issues where it wanted to go further – for instance, through the innovation of annual EMP summits at head of government/state level and the adoption of a special travel visa for business people, academics, researchers, students, journalists and trade unionists involved in Partnership activities (*Euromed Report* 41, 12 April 2002).

Particularly disappointed by the conference outcome was the Euro-Mediterranean Human Rights Network, which had expressed concerns that the new JHA agenda would lead to security priorities overshadowing EMP promotion of the rule of law and human rights [EMHRN, 2002]. The Network saw how the poor performance of many MPCs in relation to their democracy and human rights commitments failed to receive any response under the Spanish Presidency – indeed, Spanish relations with Algeria were reinforced.[4] The Commission had called for the creation of joint working groups with each MPC to focus on these issues, and for greater conditionality to be introduced into MEDA allocations. All that it secured here was a mandate for senior officials 'to study the setting up of a more structured dialogue on this sensitive topic' (Valencia Action Plan, II.3). Also ignored were some of the more challenging proposals generated by an international seminar held in Barcelona during the preparations for the Spanish Presidency: for instance, the idea of using co-operation over migration issues as an opportunity for cultural dialogue, or the proposal to establish a human rights observatory in an MPC [Generalitat de Catalunya, 2001].

It seems doubtful that the decisions taken at Valencia will bring about the kind of decentralized co-operation that is required to avoid a 'monopolisation of the Barcelona Process by governments and elites' [ibid.] and in this respect also reinvigorate the Partnership. At present, the structure of the EMP still provides ample opportunities for defensive partners to veto or water down any proposals that they find unpalatable, leaving progress towards the vision of the future embodied in the Barcelona Declaration of 1995, at best, exceedingly slow. The Valencia Conference has not dramatically altered this reality, but has created some openings whereby 'people to people' contacts could grow, gradually, first and foremost through new forms of cultural exchange.

This will be assisted by the approach adopted in relation to the youth, education and media programmes, which the Spaniards have always insisted must be based on the principle of 'voluntary participation' [Spanish Presidency, 2002a: 17], thus exploiting 'sub-regional' opportunities to overcome or bypass resistance. At least in the context of these programmes, individual countries or small groups of countries will not be able to veto initiatives taken by 'coalitions of the willing' within the EMP, that involve less than the full 27 partners. There has been no decisive shift yet in this direction, however. In its markedly inconclusive 'institutional provisions', the Valencia Action Plan (section V) noted that senior officials would study and put forward proposals leading to the holding of 'like-minded' exercises and meetings.

Thus, the steps forward taken at Valencia remain tentative and partial, and are lacking in overall strategic coherence. A start has been made to the attempt to reinforce the third basket, long seen as crucially important by many academic observers, yet it has been done in a manner that prompts many question marks and risks bringing new contradictions into the Barcelona Process. In the context formed by increased European concerns about migration issues and by the post-September 11 preoccupation with international terrorism, the simultaneous attempt to introduce a regional JHA programme into the EMP could overshadow, and ultimately thwart, the efforts being made towards civilizational rapprochement in the cultural sphere. The likelihood of this happening will be increased if the balanced approach (between security and cultural initiatives) taken by Spanish officials fails to be maintained by subsequent European Council presidencies.[5]

Moreover, in the near future, with the EU grappling with its largest enlargement since its foundation, and with most of the newcomers located in the East, it will be difficult for member states to maintain even the existing limited European consensus *vis-à-vis* the South, let alone integrate the South into the building of a broader consensus surrounding the further development of the Barcelona Process. Thus, realistically it is hard to see the good intentions surrounding the development of 'co-ownership' within the institutional structures of the EMP amounting to very much in practice.

Notes

The author is grateful for perceptive comments by Oliver Schlumberger on an earlier draft and for conversations with Spanish diplomats, especially Euro-Mediterranean ambassador Eudaldo Mirapeix, who played a central role in preparations for the Valencia Conference of April 2002.

[1] While this may be substantially true, the limits to the consensus were reflected in the lack of a common commitment in relation to the search for peace in the Middle East (referred to only in the Presidency Conclusions).

[2] Several northern member states argued that the funding for the new Foundation should be found within the existing MEDA budget.

[3] 'Bilateral' here refers to the EU-15 + individual MPC nature of the consultations. Tunisian efforts to co-ordinate the Arab MPCs also featured in this process, but it would be an exaggeration to suggest that it acquired an inter-regional dimension.

[4] Amidst much talk of enhanced co-operation in the fields of energy and security, and with Hispano-Moroccan relations extremely troubled, Spain and Algeria proceeded to sign a Friendship Treaty in October 2002 (*El País*, 8 Oct. 2002).

[5] At present the sustainability of EMP policy initiatives suffers from the current arrangements surrounding the EU Council Presidency, which rotates between member states on a six-monthly basis. There are some indications, however, that Spain's own diplomatic efforts to promote a dialogue between civilizations has persisted beyond its EU presidency on a more global level. In October 2001, Spanish officials welcomed statements by Iranian President, Mohamed Khatami, during a state visit to Spain, in which he suggested that Iran's 'democratic Islamism' could play a role in dialogue between Islam and the West (*El País*, 31 Oct. 2001). Spain is also among the EU countries that have called for Turkey to be given a target date for entry to the Union.

References

Adler, E. and B. Crawford (2002): 'Constructing a Mediterranean Region: A Cultural Approach', paper presented at a conference on 'The Convergence of Civilizations', Convento de Arrábida, Setúbal, June 2002.

Attinà, F. (2002): 'Comparing Security Building in the Mediterranean Area with Security Partnership Building in other Areas', paper presented at the Conference on 'The Mediterranean in the New Evolving International Order: Domestic, Regional and International Interests', forming part of the First World Congress for Middle Eastern Studies, University of Mainz, 11–13 Sept. 2002.

Bicchi, F. (2002): 'From Security to Economy and Back: Euro-Mediterranean Relations in Perspective', paper presented at a conference on 'The Convergence of Civilizations', Convento de Arrábida, Setúbal, June 2002.

EMHRN (2002): 'Euro-Mediterranean meeting in Valencia. The EMHRN requests that human rights are put on top of the agenda', statement issued 19 April.

European Commission (2000): Communication from the Commission to the Council and the European Parliament, 'Reinvigorating the Barcelona Process', Brussels, 6 Sept., COM(00) 497 final.

European Commission (2002): Communication from the Commission to the Council and the European Parliament, 'To Prepare the Meeting of Euro-Mediterranean Foreign Ministers, Valencia, 22–23 April, 2002', Brussels, 13 Feb., SEC(2002) 159 final.

European Council (2000): 'Common Strategy of the European Council of 19 June 2000 on the Mediterranean Region', 2000/458/CFSP, *Official Journal of the European Communities*, 22 July, L 183/5–10.

Generalitat de Catalunya (2001): Institut Català de la Mediterrània, Euro-Mediterranean Seminar on 'Ideas to Relaunch the Barcelona Process', Barcelona, 30 Nov. and 1 Dec., Policy Paper (Recommendations and Proposals for the Spanish Presidency of the EU).

Gillespie, R. (2001): *Spain and the Western Mediterranean*, Economic and Social Research Council, 'One Europe or Several?' Programme, working paper 37/01, Brighton: University of Sussex.

Gillespie, R. (2002): 'The Valencia Conference: Reinvigorating the Barcelona Process?' *Mediterranean Politics* 7/2.

Huysmans, J. (2000): 'The European Union and the Securitization of Migration', *Journal of Comon Market Studies* 38/5.

Jünemann, A. (2003): 'The Forum Civil EuroMed: Critical Watchdog and Intercultural Mediator', in S. Panebianco (ed.), *A New Euro-Mediterranean Cultural Identity*, London and Portland, OR: Frank Cass (forthcoming).

Mira Salama, C. (2002): 'Madrid and Valencia: Latin America and the Mediterranean in the Spanish Presidency: The Latin American and Mediterranean Agendas Compared', paper presented at the Conference on 'The Spanish Presidency of the European Union', Europe in the World Centre, University of Liverpool, 12 Oct. 2002 (www.liv.ac.uk/ewc).

Monar, J. (2001): 'The Dynamics of Justice and Home Affairs', *Journal of Common Market Studies* 39/4.

Montobbio, M. (2002): 'The Spanish Presidency of the Council of the European Union 2002 and the Relaunching of the Barcelona Process', paper presented at the Conference on 'The Spanish Presidency of the European Union', Europe in the World Centre, University of Liverpool, 12 Oct. 2002 (www.liv.ac.uk/ewc)

Schumacher, T. (2001): 'The Mediterranean as a New Foreign Policy Challenge? Sweden and the Barcelona Process', *Mediterranean Politics* 6/3.

Spanish Presidency (2002a): 'Proyecto de Intervención del Secretario de Estado de Asuntos Exteriores ante la Comisión de Asuntos Exteriores del Parlamento Europeo sobre las prioridades de la Presidencia en el ámbito de las relaciones euromediterráneas (Bruselas, 24 de Enero 2002)', España 2002, Presidency website, www.ue2002.es.

Spanish Presidency (2002b): *Más Europa*, Programa de la Presidencia Española de la Unión Europea, 1–1/30-6-2002. Presidency website, www.ue2002.es.

Spencer, C. (2001): 'The Euro-Mediterranean Partnership: Changing Context in 2000', *Mediterranean Politics* 6/1.

Youngs, R. (2002): 'The European Union and Democracy Promotion in the Mediterranean: A New or Disingenuous Strategy?' in R. Gillespie and R. Youngs (eds.), *The European Union and Democracy Promotion: The Case of North Africa*, London and Portland, OR: Frank Cass.

Regional Community Building and the Transformation of International Relations: The Case of the Euro-Mediterranean Partnership

FRÉDÉRIC VOLPI

This article examines whether there exists a European approach to international relations that makes a difference to the global prospects for political co-operation between western liberal democracies and other regional and cultural groupings. More precisely, it investigates whether, and how, the European Union through its Euro-Mediterranean Partnership (EMP) can create a new type of regional community that increases security and reduces politico-cultural tensions around the Mediterranean. In particular, the article addresses the issue of how far such a 'partnership' constitutes a new approach to community building that shuns old realist approaches to international relations but creates instead in the Mediterranean region a rationale for co-operation grounded in the social constructivist notion of a 'convergence of civilizations'.

Robert Kagan recently suggested that the United States and the European Union were conducting their foreign policies in very different ways because, at heart, they possessed two very different conceptions of world order and of the mechanisms that needed to be put in place to create and/or secure this order [Kagan, 2003]. According to Kagan, the US continues to think in terms of power politics (*Machtpolitik*) because, as the sole remaining superpower and global hegemon, they *can* meaningfully think about world politics in such terms, but also because it may be the case that they *must* think in those terms for their own sake and the sake of the global community. Europeans on the other hand have developed a more 'postmodern' (for want of a better word) notion of power, based on the pseudo-Kantian 'perpetual peace' ideal of the primacy of laws and, implicitly, on a rejection of force in the international system. In the European case, Kagan argues that this situation was principally the result of policy choices that the states *had to* make after the disasters of the Second World War, but also a consequence of the fact that they *could* choose such an option safely within the confines of Western Europe, thanks to US protection.

Kagan's perspective on international politics turns on its head another relatively fashionable view of world politics based on cultural-ideological oppositions, the

Huntingtonian suggestion that the relationship between western democracies and non-western polities (especially Muslim polities) are principally defined by 'civilizational' oppositions – and particularly the clash between Islam/Islamism and western liberalism [Huntington, 1996]. From Kagan's perspective, far more than an inter-civilizational opposition, it is an intra-civilizational difference within the 'West' that is relevant for (re)shaping the international system. But is there a 'European way' that really makes a difference to the global prospects for political and cultural dialogue between western liberal democracies and other regional and cultural groupings?

On this issue, Kagan makes much of the lack of popular enthusiasm in European countries for direct military action and regime change in the case of the US-led interventions in Afghanistan and in Iraq. He points out that although the European governments and the US administration may have shared the same long-term views on the future of those countries, they disagreed on the means that could legitimately be used to secure these objectives. (Typically, Europeans stressed the inconsistency of the notion that an ad hoc use of force by the US was the best way to establish a more law-abiding international community.) But how far has the EU itself being able to practise what it preaches (to the US and the rest of the world)? John Ikenberry criticizes Kagan for ignoring 'the fact that the United Kingdom and France retain great-power identities and a willingness to use military force' [Ikenberry, 2003]. Yet, might it not be the case that the international behaviour of these two former great powers is increasingly becoming anachronistic and unfashionable in contemporary European politics? Is the EU approach towards the Muslim world increasingly moulding a new type of international political order?

What follows is an analysis of the political practices of the European Union (and EU member states) that are developed in Europe's own backyard: the Mediterranean region, and particularly towards the states on the southern shores of the Mediterranean. In the following section, I sketch the main tenets of the EU programme designed to establish an integrated regional community around the Mediterranean: the Euro-Mediterranean Partnership (EMP). After that, I address the issue of how far this 'partnership' constitutes a 'new' approach to community building that shuns traditional *Machtpolitik* approaches to international relations. Finally, I examine some of the main drawbacks to the EMP approach to regional integration and the unintended consequences of this process for politico-cultural conflict in the region.

The Euro-Mediterranean Partnership (EMP)

The EMP was officially launched at the Euro-Mediterranean conference held in Barcelona in 1995 – hence, it is also known as the Barcelona process [European Union, 1995]. It was designed as a standard framework for agreements between the European Union member states and the Mediterranean 'partner countries' – Morocco, Algeria, Tunisia, Egypt, Israel, Jordan, the Palestinian Authority, Lebanon, Syria, Turkey, Cyprus and Malta. (Libya only has an 'observer' status so far, but the recent lifting of international sanctions on the country may pave the way for greater participation in the EMP in the near future). Bilateral association agreements between individual 'partner countries' and the EU have been negotiated under this framework ever since. Morocco, Tunisia, Israel and the Palestinian Authority became the first signatories of these agreements. Egypt concluded its bilateral negotiations in 1999, Algeria in 2001, Lebanon in 2002 and Syria is still negotiating at the time of writing. For the remaining countries, the EMP has been superseded already by other agreements, such as the customs union signed between Turkey and the EU of 1996, and the accession treaty (for EU membership) for Malta and Cyprus.

Essentially, the EMP is an ambitious regional co-operation programme covering all aspects of the social, economic and political relations between the EU and the states on the southern shores of the Mediterranean. In practice, this partnership is organized into three 'pillars' or 'baskets' covering (i) political and security partnership, (ii) economic and financial partnership and (iii) partnership in social, cultural and human affairs. In this framework, the political and security partnership aims at 'establishing a common area of peace and stability', the economic and financial partnership is designed for 'creating an area of shared prosperity', whilst the social and cultural partnership is the means of 'developing human resources, promoting understanding between cultures and exchanges between civil societies' [European Union, 1995].

At one level the EMP can be conceived merely as a technical attempt at rationalizing the various pre-existing treaties and agreements – particularly in the economic and financial domains – signed between the EU and countries on the southern shores of the Mediterranean, as well as providing a unified framework of reference for new agreements. (This has generally been the official European position, which only partially reflects the fact that there are ongoing disagreements amongst both politicians and analysts about the coherence of the various components of the programme).[1] It brings together under a single roof, in a manageable institutional agenda, preexisting security initiatives both large and small – for example, the Italo-Spanish proposal for a Conference on Security and Co-operation in the Mediterranean (1990), the French-inspired Western Mediterranean Security Forum (1991, revived in 2001) and the Mediterranean Dialogue programme (1994). However, besides this technical exercise, the EMP can also be seen as a vehicle for a new kind of regional community building because it sets forth an ambitious set of political and cultural objectives. In particular, the proposition to 'develop the rule of law and democracy' in the 'partner countries', and the declaration that this partnership will 'encourage actions of support for democratic institutions and for the strengthening of the rule of law and civil society' [European Union, 1995], outline a course of actions that could directly undermine the political systems of most North African and Middle Eastern countries and introduce a new model for politics in the region.

In the case of the EMP, however, as so often with EU programmes and policies, the devil is in the detail. Despite giving political, security, economic and cultural aspects the same official recognition, the EU has provided varying amounts of support for the different programmes of the EMP, and particularly funding through the partnership's financial protocol (MEDA). For example, Richard Youngs notes that 'funds allocated for democracy assistance over the latter half of the 1990s amounted to less than 0.5 per cent of all aid in the region. Over 200 times more money was given under the main MEDA budget for assisting the process of economic restructuring' [Youngs, 2002]. Indeed, during this period, under this grand EMP scheme, democratic assistance efforts in the Mediterranean region only amounted to 14 per cent of the Commission's overall democratic assistance budget, which was less than the assistance provided to less strategically located regions – such as Latin America, which received 17 per cent of these funds. Furthermore, in 2001, the democracy promotion fund of the EMP was disbanded as a distinct regional programme and merged into the overall democracy promotion programme of the Commission. These issues notwithstanding, at the ministerial conference of Valencia in 2002 the EMP promoters in the EU – the Commission and the Parliament – boldly stated their ambition to increase their support for democratic reforms and the defence of human rights in the region by proposing to link a proportion of the MEDA funds to such political conditionality from 2005 onwards [Commission of the European Communities, 2003a].

Regarding the exchanges in the field of culture and human affairs, the EMP programme can be described at best as rather tame. First, the EU has been reluctant to engage directly with civil society associations engaged in political activities, including most Islamic associations. Since the Islamic associations constitute the backbone of any non-governmental and 'civil society'-type activities in the Middle East and North Africa [Volpi, 2003], it is difficult to conceive how the cultural and human affairs component of the EMP programme could ever have much of an impact. Secondly, even when the partnership involves civil society organizations in these countries, it is generally the case, as Annette Jünemann points out, that the powers that be in the region are quite capable of setting up their own pro-govern-mental 'civil society' associations and NGOs (the so-called 'GONGOs') to siphon off these EU funds [Jünemann, 2002]. In this situation, considering the reduced amount of attention given so far to the political (read: democracy promotion) and cultural (read: Islamic/liberal social dialogue) elements, it may be tempting to describe the EMP as nothing more than a glorified trade agreement. Yet, as Peter Burnell emphasizes, some social outcomes simply cannot be imposed from the outside by a calculated utilization of aid-linked political conditionality; and in these cases the more economistic and apparently value-neutral incentives provided by the EU may have a greater impact on the domestic situation of these countries than an immediate cost-benefit analysis can reveal [Burnell, 2003].

Although most European efforts since the launch of the EMP have been spent on crafting economic and financial agreements, the incremental impact of the partner-ship on the region remains difficult to estimate even in such 'narrow' economic terms [Philippart, 2003]. The stated ambitions of the economic programme of the EMP were to introduce liberalization in the countries of the South, to facilitate North–South exchanges and to promote development. Unsurprisingly, therefore, the bulk of the MEDA funds primarily went to financing public infrastructure, public administration reform, public sector reform and social development projects. This effort, however, does not appear to have significantly affected the levels of foreign direct investment (FDI) and the social and economic development indicators in those countries, except in the hydrocarbons sector [Dillman, 2002]. In particular, it is clear that private investors from the EU remain reluctant to invest significant amounts of money in the countries of the Middle East and North Africa, principally because of the inherent instability of these domestic economies, which are controlled (albeit indirectly) by a state oligarchy. Bradford Dillman notes that in these polities,

> state elites have accessed resources from the international economy to implement partial economic reform that sustain their distributional coalitions and thereby inhibit far reaching political reform [. . .] By preserving their states as the necessary intermediary between international and domestic economic actors, they have been able to construct and reshape patronage networks in such a manner as to maintain, if not reinforce, their own economic and political power [Dillman, 2002].[2]

Thus it appears that the resources made available by the EMP to the states on the southern shores of the Mediterranean have the potential to reinforce the existing political and economic status quo.[3]

In this context, how meaningful is it to present the EMP as a process that brings something qualitatively and quantitatively new to the ideal and practice of governance and institutional reform? Something which, if used competently, could help to avoid an entrenchment in the Mediterranean region of the kind of politico-cultural quagmires that we witnessed recently in countries like Iraq and Afghanistan. Despite its inadequacies, one could argue that at the very least the EMP has succeeded in maintaining a working regional institutional framework [Philippart, 2003]. But can we go further and argue with commentators like Emanuel Adler and Beverly Crawford that this partnership can be viewed as 'the corollary of the step-by-step creation of the EU on the rubble of World War II' [Adler and Crawford, 2002)].[4]

Realism and Social Constructivism in the EMP

To assess whether a balance-of-power approach to regional integration or clash-of-civilizations views of international relations across the Mediterranean are being superseded by a constructivist or 'postmodern' approach to power, it is important to look at how 'realists' and 'constructivists' explain the successes and failures of the EMP [e.g. Attina, 2003]. Evidently, these two approaches to international relations are not mutually exclusive, but because they emphasize different types of cost-benefit structure and rationale, it is helpful to treat them as two analytically distinct perspectives on political order.

The Realist Interpretation

Up to the end of the Cold War, there can be no doubt that most of the dealings across the Mediterranean were built on a solid realpolitik basis, albeit in the context of a backwater. North African and Middle Eastern countries played the US and its European allies off against the Soviet bloc for their own benefit; and the 'West' and the communist bloc rewarded them according to these countries' strategic value on the regional stage [Richards and Waterbury, 1990]. This approach was reassessed at the end of the Cold War, though for a while regional players appeared to be unsure of what ought to be the basis of their relations, or whether there was a distinct Mediterranean community that warranted specific regional policies [Calleya, 1997]. The idea to create the EMP surfaced as early as 1989, but it was not until 1992–93 that EU member states began to make concrete plans for its implementation, in the face of rapid and unexpected political transformations in North Africa (collapse of the Algerian democratic transition) and in the Middle East (signing of the Oslo agreement between Israel and Palestine). This renewed European interest was accompanied by new security concerns over the region in the US and the launching of the North Atlantic Treaty Organization's (NATO's) Mediterranean Initiative in 1994 [Larrabee et al., 1998].

The beginning of the civil conflict in Algeria in 1992, and the flow of refugees that reached Europe as a result, quickly led the southern members of the European Union to propose joint European initiatives to tackle the security and socio-economic challenges that erupted on the southern flank of the EU. From a security perspective, therefore, the Euro-Mediterranean Partnership retained the realpolitik outlook that had prevailed during the Cold War – except that this time competing against the US was becoming a predominant consideration for some members, such as France [Petras and Morley, 2000]. In this post-Cold War context, communist takeovers were no longer on the cards but Islamist challenges were to be taken very seriously [Fuller, 1996; Willis, 1996]. Furthermore, if direct military threats were thought to be near immaterial in the short term, the EU increasingly considered illegal trafficking, migration and terrorism as extremely serious problems. Indeed, Javier Solana, then secretary-general of NATO, declared in 1997 that 'most security challenges in the Mediterranean arise from worsening socio-economic conditions and fragmentation, not from military risks' [quoted in Pugh, 2001: 7].[5]

From this realist perspective, the framework of the EMP can be presented in a relatively coherent, albeit restricted manner. (I must stress that the realist sketch that I provide here only serves to illustrate an ideal-type realist response that one could invoke in order to rationalize the behaviour of the EU in specific instances. I do not assume that, on its own, such a crude realist perspective does allow us to understand and explain EU policies in their entirety or invariably). The assessment of the EU would be that stable regimes running their national economy efficiently in the Middle East and North Africa provide the best means of obtaining a well-policed zone of regional security and prosperity. Therefore, the partnership underscores the status quo in so far as it strengthens, or at least does not undermine, the regional interests of the EU. The case of EU–Algerian relations could be cited as a good illustration of this approach. In this context, MEDA funds were provided to the military-backed Algerian regime despite the latter's flagrant violation of the democratic and human rights clauses of the EMP agreement. (Only during the period 1997–99 did the EU briefly stop providing MEDA funds due to blatant election-rigging in the country, but funding resumed after the 1999 election despite further irregularities on a similar scale). This state of affairs led some commentators to suggest that withdrawing funding was not directly connected to democracy promotion, but rather part of an elaborate plot to extract more economic concessions from the Algerian regime at a time when it was negotiating the terms of a bilateral trade agreement with the EU [Roberts, 2003]. From this perspective, political and security challenges are directly linked to socio-economic issues, and by improving the socio-economic conditions of the countries on the southern shores of the Mediterranean the EMP directly contributes to resolving whatever security problems there may be.[6] As French prime minister Juppé explained to the French Parliament at the height of the Algerian civil conflict, 'under-development provides a fertile terrain for the growth of pernicious ideologies' [quoted in Césari, 1994–95: 179]. Unsurprisingly, therefore, financial support for the incumbent military regime in Algeria could be perceived as the best way to resolve the crisis.

If we take the view that these dealings with Algeria encapsulate the realpolitik rationale of EU actions in the region, there is little to be said in favour of the constructivists' suggestion that this partnership across the Mediterranean may create a new type of international order. In the aforementioned realist scheme, political and economic development in the 'South' is only encouraged in so far as it props up economic and security indicators in Europe. It is not promoted for the sake of individual countries in the Middle East and North Africa, nor for the sake of a cohesive regional community. The Mediterranean partnership is not therefore a stepping stone to full EU membership or the beginning of a new regional community of the same standing as the EU. It is very much a process and an ideal *subservient* to the process of community building in Europe. Even though some countries like Turkey, Cyprus or Malta may be able to upgrade from one type of membership to another, the remaining polities are simply excluded from this more complex community-building process because of their geographical location. (When Morocco asked to be considered as a potential EU member, the EU flatly rejected this request on the grounds that Morocco was not a European country).

I must emphasize that this rather crude description of realism and national interest points to an 'ideal type' realist response that is unlikely to exist in such an unmitigated form in practice, or for very long. However, for this realist rationale to shape regional co-operation it is enough that at least one of the participants perceives (or chooses to present) this relationship in those terms. Thus, if such realist views actually underpin, or are perceived to underpin, the EMP it is unsurprising that the construction of a regional partnership should lead to conflict with, and within, the southern 'partner countries'. In this context, cultural oppositions to regional institution building can be presented merely as a rephrasing of national interests. Support for, or rejection of, the EMP programmes by the governments and societies of these North African and Middle Eastern countries is therefore dictated principally by domestic political concerns and calculations. No one 'really' believes in the construction of an EU-like community across the Mediterranean, but everyone will be willing to engage with this institutional framework if it provides them with some tactical advantages over their domestic opponents. From this (purposely stark) realist perspective, therefore, whatever the EMP impact on culturally-phrased political oppositions around the Mediterranean might concretely be/become, its rationale ought to be conceived and measured in terms of the particular interests of the EU and of its 'partner countries'; not in terms of an implicit regional community (and the greater good that it represents).

The Social Constructivist Turn

Some commentators like Emanuel Adler and Beverly Crawford insist that despite its initial realist rationale, the EMP can lay the foundations for a far-reaching transformation of the Mediterranean region based on the production of new norms, values and practices, which have the potential to generate a 'convergence of civilizations' [Adler and Crawford, 2002].[7] They argue that even though the EMP was born out of instrumental calculation by the EU, and even though the creation of an EU-like security community is not the explicit aim of the EMP, this process may eventually transform the Mediterranean region into such a community because the policy makers involved in this process are duplicating the mechanisms that were used to create the EU and the Organization for Security and Co-operation in Europe (OSCE). Adler and Crawford point out that because this process has been 'framed around pluralistic security community processes, institutions, and practices [. . .] security community building already has consciously or unconsciously become part of Mediterranean integration practice' [Adler and Crawford, 2002: 14–15].

The proposition that the norms and principles of the EU will slowly colonize neighbouring institutional frameworks via the implementation of the EMP agreements is an interesting one – even though there may be an odd Hegelian 'history-working-behind-the-backs-of-men' flavour to this argument. In this kind of social constructivist approach, which Adler has been developing for quite some time now, one expects to see a slow – and even unexpected at times – change in the identity and interests of the community members [e.g. Adler, 1997a; 1997b; Adler and Barnett, 1998]. These changes of perspective, in their turn, become institutionalized in the practices of the community. In the present situation, the process that Adler and Crawford describe would involve firstly the creation of a Mediterranean narrative based on 'shared normative and epistemic understandings and meanings about political, economic, and social life, for example, about social order, the rule of law, human rights, social and political justice, peace, and security' [Adler and Crawford, 2002: 25]. This shared narrative would then provide the infrastructure for actual practices, policies and institutions of a truly regional character. From this security community angle, therefore, the process of institutionalization would be largely antithetical to the balance-of-power mechanisms that underpin the above-mentioned realist model of international relations [Adler and Barnett, 1998]. Obviously, there may be some serious obstacle to this process – in particular regional confrontations such as the Israeli–Palestinian conflict can cause serious problems – and some of the results obtained in a specifically European context may not be replicated elsewhere. But these practical difficulties need not pose a fundamental threat to the long-term development of a meaningful security community and regional identity [Adler, 2001].

How well does such a social constructivist approach reflect contemporary transformations in the Mediterranean region? In practice, it is difficult to see any real progress being made on the discursive front, let alone at the institutional level. Of course, the construction of a regional narrative, of regional institutional practices and of a security community is necessarily a slow, long-term process and it might be unfair to discard these propositions on the grounds that there is little tangible evidence of success thus far. Many commentators recognize that the EMP has had a sluggish start – perhaps even a false start – because it focused too much on form and procedure and too little on content [Gillespie and Whitehead, 2002; Joffé, 2000]. But lack of political commitments and tangible results notwithstanding, one may ask whether this process of construction of an all-encompassing community is entirely satisfactory from a theoretical perspective.

One of the main conceptual stumbling blocks of these constructivist schemes (and other similar deliberative models) is the description of the relationship between the causal relevance of new norms and identities, on the one hand, and the rationale for the acquisition of these very norms and identities.[8] Implicitly or explicitly, their fallback position is to establish a connection between the 'truth' of the norms and values proposed – and their associated practices – and the capability of these concepts to spread to other individuals and communities. In other words, by operating within a Habermasian framework, it can be argued that because people recognize the same 'truth', after deliberation they may come to accept it. Thus, Adler and Crawford indicate that 'the potential of social communication to change identities, promote trust, and help change interests in the direction of security and peace, relies on social communications' effect on people's practices' [Adler and Crawford, 2002: 6].

In practice, many proponents of such constructivist approaches to international/ regional relations tend to say that the diffusion of norms, values, practices and insti-tutions is principally one way – from well-established liberal democracies in the 'North' towards countries of the developing world in the 'South'. (There is of course the theoretical possibility that the 'South' can help the 'North' to develop better social, political and economic ideas and practices, but in the everyday running of contemporary world affairs, one can witness very few clear-cut instances of this process happening thus far). Thus, in the Mediterranean context, Adler and Crawford assert that 'the identity that the theory of pluralistic security communities predicts as a key ingredient in "region-building" is distinctly derived from Western Enlightenment principles and values. It depends not only on shared norms that create a civil and tolerant culture, but also on institutions that embody those norms with the backing of materially powerful states' [Adler and Crawford, 2002: 23].

Whilst there can be few doubts that powerful players on the international stage could impose their institutional arrangements, it is far less evident that, new institu-tional frameworks notwithstanding, a liberal-democratic ethos should pervade and underpin this process of (international/regional) community building. Any sugges-tion that a civil society and civil beliefs derived from the Enlightenment are neces-sary components of region-building rests on very flimsy epistemic foundations. From an epistemological perspective, the current dominance of a liberal world-view in politics and economics may be recognized pragmatically as a 'matter of fact', but one ought not to equate this visible dominance to proof that liberal norms and prac-tices have therefore more solid epistemic foundations or are closer to any kind of 'truth' than other world-views [Rorty, 1998].[9] (And it seems to me that Islamist ideologues, should they choose to do so, could devise a Mediterranean community-building rationale based on Islamic principles and practices – thereby Islamicizing Liberalism instead of liberalizing Islamism [Volpi, 2002; Bielefeldt, 2000]. Indeed, one could even argue that since Muslim communities are growing apace inside European democracies it might be easier to create a civilizational convergence by Islamicizing the North instead of liberalizing the South.)

In other words, there is no compelling theoretical reason to believe that people all around the world should 'logically' come to similar views should they open channels of communication with the liberal world, let alone construct a regional community based on this liberal model. This does not mean that a cohesive Mediterranean community will never be created; it simply means that this constructivist project is far more open-ended than we had thought [e.g. Rumelili, 2003]. Obviously, once one takes a more sceptical approach to the alleged epistemic supremacy of the liberal democratic discourse, it becomes more difficult to unambiguously rate the success or failure of the process of replication of its institutions and practices. Agents may build similar institutions and agree on practising the same practice for very different reasons indeed; and with the view of achieving very different, and even antagonistic objectives.

The EMP and the Sources of Politico-cultural Conflict in the Mediterranean

There are at least three main problems associated with the formation of a more cohesive Mediterranean community via the EMP programmes. First, there are important issues (and conflicts of interest) that remain primarily conceived in terms of national interest – for example, migration – and that generate mutually negative perceptions of the 'other', on both shores of the Mediterranean. Second, the liberal promoters of this regional community themselves face a number of contradictions in their political practices, as they seek to advance their liberal ideals whilst fighting off the dangers of terrorism in a sometimes less than liberal fashion [Amnesty International, 2000]. Third, even where the EMP has the opportunity to push forward its ambitious regional agenda, its institutional model is undermined by the poor practices deployed on its behalf. Let me develop these points one by one, and highlight their cumulative impact on regional politics.

First, an issue such as migration control has been at the heart of the EMP from the very start of the process. For domestic reasons, the EU member states, and especially southern members like Spain, France or Italy, have had to politicize the issue of the migrant workers from the countries of North Africa and the Middle East [López García and Hernando de Larramendi, 2002; Pugh, 2001]. In practice, whilst the EU as a whole is keen to have an influx of educated and trained workers from these countries, most member states are unwilling to receive unskilled job seekers, who are widely portrayed as a drain on the welfare system. (In effect, some countries also need an unskilled labour force for their primary sector, but there remains cultural and political opposition, particularly on the far right, to having migrants from the Middle East or North Africa). However, on the southern shores of the Mediterranean, countries face similar problems in coping with large numbers of unskilled job seekers, as well as being unable to retain their most qualified workers who join the brain drain. In a nutshell, across the region all the parties to the EMP want to acquire and/or retain employable qualified workers, whilst none of them wish to welcome and/or keep untrained job seekers, all for the sake of their national economy. Hence, the EU repeatedly encourages its southern 'partner countries' to adopt new border control agreements, and provides them with funds for policing borders and for local development initiatives [Youngs, 2003]. However, as Abdelaziz Testas points out, whilst North African and Middle Eastern countries formally agreed to the terms of the EMP and receive funds to this effect, they have tended to respond to these EU initiatives on migration by wilfully (though not explicitly) failing to implement the required reforms [Testas, 2001].

Because the southern partners of the EU estimate that migration is crucial to ease the pressure on their domestic labour markets and generate cash remittances, they have a strong incentive to play the 'inefficiency card' in this domain. Testas concludes that they will continue to 'find it unattractive to co-operate with their EU partners over migration as long as they expect significant benefits to be reaped from it' [Testas, 2001: 68].[10] Thus, on this (perceived) critical matter, the EMP appears to have little to offer to the formation of a regional community because the participants appear to be unable to conceive their relationships in non-exclusionary terms. One may perhaps see a glimmer of hope in the introduction of the 'Wider Europe' frame-work by the European Commission in 2003. This new programme is designed to facilitate the movement of goods and persons between the EU and neighbouring non-EU countries (east and south). The Commission indicates that 'the EU is currently looking at ways of facilitating the crossing of external borders for bona fide third-country nationals living in the border areas that have legitimate and valid grounds for regularly crossing the border and do not pose any security threat' [Commission of the European Communities, 2003b]. It might therefore indicate the beginning of a change in attitudes towards migration. At the same time, however, it makes (or re-establishes) a direct link between migration and security risks. Hence it may merely be a rephrasing of this exclusionary mindset, not on economic grounds (rich versus poor) but on security grounds (secure versus insecure).

Second, the promotion of a regional security community has been problematic for the EMP process principally because it remains unclear, even for its European promoters, whether liberal democratic ideals ought to be advocated across the board, or whether some issues such as security ought to be insulated from the rest of the debate [Youngs, 2003]. In the post-9/11 context, the renewed concerns not only with state security but also with the securitization of society are often at odds with the earlier EU discourse on liberalization and democratization. The discourse on democ-ratization has not been waived altogether as western democracies still perceive the spread of liberal democracy not only as a good in itself for the recipient countries, but also as the best long-term opportunity to reduce international conflict.[11] In the post-9/11 order, however, these calls for political reform in North African and Middle Eastern countries have been supplemented by new demands for tighter control of the terrorist elements that may actually or potentially exist in these polities. Critically, however, there is a tension between democratizing and liberalizing political activities on the one hand, and carefully monitoring the activities of potentially subversive social and political movements, on the other. Indeed, as Richard Gillespie points out, 'in the context formed by increased European concerns about migration issues and by the post-September 11 preoccupation with international terrorism, the simultaneous attempt to introduce a regional JHA [Justice and Home Affairs] programme into the EMP could overshadow, and ultimately thwart, the efforts being made towards civilizational rapprochement in the cultural sphere' [Gillespie, 2003: 34].

It is a well-known conundrum of liberalism that there is a loophole in the theory that allows the powers that be to justify in principle the imposition of restrictions on civil and political liberties today if this is needed in order to secure them for future generations – and challenges to state security point to a clearly defined political good that must be secured in order to allow future citizens to enjoy these liberal freedoms. The substance of the message that is coming out of both the executive and legislative branches of the governments in Europe (and the US) in the wake of 9/11 is that the new powers given to security agencies to tackle terrorism, as well as the new security-linked decrees and legislation, temporarily impinge on some civil liberties with a view to protecting other more important civil and political liberties that are under lethal threat from terrorism. Allegedly, the political leaders making this argument have the most benign intentions. But the purportedly excellent intentions of these rulers notwithstanding, the implementation of these policies is bound to be problematic, firstly because of the ad hoc nature of the decision-making process invoked and secondly because of the nature of the political commodity involved – *trust* [Warren, 1999; Gambetta, 1988].

At the regional level, whatever kind of security community one is trying to create in the Mediterranean on the basis of these shared liberal democratic values and practices, policy makers generally accept the idea that one might have to turn to other, non-liberal democratic means that are more expedient in the case of issues like national security.[12] Unsurprisingly, North African and Middle Eastern regimes have jumped on this bandwagon and carefully cordoned off large areas of political activities on grounds of national security. As Daniel Brumberg points out, this new emphasis on security in the region generally means an entrenchment of 'liberalised autocracies' [Brumberg, 2002]. (Again, the case of Algeria, from the 1992 military coup to the conclusion of the EMP bilateral agreement negotiations in 2001, is a dramatic illustration of this scenario [Volpi, 2003; Roberts, 2003]). Ultimately, these policies underpin the incremental entrenchment of two largely incompatible political rationales – one of greater liberalization, the other of greater autocratic power accumulation – at the heart of Middle Eastern and North African polities, and are setting the stage for a future confrontation across the Mediterranean.

Third and finally, the EMP has been unable to function satisfactorily as a community-building mechanism because of the tension that exists between its declarative content and its performative impact.[13] Whatever EU officials may declare about the positive relationship between economic reforms, growth and political liberalization, their policies can be perceived not only as failing to have a significant impact on the socio-cultural, economic and political situation of the southern Mediterranean region, but also as entrenching existing inequalities. It is commonly argued by governmental and civil society agents that the EU has been taking advantage of its dominant economic position to set the terms of the EMP with its 'partner' countries in the Middle East and North Africa [El-Sayed Selim, 1999]. The issue of how far this description is accurate ought not to detract our attention from the fact that whatever kind of regional community the EMP is trying to create in the Mediterranean, the position of strength of the EU in the economic field and the way it uses this power to promote its economic, socio-cultural and political views will set the tone for the kind of international behaviour that is deemed acceptable and appropriate in the region. In particular, if one considers seriously the implications of a social constructivist perspective and not merely mechanically reiterates the value of a liberal vision for the region, one could easily identify a second order discourse for the EMP, expressed in the idiom of unilateral securitization, financial orthodoxy, cultural ascendancy and technocratic decision-making. This perfomative discourse not only undermines the declarative content of the EMP vis-à-vis liberalization and democratization, but also lays the ground for an alternative regional political ethos. It produces learning outcomes that reinforce the autocratic tendencies of the leaders and citizens of the countries of the southern shores of the Mediterranean.

Conclusion

Can the European Union create, through its Euro-Mediterranean Partnership, a new kind of regional community that increases security and reduces politico-cultural conflict in the Middle East and North Africa? That many European policy makers view the rationale for this North–South co-operation in the Mediterranean region in terms of an idealized social constructivist approach to global political change is made clear by the ambitious plans revealed in a series of documents from the Barcelona Declaration (1995) to the Common Strategy on the Mediterranean (2000) and finally to the Wider Europe framework (2003). In practice, however, it could be argued that the present outcomes of the EMP initiative appear to differ little from the results obtained by countries using a more traditional ('realist') approach to international relations – for example, the Unites States in Iraq and Libya. There are at least three main reasons for this state of affairs.

Firstly, there is the fact that crucial regional issues, such as migration, remain primarily viewed in terms of national interest, and national governments (and parts of civil society) tend to be unwilling to recast the problem in a truly regional perspective. Secondly, under the post-9/11 order particularly, there are obvious tensions between the long-term strategic aims of the EU engagement with its Mediterranean partners and its tactical security choices. (On the one hand, the EU is attempting to strengthen existing illiberal state institutions in North African and Middle Eastern countries in order to gain more effective co-operation on security/anti-terrorist policies; on the other hand, it is keen to promote power-sharing and good governance in countries that function essentially on a non-democratic basis). Lastly, the various national, sub-national and supranational institutions involved in the EMP programme are often unable to address the challenges of multi-layered transnational governance in a coherent way. In particular, the EMP finds it extremely difficult to promote the 'right' kind of political ethos and the EU partners are left to interpret an ambiguous combination of discourses and practices that repeatedly contradict one another.

In this context one may contemplate three scenarios for the political future of the Mediterranean region. First, it may well be that the EMP process is largely irrelevant to the issue of regional community building. The European Union is not the political and military heavyweight that some imagine it to be, and the economic weapons that it possesses are only truly relevant for economic liberalization. Political and security issues in the Middle East and North Africa are massively over-determined by domestic political issues (such as Islamist challenges), the regional balance of power and the actions of the sole remaining superpower – the US. Any progress or conces-sion that may be made to the EMP to please European governments and European public opinion is made for purposes of expediency, and actual implementation (or the lack of it) is determined by the above-mentioned factors. The EMP is at best a piecemeal process that does not have a momentum of its own, and its impact is mostly cosmetic. This, in my view, is fairly indicative of the present situation in the region.

The second scenario is that current European efforts to promote liberalization and to establish more secure relations with countries on the southern shores of the Mediterranean are, *pace* Kagan, a subtle rephrasing of realpolitik. Policy makers may voice their support for (and perhaps even believe in) liberalization and democ-ratization, but policies are primarily devised to maintain the position of strength of the EU in the region. Sophisticated rephrasing of modernization theory suggesting that authoritarian political orders might represent the best option for these southern 'partner countries' during a period of international instability and global socio-economic transformation, and the best way to avoid falling into the depths of anarchy, in fact underpin the EMP approach. After 9/11 in particular, those European policy makers concerned with fashioning a new world order in the image of the most successful western political and economic institutions have come to view culturally phrased – read Islamic – political opposition as a main source of instability in the region. As a result, democratization is seen as an ambiguous process and political good. The assumption that political liberalization does not pose a major threat to political order but rather is a prerequisite for a functional political and economic system is placed under scrutiny. In this context, EMP policies on democracy promo-tion and the strengthening of civil society, which objectively appear to be failing or proving counter-productive, may in fact be performing their function appropriately in a situation were the furtherance of the status quo is given a greater priority than liberalization.

Thirdly and finally, from a constructivist perspective, regional co-operation and reforms need to be pushed forward despite these initial setbacks because long-term gains for all those involved in this process cannot be secured without the tentative build-up of a necessarily imperfect institutional platform. The main challenge for the proponents of this approach is to gain a reasonably accurate picture of the kind of epistemic community that is being constructed around the Mediterranean, and the kind of political learning that is actually being promoted by the EMP. The principled opposition between the EU and the US on how to behave in international relations that Kagan stresses in his book, even if true, does not necessarily translate into the construction of different international orders. What constitutes a regional order is a particular combination of political principles (ethos) and practices (techne). In the Mediterranean region, however, the EU finds it difficult to link these two components in a coherent framework. As a result, despite the best intentions of its European promoters, the practical inadequacies of the EMP may corrupt its declarative intent and redirect the process of region-building away from an imagined Kantian community and towards a more 'realist' international order.

Notes

[1] Compare the assessments obtained in the Euro-Med official documents (available online at ⟨http://europa.eu.int/comm/external_relations/euromed/doc.htm⟩) with that of Joffé [2000], Spencer [2001] and Gillespie [2002].

[2] Dillman concludes that economic liberalization did not spill over to political reforms in North Africa because authoritarian regimes have been able to use these reforms to strengthen their position by dictating the winners and losers in the first stages of economic liberalization – see also Volpi [2003].

[3] Looking at some of the very first signatories of the EMP, Morocco and Tunisia, which are also some of the largest recipients of MEDA funds, the picture is mixed at best. If Morocco has made some small but significant steps towards political liberalization, its actions in the Western Sahara meant that it was rated as one of the worst authoritarian regimes in the world by the Freedom House survey [Freedom House, 2003]. Regarding Tunisia, most commentators agree that it is today a far more tightly state-controlled polity than it was a decade ago [e.g. Sadiki, 2002].

[4] Adler specifies the historical framework that he has in mind in another paper by warning that 'if you wish to apply European experience to today's Middle East, do not think EU, rather, think July 1914' [Adler, 2001: 1].

[5] Pugh points out that in the last decade, a country like Spain intercepted up to 7000 illegal migrants per year passing through the Strait of Gibraltar. This influx of people from North Africa is not limited to southern European countries, as the UK also witnessed a dramatic surge in the number of asylum seekers from Algeria, which ranked seventh highest in its list of countries of origin of asylum seekers in 1995 [Information Centre about Asylum and Refugees in the UK, 2003].

[6] Some commentators, such as Lia [1999], correctly detect a crypto-Marxist argument underpinning this rationale.

[7] This idea was also the general theme of the regional conference that they organized in Portugal in 2002, and which was entitled: 'The Convergence of Civilizations? Constructing a Mediterranean Region'. It must be noted however that since then, Adler and Crawford have developed and refined several of the arguments and claims that they made in their original conference paper.

[8] See Sending's [2003] helpful description of this inconsistency in terms of the 'logic of appropriateness' and the 'logic of arguing'.

[9] In fairness to Adler, it must be stressed that his own explanatory framework makes strenuous effects to ground this account on a pragmatic approach to political understanding.

[10] Testas points out that over 90 per cent of Algerian and Tunisian expatriates and over 80 per cent of Tunisian expatriates reside in Europe, and it is estimated that 95 per cent of remittances transferred to the Maghreb originate there.

[11] The last assessment is based largely on the controversial claims made by democratic peace theory [cf. Barkawi and Laffey, 2001].

[12] For example, the new provisos of the UK immigration act mean that the security and justice apparatuses do not use the same procedures and justifications for their own nationals and for foreign terrorist suspects [Grimwood and Miller, 2001].

[13] The issue of the declarative and performative aspects of speech acts has been particularly well explored by Austin [1975] and by Skinner [in Tully (ed.), 1988].

References

Adler, E. (1997a): 'Seizing the Middle Ground: Constructivism in World Politics', *European Journal of International Relations* 3/3.

Adler, E. (1997b): 'Imagined (Security) Communities: Cognitive Regions in International Relations', *Millennium* 26/2.

Adler, E. (2001): 'A Mediterranean Canon and an Israeli Prelude to Long Term Peace', Jean Monnet Working Paper 34, University of Catania.

Adler, E. and M. Barnett (1998): 'A Framework for the Study of Security Communities', in Adler, E. and M. Barnett (eds.), *Security Communities*, Cambridge: Cambridge University Press.

Adler, E. and B. Crawford (2002): 'Constructing a Mediterranean Region: A Cultural Approach', paper presented at the Conference on The Convergence of Civilizations? Constructing a Mediterranean Region, 6–9 June, Arrábida Monastery, Fundação Oriente, Lisbon. Available online at ‹http://ies. berkeley.edu/research/MeditAdlerCrawford.pdf›.

Amnesty International (2000): 'United Kingdom: Briefing on the Terrorism Bill', London: Amnesty International.

Attina, F. (2003): 'The Euro-Mediterranean Partnership Assessed: The Realist and Liberal Views', *European Foreign Affairs Review* 8/2.

Austin, J.L. (1975): *How to Do Things with Words*, Oxford: Oxford University Press.

Barkawi, T. and M. Laffey (eds.) (2001): *Democracy, Liberalism, and War: Rethinking the Democratic Peace Debate*, Boulder, CO: Lynne Rienner.

Bielefeldt, H. (2000): ' "Western" versus "Islamic" Human Rights Conceptions?', *Political Theory* 28/1.

Brumberg, D. (2002): 'The Trap of Liberalized Autocracy', *Journal of Democracy*, 13/4.

Burnell, P. (2003): 'The Domestic Political Impact of Foreign Aid: Recalibrating the Research Agenda', paper presented at the ECPR annual conference, 18–21 Sept., Marburg, available online at ‹http:// www.essex.ac.uk/ecpr/events/generalconference/marburg/papers/26/4/ Burnell.pdf›.

Calleya, S.C. (1997): *Navigating Regional Dynamics in the Post-Cold War World: Patterns of Relations in the Mediterranean Area*, Aldershot: Dartmouth.

Césari, J. (1994–95): 'L'Éffet Airbus', *Les Cahiers de l'Orient*, pp.36–7.

Commission of the European Communities (2003a): *Reinvigorating EU Actions on Human Rights and Democratisation with Mediterranean Partners*, Communication from the Commission to the Council and the European Parliament, 25 May, Brussels, Com (2003) 294 final.

Commission of the European Communities (2003b): *Wider Europe – Neighbourhood: A New Framework for Relations with our Eastern and Southern Neighbours*, Communication from the Commission to the Council and the European Parliament, 11 March, Brussels, Com (2003) 104 final.

Dillman, B. (2002): 'International Markets and Partial Economic Reforms in North Africa: What Impact on Democratization?', in Gillespie and Youngs [2002].

El-Sayed Selim, M. (1999): 'Arab Perceptions of the European Union's Euro-Mediterranean Projects', in S.J. Blank (ed.), *Mediterranean Security into the Coming Millennium*, Carlisle: Strategic Studies Institute.

European Union (1995): *Barcelona Declaration*, text adopted at the Euro-Mediterranean Conference on 28 Nov. Available online at: ‹http://europa.eu.int/comm/external_relations/euromed/bd.htm›.

Freedom House (2003): The World's Most Repressive Regimes 2003: A Special Report to the 59th Session of the United Nations Commission on Human Rights, Geneva.

Fuller, G.E. (1996): *Algeria: The Next Fundamentalist State?*, Santa Monica, CA: RAND Corporation.

Gambetta, D. (ed.) (1988): *Trust: Making and Breaking Cooperative Relations*, Oxford: Blackwell.

Gillespie, R. (2002): 'The Valencia Conference: Reinvigorating the Barcelona Process?', *Mediterranean Politics* 7/2.

Gillespie, R. (2003): 'Reshaping the Agenda? The Internal Politics of the Barcelona Process in the Aftermath of September 11', *Mediterranean Politics* 8/2–8/3.

Gillespie, R. and L. Whitehead (2002): 'European Democratic Promotion in North Africa: Limits and Prospects', in Gillespie and Youngs [2002].

Gillespie, R. and R. Youngs (eds.) (2002): *The European Union and Democracy Promotion: The Case of North Africa*, London: Frank Cass.

Grimwood, G.G. and V. Miller (2001): 'The Anti-Terrorism, Crime and Security Bill. Immigration, asylum, race and religion: Bill 49 of 2001–2002', London: House of Commons Library.

Huntington, S. (1996): *The Clash of Civilisations and the Remaking of the World Order*, New York: Simon and Schuster.

Ikenberry, J. (2003): 'Review of Robert Kagan's Paradise and Power: America and Europe in the New World Order', *Foreign Affairs* 82/2.

Information Centre about Asylum and Refugees in the UK (2003): 'Algerian Asylum Applications to the UK', Statistical Snapshots Series 2003. Available online at: ⟨http://www.icar.org.uk/content/res/stats/papers.html⟩.

Joffé, G. (2000): 'Europe and the Mediterranean: The Barcelona Process Five Years On', *Royal Institute of International Affairs Briefing Paper* 16.

Jünemann, A. (2002): 'From the Bottom to the Top: Civil Society and Transnational Non-Governmental Organizations in the Euro-Mediterranean Partnership', in Gillespie and Youngs [2002].

Kagan, R. (2003): *Paradise and Power: America and Europe in the New World Order*, London: Atlantic Books.

Larrabee, F.S., *et al.* (1998): *NATO's Mediterranean Initiative: Policy Issues and Dilemmas*, Santa Monica, CA: RAND Corporation.

Lesser, I.O., *et al.* (2000): *The Future of NATO's Mediterranean Initiative: Evolution and Next Steps*, Santa Monica, CA: RAND Corporation.

Lia, B. (1999): 'Security Challenges in Europe's Mediterranean Periphery – Perspectives and Policy Dilemmas', *European Security* 8/4.

López García, B. and M. Hernando de Larramendi (2002): 'Spain and North Africa: Towards a "Dynamic Stability2"', in Gillespie and Youngs [2002].

Petras, J. and M. Morley (2000): 'Contesting Hegemons: US–French Relations in the "New World Order" ', *Review of International Studies* 26/1.

Philippart, E. (2003): 'The Euro-Mediterranean Partnership: A Critical Evaluation of an Ambitious Scheme', *European Foreign Affairs Review* 8/2.

Pugh, M. (2001): 'Mediterranean Boat People: A Case for Co-operation', *Mediterranean Politics* 6/1.

Richards, A. and J. Waterbury (1990): *A Political Economy of the Middle East: State, Class and Economic Development*, Boulder, CO: Westview Press.

Roberts, H. (2003): *The Battlefield Algeria 1988–2002*, London: Verso.

Rorty, R. (1998): *Truth and Progress: Philosophical Papers*, Vol. 3, Cambridge: Cambridge University Press.

Rumelili, B. (2003): 'Liminality and Perpetuation of Conflicts: Turkish-Greek Relations in the Context of Community-Building by the EU', *European Journal of International Relations* 9/2.

Sadiki, L. (2002): 'Political Liberalization in Bin Ali's Tunisia: Façade Democracy', *Democratization* 9/4.

Sending, O.J. (2002): 'Constitution, Choice and Change: Problems with the "Logic of Appropriateness" and its Use in Constructivist Theory', *European Journal of International Relations* 8/4.

Spencer, C. (2001): 'The EU and Common Strategies: The Revealing Case of the Mediterranean', *European Foreign Affairs Review* 6/1.

Testas, A. (2001): 'Maghreb-EU Migration: Interdependence, Remittances, the Labour Market and Implications for Economic Development', *Mediterranean Politics* 6/3.

Tully, J. (ed.) (1988): *Meaning and Context: Quentin Skinner and His Critics*, Cambridge: Polity Press.

Volpi, F. (2002): 'Language, Practices and the Formation of a Transnational Liberal-Democratic Ethos', *Global Society* 16/1.

Volpi, F. (2003): *Islam and Democracy: The Failure of Dialogue in Algeria*, London: Pluto Press.

Warren, M. (ed.) (1999): *Democracy and Trust*, Cambridge: Cambridge University Press.

Willis, M. (1996): *The Islamist Challenge in Algeria: A Political History*, London: Ithaca.

Youngs, R. (2002): 'The European Union and Democracy Promotion in the Mediterranean: A New or Disingenuous Strategy?' in Gillespie and Youngs [2002].

Youngs, R. (2003): 'Strengths and Weaknesses in the Evolution of European Political Aid, paper presented at the ECPR Conference, 18–20 Sept., Marburg. Available online at: ‹http://www.essex.ac.uk/ ecpr/events/generalconference/marburg/papers/26/4/Youngs.pdf›.

The Use of Conditionality in Support of Political, Economic and Social Rights: Unveiling the Euro-Mediterranean Partnership's True Hierarchy of Objectives?

DOROTHÉE SCHMID

For about a decade the European Union has imposed conditions on the delivery of financial aid to third countries in order to promote economic, institutional and political reform. This approach has also been applied to the Euro-Mediterranean Partnership, which provides rather sophisticated legal and institutional resources to organize political conditionality. Whilst the general advancement of human rights remains a major topic for Euro-Mediterranean co-operation the efficiency of the conditionality methodology in supporting social and economic rights, as compared to strictly political rights, remains uncertain. This study examines the actual enforcement of such social conditionality in the case of two test countries, namely Morocco and Turkey.

The Euro-Mediterranean Partnership between Economic, Political and Social Concerns

After eight years of unequal progress, it is becoming less and less easy to draw a balanced image of the Barcelona process and to account fairly for its successes and shortcomings. One way of clarifying the debate might be to decide whether the Euro-Mediterranean Partnership (EMP) is essentially more of an economic, a social or a political project. In the words of the Barcelona Declaration, the new Mediterranean initiative is characterized as 'strategic', suggesting that the main ambition of the Partnership lies even beyond the simple political realm. One must also keep in mind that the preamble of the Barcelona declaration itself mentions 'the strengthening of democracy and respect for human rights' as 'essential aspects of the Partnership'.

Yet concrete daily management of the Partnership is very much focused on the advancement of the Euro-Mediterranean Free Trade Area (EMFTA) project, which continues to proceed at quite a steady pace. Consequently, the economic side of liberalism appears to increasingly gain precedence over the political ideal which initially inspired the EMP. This soft 'perversion' suggests a need to intensify reflection on the economic and social impacts of European co-operation in the Mediterranean Partner Countries (MPCs), which is the aim of this study.

The democratic side of the European project is by now rather well documented [Youngs 2001, 2002]. Human rights are a growing concern to researchers who can draw on non-governmental organiztions' (NGOs') data to shore up a rather pessimistic view about the true political outcomes of the Partnership. Yet, to date, the analysis has very much focused on the first generation of civil and political rights, rather than the development of the second generation of social and economic rights. This omission is all the more conceptually problematic given the fact, that, as emphasized above, the EMP is becoming increasingly economy-oriented. Therefore, in order to be productive, any future pragmatic analysis of human rights matters within the Euro-Mediterranean framework is best served by primarily studying economic and social rights.

The Benefits of Conditionality within the Partnership

Conditionality, which is the central concept examined in this study, is a classical management instrument used to help foster change in a predetermined reform process. Concretely, it is one of the methods that allow managers to obtain targeted, pre-established results within a financial co-operation framework and can be basically defined as establishing an explicit link between the delivery of financial or technical aid and the realization of certain mutually pre-agreed reforms. Karen E. Smith gives the following description of *political* conditionality in a text dealing with the European Union's (EU's) conditionality policies: it is 'the linking, by a state or an international organization, of perceived benefits to another state (such as aid), to the fulfilment of conditions relating to the protection of human rights and the advancement of democratic principles' [Smith, 1998: 256]. This narrow definition can be enlarged to take into account other types of conditionalities, such as those relating to institutional or economic reform.

These three goals – economic, institutional and political – have been successively advanced as the concept of conditionality has historically evolved, although, generally speaking, most operational conditionalities are in practice economy-oriented. 'Social conditionality' as such is not really a widespread notion, even though it is occasionally used by the European Commission itself with respect to the Mediterranean Partners Countries (MPCs) [European Commission, 2003a: 2]. On the other hand, political conditionality usually includes mechanisms designed to ensure the respect of human rights, including those potentially of a social and economic nature.

In the wake of a recent trend by the International Financial Institutions (IFIs) to re-establish governance issues as the key to economic development, the widely praised UNDP Arab Human Development Report of 2001 emphasized the key role of human rights and democracy in developing the Arab world [Fergany ed., 2001]. However, this global notion of 'human rights' can in fact be split into different operational categories. For example, an inquiry on the use of conditionality in the

Euro-Mediterranean framework, would begin by inclining to believe that special significance should be given to social and economic rights, in so far as their connection to economic performance is more easy to establish than political rights. The development of the 'twin liberalization' scheme[1] would indeed be improved if social and economic rights were seen to be a necessary link between economic and political autonomy for the individual. Paradoxically, and given the failure of political conditionality mechanisms within the EMP, social and economic rights could thus be identified as relevant criteria for underpinning the success of the waning, theoretical Euro-Mediterranean liberal plot.

Comparing Turkish Performance to Moroccan Resistance: The Paradoxical Course of Social and Economic Rights within the EMP

The present essay, based on extensive field research,[2] aims at testing the effective enforcement of different types of European conditionalities applied to two test countries, and to assess the impact they have had on economic and social rights. The two case studies selected, namely Morocco and Turkey, exemplify two rather different types of relationship with the European Union moving in parallel. Hence, this study does not suggest that straight comparisons between the two can be made.

The two countries have manifested contrasting types of reactions towards European conditionalities. Drawn by the prospect of joining the EU, successive Turkish governments have chosen to somewhat anticipate European conditionalities, whereas Morocco seems to manifest a relative degree of independence with respect to European exigencies. However, both countries do seem to unite in a common search for autonomy in dealing with external demands and trying to liberate themselves from an externally imposed scheme, one by endorsing it as if it were an internally produced constraint, the other by keeping it at a distance. In this context, the impact of European conditionalities, as applied to economic and social rights, essentially reflects each government's respective hierarchy of priorities.

Targeting Aid to Support Economic, Social and Political Reform: The Recent Emergence of an Inclusive Practice of Conditionality

An Economic Tool Escaping the IFIs' Sphere

During the last decade the concept of conditionality, which is given a common sense meaning throughout this study, underwent a re-elaboration that very much contributed to its rising credit among political scientists as it extended its influence progressively from the specialized field of applied economics, where it was initially developed, to the discipline of political science.

The original conception of conditionality is attributed to economists. Since the 1950s the concept has been continually elaborated by the International Monetary Fund (IMF) and the World Bank (WB) and was especially popular among macroeconomists during the 1970s. The first concrete experiences with conditionality relates to the IFIs' operating contracts with beneficiary countries, including specific mechanisms for the assessment of correct implementation of development policies.[3]

Conditionality has thus been on the management agenda of IFIs for about 50 years. Structural conditionality was systematically imposed through increasingly complex mechanisms on non-industrialized countries, and reached its highest degree of sophistication in 1986, with the introduction of the IMF's Structural Adjustment Facility (SAF). The mere mention of SAF immediately brings to mind the associated debates about the legitimacy of intervening in recipient countries' internal affairs. In fact, during the 1980s a gradual shift was observed from strictly economic to more institutional conditionalities, thereby creating a new usage for this technocratic management tool, perceived so far as a rather neutral device.

The Rise of the 'New Conditionality'

The generalization of political conditionality could be observed at the end of the twentieth century as a gradual process, which was given a decisive momentum after the end of the Cold War.[4] After two decades of rather narrow practice of macro-economic and financial conditionality, the agenda of the major donors progressively evolved to integrate new priorities. In the 1990s, there was a new focus on poverty. A second important set of goals, dealing with the global concept of 'governance', was reintroduced subsequently into co-operation frameworks. This can be considered as the turning point for the late emergence of the institutional and political version of conditionality. Joan Nelson and Stephanie Eglington thus remark that, following the primacy of economic austerity in the 1980s, issues such as poverty reduction, governance, democracy and the environment gradually became central pillars of many foreign assistance programmes [Nelson and Eglington, 1993: 46].

A new direction was then imposed for the use of classical conditionalities, ultimately formalized as what has been globally termed the 'new' conditionality [Uvin and Biagiotti, 1996]. This expansion developed in parallel with an increasing acceptance of a broader concept of development: economic analysts began to admit that, in the long run, economic growth is neither sustainable nor desirable unless it is accompanied by environmental protection and reduced poverty; the quality of governance and the pace of institutional and political reform affecting all three goals simultaneously. Finally, Peter Uvin and Isabelle Biagiotti conclude that:

> Political conditionality (. . .) may be defined as a set of specific state behaviors – respecting Human rights, organizing multi-party elections, working in a good governance mode, and cutting military spending – that are internationally upheld as conducive to development and whose realization is promoted, *inter alia*, through that leverage instrument, i.e. the withholding of development assistance, or the threat thereof. [Uvin and Biagiotti, 1996: 378]

The international community at large, including policy makers from industrialized countries, and not merely macroeconomists, consequently began to show an interest in political conditionality. The concept reached its highest peak of popularity after the end of the Cold War, when conditionality joined the practical list of foreign policy tools of most western powers [Crawford, 1997: 69]. Democratic governments from northern nations gradually took to imposing general institutional and/or political conditions upon the granting of development aid to emerging countries in order to normalize them into a purportedly balanced pattern of political, economic and social development.

Multiple Devices

The mechanism to enforce conditionalities can be described as two-fold. First, sound, explicit and pre-agreed norms are an essential prerequisite to establish an efficient system of conditionality. These norms can be universally agreed upon, or enshrined in a particular agreement. The human rights regime, central to our demonstration here, is usually considered as a reasonably well-codified international domain.[5] Second, some specific device has to be established to ensure respect for the norm.

This device can be used only if the two partners – donor and recipient – are linked by a form of contract. Karen E. Smith thus enumerates the various type of relationships and associated contracts that might allow the Europeans to politically condition their relationships to third countries: these involve the granting of trading preferences, the signing and implementation of co-operation and association agreements, the deliverance of financial aid, and, finally, awarding diplomatic recognition or eventual EU membership [Smith, 1998: 253]. These are all configurations in which the EU is in a position to deal a specific advantage against some targeted efforts. In all these cases, the donor can provide incentives – increasing assistance, or the *positive* side of conditionality – or define sanctions – suspension of aid being the most immediate *negative* interpretation of conditionality – that concretize the enforcement of pre-fixed requirements vis-à-vis the recipient country.

The initial concept of conditionality essentially developed a punitive vision, relying on threat and effective sanctions to force the recipient country into complying with the commonly established scheme. Yet, a gradual shift was observed during the last decade, from negative to positive conditionality, the latter being understood as part of a more co-operative approach. Both approaches have their advantages and specific flaws, which must be carefully appraised in consideration of the particular environment in which they will be enforced [Crawford, 1997]. The European Union's culture of conditionality has to date always emphasized the principles of positivity and proportionality [Schmid, 2003: 28 – 9].

Conditionality and Human Rights: The Place of Economic and Social Rights

One of the applications of political conditionality is obviously the promotion of human rights in all their different manifestations. However, it is also necessary to acknowledge here that the record concerning the efficiency of this instrument to foster political reform, and more precisely to diffuse democratic norms, is not completely convincing [Stokke, 1995; Carothers, 2002; Santiso, 2003].

The first undoubted reason for this mitigated success is the technical specifications that practically constrain the enforcement of conditionalities. In reality, many different features have to be taken into account in order to design an adequate conditionality system. The feasibility of objectives, proportionality of envisaged measures, together with the existence of sound and credible indicators are all strong elements whose aggregation increases the effectiveness of the system. For example, it has been proven that, generally speaking, multifaceted conditionality is less efficient than very targeted mechanisms [Nelson and Eglington, 1993]. The inertia of the donor's bureaucracy also frequently seems to be responsible for what could be considered as excessive complacency confronting the repeated failures of the recipients [Dreher, 2002]. In addition, as will be developed here with the study's two case studies, other political considerations can intervene which can explain occasional or repeated indulgence on the part of donors.

The second restriction weighing upon the use of conditionality in support of human rights policies relates to the definition of human rights itself. 'Good governance' is certainly a rather vague notion, even when it is coupled with a reference to the 'Rule of Law', or 'democracy' at large. Whilst 'human rights' might sound more explicit, their concrete interpretation is also controversial as between political, economic and social rights. In this context, the possibility of adhering to some form of practical hierarchy of importance is questionable. The choice of placing an emphasis on political pluralism and elections ahead of defending the upgrading of working conditions or the social benefits generally associated with the welfare state, in fact reveals a conceptual bias concerning the meaning of democracy.[6] Economic and social rights were historically second to be legalized in our western societies. Their progress roughly went ahead after the emergence of political rights and the consolidation of democratic institutions. Putting political rights on the first place on the agenda then means exporting the democratic process, just as westerners experienced it in the eighteenth and nineteenth centuries.

Arguably, the heart of the debate is whether the different expressions of human rights, as consecrated by the Universal Declaration of Human Rights, can, or should be consciously separated in practice. Leaving aside the ethical aspects of the question, and the associated debate concerning subjective responsibility, simply concentrating on the observation of existing institutional apparatuses reveals that the promotion of the whole range of human rights has hardly ever been a unified process. In this context, can the conditionality system efficiently contribute to the promotion of economic and social rights? The answer reasonably depends on the final selected goals of a given aid system. On the one hand, donors often favour economic development as an end in itself, political and institutional environment being in this case seen only as one element of support for economic growth. On the other hand, political liberty is sometimes erected as a single goal, political convergence thus being established as a prerequisite for the very delivery of financial assistance. In the first case of privileging economic development economic and social rights are a potential, but not compulsory, institutional element of the game. In the second case, these rights have to be explicitly inserted in the list of human rights to benefit from targeted support. However, in neither case do they appear as immediately indispensable for the fulfilment of the programme.

At this stage, this essay would like to propose that the Euro-Mediterranean Partnership scheme could open a third, intermediate path where it clearly links the occurrence of political reform to the amelioration of economic performance. Social and economic rights can, indeed, be considered as the 'missing link' towards the emergence of political rights in developing countries benefiting from external aid.[7] In turn, the logical relevance of economic and social rights in the process of creating political awareness is very clear and is one of the sophisticated mechanisms contributing to the twin liberalization plot of the Barcelona process.

Conditionality in the Euro-Mediterranean Partnership Context

Growing confusion has recently arisen in the debate about European conditionalities applied to MPCs. Public disappointment is frequently expressed about Europe's supposed indifference towards non-compliance or even violation of bilaterally pre-agreed rules, especially concerning human rights. Such a discussion actually brings together very differing levels of analysis, suggesting at the outset the necessity of clarifying the associated legal and technical contexts.

The Barcelona Plot: Conditionalities as a Pedagogy

It is very easy to conceive the function of conditionality if one keeps in mind the original liberal design that inspired the EMP initiative. Conditionality can truly be advocated as an ideal tool to support the realization of Europe's comprehensive ambition to uphold an area of combined economic and political freedom.

Considering the slow pace of reform in most MPCs, some incentives to move forward might indeed prove extremely useful. One advantage of the conditionality instrument is that it is rather painless and relatively cheap; as an instrument for intervention it also respects the new philosophy of responsibility and ownership embodied by the spirit of 'Partnership'. Conditionality thus naturally belongs to the new pedagogy that informs European initiatives vis-à-vis the Mediterranean region: Persuasion is the rule, not coercion. For their part, partner countries should be a priori quite receptive to an open process that leads to gradually contractualizing their relationship with Europe. Understandably enough, the notion of positive conditionality is especially popular among bureaucrats and scholars from the eastern and southern part of the Mediterranean.[8]

The Classical Way: Bilateral Macro-Economic Conditionalities

Classical conditionalities, in the traditional IFIs' sense of financial aid against completion of pre-defined economic and institutional objectives, do exist in the EMP's context. They are put into force through bilateral co-operation with each Partner Country. The triennial National Indicative Programmes (NIPs), which are jointly elaborated by the European Commission and the relevant southern authorities, determine the priorities for co-operation and the amount of financial aid to be allotted to meet respective needs. In conformity with Article 5 of the MEDA financial regulation, the measures to be financed are decided according to five different criteria: the beneficiary's priorities; their evolving needs; their absorption capacity; progress accomplished towards structural reform and an evaluation of the effectiveness of the measures taken to meet agreed priorities.

The last three criteria are considered to form the legal basis for the economic conditionality of the Partnership [Mekaoui, 2000; Lannon, Inglis and Haenelbacke, 2001]. Practically, the Commission establishes effective lists of conditionalities to be fulfilled in the enforcement of NIPs. They resemble very much the multilateral donors system, also in their tendency to include not only economic indicators, but increasingly more institutional prerequisites ('good governance'). Social and economic rights could easily be inserted into this comprehensive frame for reforms.

The Human Rights Clause: A Case for Political Conditionality

The most well-known mechanism providing room for political conditionality within the Euro-Mediterranean Partnership is certainly the 'article 2 clause'. All bilateral agreements signed with the MPCs now include a clause explicitly urging respect for human rights and democratic principles.[9] The redaction of all agreements opens the possibility for the EU to take 'appropriate measures' where there is a violation of an 'essential clause of the agreement', in this context 'respect for human rights and democratic principles'. A suspension of the co-operation agreement could ultimately be considered under certain circumstances.

However, the operability of this human rights clause is open to doubt. Whilst it remains a fundamental principle or dream for political activists, it has, to date, never been activated. Although reference to the clause has been raised on a number of occasions since the Barcelona Declaration was adopted, the specific political constraints of European decision making, combined with the very particular spirit of consensus that informs the EMP, makes it very difficult to bring about any coercive measure sanctioning abusive behaviour.[10] Strictly defined political conditionality is not a reality within the EMP's framework, with the result that it cannot be used to effectively defend human rights.

The Copenhagen Criteria: An Inclusive Frame for Candidate Countries

Another set of particular constraints affects only a very specific category of Mediterranean Partners, namely future member states of the European Union. The June 1993 Copenhagen European Summit laid out a list of criteria to be gradually fulfilled by applicant countries in the period between the opening of accession negotiations with the EU and their effective adhesion. These criteria are threefold. First, the economic criteria contain indicators to be met in order to ensure economic convergence with present members of the EU. Second, the political standards include the stability of institutions ensuring democracy, the rule of law, human rights and the protection of minorities. The third criterion is legal and relates to the adoption of the Acquis communautaire within the internal legislation of future members.

One MPC only, namely Turkey, is currently concerned with fulfilling this particular set of obligations, which were initially fixed with reference to Eastern European countries. The Copenhagen criteria have been practically transformed into a rather severe contract, defining the contours of a very global, inclusive conditionality system [Van Westering, 2000]. A sophisticated monitoring procedure has been organized to follow up the candidates' progress. However, such benchmarking still fails to enhance the credibility of the narrowly defined Euro-Mediterranean system of conditionalities hitherto described.

One can thus appreciate the wide range of instruments available to organize conditionality in the Euro-Mediterranean context. Turkey is probably responding to the most sophisticated cascade of obligations, starting with the global political conditionality of the 'second type' Copenhagen criteria, and proceeding with different kinds of fine prerequisites inserted in sectoral co-operation programmes.

The Turkish and Moroccan Experience of European Conditionality: Contrasting Profiles

Having described the procedures, this essay now focuses attention on the actual contents of existing Euro-Mediterranean conditionalities. It will essentially try and clarify the rank of social and economic rights vis-à-vis the most common type of conditionalities, these being, respectively, economic reforms and/or civil and political rights.

It is first useful to briefly sketch out the profiles of reaction of our two test countries towards external donors' pressure, as this should help in interpreting the specific failures encountered in examining the promotion of economic and social rights. Although they both participate in the EMP multilateral adventure, Morocco and Turkey widely differ in their geopolitical position, socio-economic structures and political and institutional cultures.

Long-Standing, Active Friends

The two selected countries enjoy a special relationship with Europe. Morocco and Turkey are both old and pro-active partners with the EU. The two countries have signed up to a renewed co-operation framework and both regularly demonstrate their motivation to reinforce their bilateral connections with the EU. The bureaucracy in both states has remarkably accommodated a new institutional configuration, whilst at the same time looking to exercise influence in making compromises with Europe in their favour. Turkey is a founding member of the Council of Europe, member of the Organization for Economic Cooperation and Development (OECD) and the North Atlantic Treaty Organization (NATO), and is already included in the enlargement vision as reflected in the organization of the Commission. Morocco has a rather intense level of bilateral exchanges with Brussels and is trying to stay a leading figure in the vanguard of the EMP, fuelling the Barcelona process with new concepts and energy.

It is equally important in the interests of the analysis to select countries that show real commitment to the perspective of accomplishing internal reforms. Institutional and political change has indeed been observed in both countries over at least the last five years. Morocco and Turkey concretely seem to embody, at both extremities of the Mediterranean, the open dynamics of change advocated by the European Commission through the EMP.

The Inside/Outside Dialectic and its Effect on Bargaining Power

Turkey is still an official member of the Euro-Mediterranean club, but it actually stands on the margins of the Partnership. As a would-be member of the EU, it has never expressed real motivation to revive the EMFTA southern economic integration project. Its constant preoccupation is essentially to demonstrate at all costs that it can match the Copenhagen criteria with the same motivation and consistency manifested by the eastern European applicants, while the Europeans have lately adopted a rather critical stand towards Turkish efforts. The final date for the eventual opening of nego-tiations for accession has yet to be fixed. The key to the achievement of Turkish high, multifaceted, economic, political and cultural ambition ultimately lies in European hands,[11] and, as such, the balance of power inclines sharply to the European side.

Conversely, Morocco has had to accept for more than 15 years that is has no cred-ible prospects of ever becoming a full member of the European Union.[12] On the other hand, as a privileged partner, it ranks second in the amount of financial aid disbursed by the EU in the Mediterranean. When subjected to precise scrutiny, current economic co-operation with Morocco concretely appears to be riddled with strong political motivations. Morocco is held to be a stable regime and the one working example of democratization among Mediterranean Arab countries.[13] Since September 11, western interests globally converge on the country to keep it as a permanent and motivated ally in the enduring 'war on terrorism'. Most public donors, be they multilateral or bilateral, share and express the same concern; in the global game, Morocco is thus presently in a position of strength.

Reacting to European Conditionalities: Two Contrasted Profiles

Hence the bargaining power lying in the hands of either country when confronting the EU is not equivalent. On the one side, Turkey is very much searching for accept-ance, while Morocco is playing a multilevel diplomatic game in which the EU is cast as one single protagonist among others. These differing balance of power relation-ships reflect the way each country copes with European conditionalities.

As discussed elsewhere [Schmid, 2003], Morocco illustrates a case of relative resistance to external pressure from donors, notably expressed via the conditioning of aid. Bradford Dillman has already signalled that North African governments are globally relatively immune to conditionalities, his final statement being that 'the strings attached have not fundamentally changed economies or the autonomy of the state in them' [Dillman, 2002: 205]. Quite remarkably, Morocco has seemingly elaborated a rather sophisticated savoir-faire in dealing with different donors, building a system of multiple loyalties and reorganizing national priorities in order to gain autonomy from external pressure. Indeed, when one casts an eye over the management of bilateral conditionalities, the record is rather indulgent for

Moroccan authorities. Generally speaking, the partner country seems to be able to favour its own interpretation about the constraints to which it is opposed. For this reason Morocco can be referred to as a case of 'conditionality in reverse' [Schmid, 2003: 53].

Turkey's anxiety to respect European will stands in sharp contrast to the cool rule prevailing in Morocco. Turkish endeavours to reach political correctness are demonstrated most particularly in the field of human rights legislation [Hale, 2003] and to date have tended to anticipate most European political demands.[14] This rare example of self-discipline can inspire the expression 'self-imposed conditionality' to characterize the Turkish attitude vis-à-vis European requirements [Hale, 2003: 59]. Such observations are also strongly validated by one of Mine Eder's arguments, namely that the time frame of the conditionality system imposed on Turkey is not consistent: Turkish efforts in fact systematically precede the granting of the reward theoretically associated with the realization of the objective. In contrast to IMF conditionality, where financial aid is provided immediately after the completion of predefined exigencies, the EU system of conditionality in respect of Turkey has always suffered from a timing problem, granting benefits long after the performance was achieved. The statement is thus one of 'too little, too late' [Eder, 2003: 230].

These two greatly contrasting profiles anticipate the outcomes of social and economic conditionalities for both countries. On the Moroccan side, the product of the co-operation contract is very likely to reflect clear Moroccan internal priorities, or the order of values privileged by the Moroccan government in dealing with modernization. On the other hand, by Europe keeping a firm hand on the priorities of internal reforms the Turkish case offers a rather unique opportunity to test the true determination of the EU to defend a socially sustainable pattern of development.

The Impact of European Conditionalities on Social and Economic Rights: Confirming the Grey Zone

Before embarking on a detailed discussion of precise conditionalities, it is useful to describe the starting point, or the present status of social and economic rights in Morocco and Turkey. In essence, what sort of changes, if any, are under way in these countries concerning these issues, and what are the driving forces behind them?

Economic and social rights indicators in Turkey and Morocco are not absolutely comparable and it has to be asked whether they might indeed follow similar convergent paths. It is widely agreed that human development indicators in Turkey reach levels that are more comparable to European ones than most Arab countries. The social protection system is held to be one of the most extensive in the region. Some significant gaps can nevertheless be emphasized, especially on demographic indicators and educational needs.[15] In contrast, the level of social indicators in Morocco is among the lowest in the region.[16] The global trend is not completely positive for either country; one presently notes that the record is also becoming more contrasted.[17] It is against this nuanced backdrop that the impact of external intervention should be evaluated, distinguishing between automatic impact via the progression of the EMFTA, and the effect of conditionalities.

The Impact of Globalization on Social and Economic Rights in the Region: Evolving Indicators

Joining the EMFTA is an engagement entailing important effects on the content and quality of social and economic rights for the MPCs. Part of these effects is automatic, and part is, to a certain extent and according to certain approaches, connected to the MPCs' own reactions. These effects, be they positive or negative, actually emanate from two different processes. The first process relates to the opening up of economies and the necessity to meet the requirements of world economic competition, even if envisaged only on the Euro-Mediterranean scale. The second process depends on the particular attention being paid to economic and social rights in the execution of concrete co-operation programmes. Delivering special incentives and imposing conditionalities are two crucial instruments serving any deliberate strategy of the EU to promote social and economic rights in the MPCs. All of these elements need be taken into consideration in reaching a viable conclusion in this area.

As a first step, it is thus important to analyse the likely automatic effects of the Euro-Mediterranean Partnership, as an element of globalization per se, on the evolution of social and economic rights within the partner countries. As Mediterranean countries slowly enter the globalized system of the world economy, their agenda on economic and social rights appears to be more and more influenced by external factors, with, paradoxically, two contrasting effects. On the one hand, decision makers' attention is very much focused on economic competitiveness, entailing a strong preference for the lowering of production costs. This increasing fixation tends to have a negative impact on working conditions: commercial priorities can be held responsible for a downgrading of social and economic rights, especially in emerging countries. Low costs are more and more frequently maintained at the expense of the health and comfort of workers; whilst, at the same time, the absence of a social protection system guarantees cheaper manpower.[18] The other side of the coin involves the diffusion of an idealistic model of socially sustainable development, which is widely claimed in multilateral forums to be an ideal per se, and a necessity to counterbalance the negative human consequences of unchecked operation of the free market. This discourse is also regularly defended in the internal European context, where the enforcement of the Charter of Fundamental Rights of the European Union is a regularly debated subject [Menendez, 2002]. Exporting essential European social values to commercial partners *apparently* remains for the Union a basic objective.

Taking into account this conceptual framework, differing analyses of the impact of globalization on the development of social and economic rights in Morocco and Turkey are presented. Morocco has been implementing since 1983 the classical set of economic reforms inspired by the IMF, starting with a stabilization programme, followed by structural adjustment, limited privatization and encouragement of foreign investment [Dillman, 2001: 198] A 'post-structural agenda' has emerged since the mid-1990s to cope with globalization, including financial liberalization, and taking into account the WTO and the Euro-Mediterranean Partnership. The inclusion of external considerations on the global reform agenda is therefore quite recent for a country that for nearly two decades was granted an autonomous development model. In that context, it seems that social considerations have only recently become a chief concern for the IFIs.[19] Yet the year 2003 has been one of real advancement on social reforms in Morocco, including a decisive move for the adoption of a new Labour Code[20] and the announced reform of the status of women (*Mudawana*).

As far as Turkey is concerned the 1990s were a crucial decade of economic and social adjustment. The economy was trapped within cycles of growth-crisis-stabilization and had to endure several stabilization attempts. The government initiated a comprehensive disinflation programme in July 1998, under the auspices of the IMF and austerity has remained the guiding word ever since for a country that went through a very severe financial crisis in 2001, nearly resulting in bankruptcy. It also has to be recalled that Turkey established a customs union with the EU in 1997, and adapted rather well to this new competition framework, at least in commercial terms. However, joining the European single market was certainly a difficult aspect of the global adjustment effort performed by the Turkish private sector whilst the Turkish state has demonstrated even more difficulty in integrating flexibility into its management system. The side effects of the economic adjustment on the Turkish welfare system can, in this context, be characterized as an attempt to slowly liberalize and 'marketize' the social protection system. According to some analysts, this liberalization attempt, which implies the dismantling of currently available centralized protection systems, is leading to 'the deterioration of terms and conditions of employment and of social insurance standards, which are already very poor' [Arin, 2002: 90].

Coping with European Conditionalities: Effects on Economic and Social Rights

We shall now turn to an examination of the space devoted to social and economic rights as a specific concern for bilateral co-operation with the EU. The first matter of interest is the proportion and intensity of co-operation specifically dealing with the issue. In the case of Morocco, one has to acknowledge the existence of targeted efforts: according to field observers, the passage from the MEDA I to the MEDA II financial framework of co-operation reveals renewed attention for social issues. The social dimension is now considered to be a fundamental platform for any success in economic reforms. The list of new objectives matching this new philosophy is rather impressive and includes: institutional support to professional associations, the upgrading of technical and professional training, social housing in Tangier, health management in the eastern region, support to job creation and reforming medical insurance [Masson, 2003]. It is still too early to assess the results of this new impulse. However, classical commentaries continue to be relevant, most notably about the bureaucratic obstacles still hindering the effective disbursement of funds, making it nearly impossible to respect global schemes.[21] The main difference between the Moroccan and the European point of view on the issue is that they each regularly blame their counterpart, criticizing the slowness and complexity of each other's procedures.

In the donor's rationale, the possibility of including conditionalities in co-operation programmes is a step further in enhancing the chances of meeting specific objectives. The effects are, in fact, still rather unconvincing in the case of Morocco. As a general background, the European Commission has appeared more committed to the implementation of economic rather than political conditionalities in Morocco. The 1999 review of the 'Facilité d'ajustement structurel' can here be quoted to illustrate the cool rule spirit that permeates the Euro-Moroccan relationship: the final statement of the European Delegation in Rabat is that out of the 24 conditions, 23 have been complied with.[22] Only three conditions out of a list of 24 could be considered to really have a link with economic and social rights: the participation of private companies and NGOs in the new system of vocational training; the amelioration of the section of the 97/98 investment budget devoted to health expenses; and the presentation of an action plan for the reform of 'L'entraide et la promotion nationales', a local welfare system. One condition also was indirectly related: the necessity of providing a tentative programming of investment expenditures taking into account basic needs, notably health and education. Out of these four conditions that directly or indirectly affect the state of economic and social rights, only three were complied with. The picture is thus rather poor, as social matters are not considered as essential priorities in the co-operation contract. Yet again, one should take into account the redirection of priorities within the MEDA II financial envelope towards enhanced social conditionality.

Given the comprehensiveness of the Turkish conditionality framework, the effectiveness of European exigencies can be assessed through the regular Accession Report issued by the Commission [European Commission, 2003b]. About one-third of the report deals with the Copenhagen political criteria, this global package being split into smaller categories. The summary reveals that only two pages out of the whole 143-page report are devoted to 'Economic, social and cultural rights'. This descriptive dearth appears even more striking when one notes that, in contrast, 11 pages are dedicated to 'civil and political rights'. The record in this last sector is explicitly impressive: Turkey has received wide praise for meeting European standards on political rights. In contrast, the overall failure to address economic and social rights within the global Euro-Turkish contract results in a very meagre treatment of such matters in the Accession Report. The issues mentioned include respect for gender equality, the rights of the child and the legislation on trade unions ('right to organize' and 'right to bargain collectively'). The record is poor on all three criteria. No significant progress is reported in any of three domains, the paragraph dealing with trade unions being especially scanty. In the end, it seems likely that the EU keeps a rather low profile on these issues that are dealt with more seriously under the IFI's auspices. Social conditionality could also be tracked in the EU-Turkish relationship through the transposition of the *Acquis communautaire*; but it is widely acknowledged that social legislation has always lagged behind at the EU level. Related questions are treated under the 'Ability to assume the obligations of membership' chapter of the Report, especially in the sections concerning 'Social policy and employment' and 'Education and training' [European Commission, 2003b: 87–91, 99–101]. The paucity of hard references to economic and social rights here reflects the EU's own legal deficiencies.

In conclusion, it can be estimated that targeted European efforts aimed at supporting social and economic rights in the two test countries are insufficient. The link between possible progress towards reform and the existence of targeted conditionalities is also difficult to establish in the case of Morocco. Some explanations for this relative failure of the EU pertaining to both sides are now discussed.

Missing Link, Missing Rights: An Implicit Hierarchy of Objectives?

What is the rationale behind this relative lack of interest in the promotion of social and economic rights in the region? This study's hypothesis is that the EU is globally putting more emphasis on economic efficiency than on human rights, except when an application for membership is at stake; and that even here, in the case of would-be member countries, some categories of human rights take precedence over others.

Hierarchy of Objectives, Hierarchy of Rights

The results of our inquiry suggest that each country's reaction to different types of external conditionalities highly depends on the global cohesion of either's internal priorities. In the particular case of economic and social rights, the result is also interrelated with the cohesion of the country's socio-political frame. Some implicit hierarchy then seems to be established between the conditionalities, differing objectives being privileged by either government depending on a set of internal political constraints.

In the first place, it is clear that conditionalities dealing with the mere structure of the economy are more likely to be a top priority for both governments, firstly, because they usually meet other donors' exigencies, and also because their direct political impact is deemed to be rather low. In a globalized world, it is widely admitted that the scope of economic sovereignty has to be mutually discussed with donors. Both countries then agree to trade off part of their economic sovereignty against aid, but resist when it comes to political sovereignty.[23] The trade-off is conceivable only where national sovereignty itself is considered as a good that can be potentially exchanged for a reward. In the case of Turkey, the prospect of joining the EU is significant enough to trigger a painful redirectioning even of internal political priorities. The emphasis on economic standards was all the more essential as the country went through a real depression, endangering its ability to meet the Copenhagen criteria. At the same time, civil and political rights were certainly perceived as the number one issue feeding the hostility of European public opinion towards the Turkish candidacy [Hale, 2003]. The nation's choice was then to insist on the political criteria and to tackle the more high profiles issues such as the death penalty and the rights of the Kurdish minority.

By contrast, respecting more socially-oriented conditionalities is less immediately acceptable for recipient countries, because it may have uncontrolled political effects. In the case of Morocco, the permanence of social arrangements is very difficult to challenge and the social landscape is in a political deadlock. In summary, if it is not in the interest of ruling elites to improve social rights protection, then all efforts from outside powers to impose sound social reforms will fail.[24] The weight of internal political constraints is reflected in the shifting priorities of the Moroccan government, slowly rediscovering the importance of the missing social link. The adoption of the new labour code thus reveals the emergence of a new consensus between the trade unions, struggling for the advancement of social rights, the employers, who pay renewed attention to the issue of social peace, and the government, which is chiefly interested in normalizing labour legislation in order to attract foreign direct investment.

A Hidden European Responsibility

There also exists a growing European responsibility for the solidification against social conditionalities. Firstly, the EU has never really manifested its disagreement with the implicit benchmarking leading to discrimination between different layers of human rights in the internal priorities of Partner countries. Furthermore, some analysts also underline that a gradual perversion of the European vision is perceptible in the way the Copenhagen criteria have been implemented in Turkey. According to Mine Eder, the European project embedded in the Copenhagen criteria has in fact slowly shifted from a fundamentally Keynesian strategy, emphasising regional and social integration and cohesion, to a neoliberal agenda [Eder, 2003: 232]. In other words, Europe has become obsessed with competitiveness over the last decade, and progressively streamlined its integration project in order to make it meet the globalization agenda. Consequently, the EU has implicitly renounced an ideal of social harmonization, with common health and labour standards.

Mostly focused on macroeconomic criteria, all accession reports nonetheless reveal that the Commission still keeps an eye on social standards and regularly insists on the fundamental need to reduce regional and social inequalities in Turkey. Yet apart from simple encouragements, no particular guidelines are set out to help or eventually force the Turkish government into reconsidering its budgetary choices.

Ultimately, the practical ignorance of social and economic rights, or their downgrading to secondary objectives in the contractual relationship established with Europe, rests on a sort of implicit gentlemen's agreement. On the one side, Mediterranean governments may have no spontaneous conscience or interest in the potential of these rights to start a virtuous economic development cycle, or they might not be prone to encourage the rise of human claims anyway. On the other side, the EU favours a bluntly neoliberal pattern of development, occasionally mitigating it with targeted measures aimed at promoting, primarily, civil and political rights.

Social Relays for Social Rights: The Ownership Problem

In the conditionality theoretical framework constructed by the IFIs in the 1980s, ownership is a master concept supporting the viability of reforms. It is always important to remember that European intervention in the internal affairs of the partner countries can always be viewed with suspicion, due to its external nature. This is why the need to build a consensus in the recipient country over the objectives of reform is so important.

In some instances, one can discern a slow awakening of decision makers over the importance of the issue of economic and social rights. Eder thus states that 'Turkey's prospects for converging with the EU will depend on the economic and social reforms that the country is able to undertake on the domestic front' [Eder, 2003: 223]. Even if central governments do not make brave moves to systematically support social and economic rights, especially in times of political doubt or economic crisis, one could thus hope to find other social relays to spread the word of welfare and equity.

Business organizations might be the right relay. This direction of thought is especially promising in the Turkish context, where, from the beginning business unions have endorsed the risk of reforms. Reflecting on the potential role of TÜSIAD, Turkey's main business organization, Ziya Önis and Umut Turem rightly record that business interests have given growing support to liberal democracy and political pluralism in recently emerging second and third wave democracies, and go on to deliver a detailed account of TÜSIAD's very consistent commitment in favour of the promotion of civil and political rights. But at the same time, the authors admit that 'There is little room for income redistribution and the provision of social safety nets in TÜSIAD's vision of the optimal state' [Önis and Turem, 2002: 445, 450].

In most Maghreb countries, from the outset, businessmen viewed liberal economic reforms with suspicion, as they suspected that legal changes would hurt their companies. Moreover, in the case of Morocco, the country's professional organization of businessmen, the Confédération générale économique marocaine (CGEM) is a traditional partner of the King; it does not dare to carry out any autonomous moves [Dillman, 2002: 211] and does not provide the systematic 'counter-power attitude' that TÜSIAD assumes in the Turkish context. Yet occasional alliances may arise between different social forces, as in the convergence of priorities between the throne, the business community and the unions in the case of the promulgation of the new labour code.

The 'New Neighbourhood' Initiative: Some Room for Improvement?

The definition of a new 'proximity policy' in a joint move by the European Commission and the Council [European Commission, 2003c] sheds new light on the issue of conditionality. The 'Neighbourhood' initiative seems to confirm the normalization of the EMP, which is explicitly embedded in a wider foreign perspective. At the same time, conditionality is presented as a key instrument to accelerate convergence between all neighbour countries. Does this new scheme provide a clear set of values and operational standards?

Valued Borders, Blurring Values

The 'new Neighbourhood' initiative gathers in a single perspective very different countries that happen to share a geographical border, or quasi-border – namely, the Mediterranean Sea in the case of most MPCs – with Europe. The new framework thus places the MPCs on an equal footing with European countries which already are, or are likely to enter, the EU. When one reflects thoroughly on the Neighbourhood project, the coherence of its scope seems weak. The issues at stake are obviously not the same for all countries; the MPCs admittedly joined the list of targeted countries rather late, in order for the EU to attain the appearance of global balance that actually does not rest upon sound economic or political fundamentals.

The content of the new neighbourhood project is very close to the former Single European Market scheme: the EU essentially encourages partner countries to converge on European legal standards. Merging the EMP into the new Neighbourhood thus means exporting, more explicitly than in the past decade, the historical pattern of European construction to the Mediterranean. However, when compared to the terms of the Barcelona Declaration, the strategic ambition of the project appears rather diluted. Therefore, it is quite hazardous at the moment to predict that the enforcement of the 'new Neighbourhood' initiative implies a spectacular shift in favour of the external promotion of economic and social rights. Consequently, and as stated before, it is becoming increasingly problematic to systematically presuppose that the bad will of MPCs is solely to account for their failure in implementing a socially sustainable model of development.

Reflections on a Renewed Role for Conditionality

The final budgetary implications of the 'Neighbourhood' initiative are still unclear since the impact of European enlargement on resources devoted to external aid was already significant. The 'Neighbourhood' initiative now advocates for a de facto competition for financial resources between all neighbour countries. This game is risky for MPCs, which will have to demonstrate an upgraded ability to respond to external solicitations and make better use of the funds dedicated to bilateral co-operation.

Conditionality is thus presented as a fundamental instrument to discriminate between 'good' – performing – and 'bad' partners. In the vision exposed by the Commission, benchmarking becomes a key word under the renewed rule of positive conditionality. The comparison that we have tried to develop between the Moroccan system of reaction to conditionalities, and the Turkish attitude, makes real sense in this context: it is very difficult to conceive how to emphasize the MPCs' interest in reform if accession is not proposed as a final incentive in the new contract. If the same conditionalities apply to all neighbour countries, regardless of the substantial contents of their relationship to Europe, the results are very likely to be unequally rewarding. The risk is to encourage a background economic strife between supposed partners, the MPCs being in practice relegated as secondary players compared to European partners, in a neoliberal regional division of labour. Likewise, one can seriously question the efficacy of conditionality, be it positive or negative, if a decreasing budget is devoted to Mediterranean co-operation. Arguably, the capacity of conditionalities to bolster reform partly depends on, and increases, with the amount of aid that is offered. There is now a serious chance that European aid to the Mediterranean tends to diminish with the enforcement of the new Neighbourhood Policy; it thus risks being politically overlooked by MPCs in the future.

The Europeans will thus be compelled to invent fine technical solutions in order to show their ability to cope with the concrete particularities of every national context, and to prove that they can respond better to the development needs of MPCs. One optimistic solution we could suggest here is that insisting on medium range objectives is an efficient way to manage the conditionality contract and to obtain a correct input/result ratio. The diffusion of social and economic good practices could, in this case, be considered as a good intermediary target. When treated on a rather technical scale, social and economic rights are a rather painless objective to insist on. They can at least provide fuel for positive bargaining, and the side effects of such positive negotiation would be extremely valuable for the Partnership, both economically and politically.

Conditionality and the Promotion of Social and Economic Rights: An Unequally Efficient Tool for a Fragile Agenda

The relationship between economic growth and the expansion of social and economic rights is far from being demonstrated empirically. Furthermore, some authors suggest that a central paradox of democratization in the age of globalization is that democracy goes along with the expansion of certain types of individual rights, such as property rights and civil and human rights, and the contraction of other types of rights such as social rights [Önis and Turem, 2002: 452]. Increasing public consciousness of this growing dilemma has become urgent. Yet, even recognizing the growing discrepancy between the search for competitiveness and for justice, there still remains the need to devise the right instruments in order to fill the gap and ensure a constant progression of all types of human rights. Will conditionality be the right route?

Following the end of the Cold War, conditionality concretely joined the extensive set of foreign policy tools available to the state. It has emerged from its narrow economic usage to endorse new political functions. This evolution could be compared to the widening of the notion of human rights, from the strictly defined civil and political rights to the 'new' social and economic rights. Yet if we transpose these two processes into a single chart, they do not coincide chronologically. Strangely enough, social and economic rights have had the opportunity to figure on the agenda of classical economic conditionality; but they do not match the trajectory of political conditionality yet. Political conditionality usually sticks to a rather traditional definition of human rights, probably in order not to cast any doubt on its final goal and inspire any bargaining on the part of the aided country.

Moreover, one needs to acknowledge the global disappointment about the use of conditionality at large. This deception does not concern the contents of conditionalities, such as its neoliberal orientation that have inspired very severe comments since the end of the 1980s. Neither is it about the inevitable asymmetry of the conditionality mechanism, reinforcing the theoretical material domination of the donor upon the recipient. Rather, the present lack of understanding essentially concerns the technical performances of conditionalities. New essential critics deal with assessment methods, the framing of indicators, the efficiency of incentives as compared to sanctions, or the organization of the decision-making process that could trigger potential sanctions. So many different systems can indeed be imagined that it becomes hardly possible to compare one apparatus to another. To choose the right system, one has to prove a thorough understanding of field data. We have tried to demonstrate through our two case studies that the EU can be unequally successful in applying different systems of conditionality to different Mediterranean countries. Success partly depends on the final incentive for fulfilling the contract, on the balance of powers between the donor and the recipient, and also on the recipient's willingness or capacity to internalize the EU's own agenda of reforms.

But in any case, the agenda on social and economic rights does not seem to be really supported by the EU in its dealing with the MPCs. Downgrading partial economic rights; lagging behind on social rights; abandoning initial political ambitions: this could be a laconic résumé of the new neoliberal philosophy permeating the present practice of the EMP. If the political will emerges to move back in the initial direction and restart the 'twin liberalizations' engine, conditionality could still intervene as a good formula to give to the Partnership the time markers it has always lacked. Far from the liberal mythology and the belief in universal and automatic progress, conditionality remains a very practical and rather fair method to restore dialogue between partners from the North and from the South over the final objectives of the Barcelona Process. It is an interesting opportunity to restart working together practically on mutually-agreed objectives, within a time-consistent frame of work.

Notes

[1] This expression resumes the theoretical link established by European bureaucrats between economic and political liberalization. The concept is especially present in the Euro-Mediterranean co-operation frame [Schmid, 2002: 11].

[2] The concepts and data combined in this paper partly derive from an extensive field study completed in Morocco, Turkey and Brussels in 2002–03, which inspired a full report [Schmid, 2003]. Actualization of the data was performed mainly through interviews completed in Brussels and Paris in 2003–04.

[3] The first programme with binding performance criteria initiated by the IMF in 1958 concerned Portugal [Dreher, 2002].

[4] The rationale behind political conditionality was actually observable under bilateral co-operation frameworks in the past; American external aid has for instance been traditionally more politicized than multilateral donors' interventions, especially during the Cold War. Yet the enlargement of the geographical and functional scope of conditionality is historically linked to the collapse of Eastern Europe's socialist economies after 1989, empirically demonstrating the organic link between economic systems and the political regimes.

[5] Starting with the 1948 *Universal Declaration of Human Rights*, that generated afterwards a sophisticated legal apparatus dealing with more specific issues including the two Covenants on Economic, Social and Cultural Rights and Civil and Political Rights (1966); the Convention Against Torture (1984) and Conventions on the Rights of the Child (1989); Discrimination Against Women (1979) and Racial Discrimination (1966).

[6] Careful scrutiny of the IMF rationale suggests that the IFIs had to cope gradually with collective claims on social and economic rights in countries impoverished by structural adjustment programmes; these claims actually emerged before political demands. See *Revue nouvelle* [1999].

[7] We owe this important remark, that sets the basis for further essential reflection on the political scope of the Barcelona process, to Iván Martin [2004].

[8] This general impression derives from conversations held principally with Egyptian and Moroccan experts.

[9] Such clauses are not exclusive of the Euro-Mediterranean regime: they have by now been generalized to practically all bilateral external agreements signed by the EU. For a thorough legal discussion of the inspiration and implications of these article 2 clauses in all external agreements completed with the EU, see Fierro, [2001]; for a special focus on the Euro-Mediterranean case, see Bartels, in this issue.

[10] Sanctions have to be decided by the European Council at a qualified majority, upon a proposal made by the Commission. Such a process was never completed to date. The most publicized and controversial case concerned the possibility of taking sanctions against the State of Israel to condemn its policy with regard to the Palestinian population in the Occupied Territories in Spring 2002, but no sanction was decided. At this stage of implementation, the Barcelona framework thus seems to be paradoxically enough less severe than the previous Euro-Mediterranean regime, which allowed the European Parliament to block aid on several occasions on violation of human rights grounds.

[11] One late yet growing preoccupation among Turkish decision makers is the attitude of European public opinion and politicians with respect to the Turkish candidacy. In view of that, Müftüler-Bac and MacLaren, [2003] praise the emergence of a 'dynamics of inclusion', succeeding the 'dynamics of exclusion'.

[12] The late King Hassan II issued an official demand for Morocco to join the European Economic Community (EEC) in 1987. He was afforded no encouragement on this issue at the time.

[13] Such a positive appraisal of the Moroccan political reform process could certainly be disputed; yet what we want to underline here is that this optimism has become the common mood of most actors at the Commission and inside the bureaucracies of the most involved member states (especially France).

[14] We intentionally use the expression 'political correctness' in order to draw the reader's attention to the formal consistency of this reform process: legal reforms concerning human rights in Turkey should of course be carefully scrutinized and confronted to practice within the coming years [Emerson, 2004; IKV, 2004].

[15] For a review of all data according to the Copenhagen criteria framework, see the European Commission [2003b].

[16] For reliable data, see Fergany [2001].

[17] Written work dedicated to the situation of economic and social rights in Turkey is rather scarce, compared to the literature dealing with political rights; see Arin [2002]; Akkaya [2002]. To gather updated, accurate data and analysis concerning the state of social legislation in Morocco, please see the bulletin regularly issued by the Social Department at the French Mission Economique et Financière in Rabat, *Actualités sociales Maroc*.

[18] On the connection between globalization and the treatment of human rights, specifically the evolution of social and economic rights, see, for example, Kapstein and Milanovic [2001]; Flauss [2002]; Wai [2003].

[19] The economic press itself regularly echoes this concern by now. See *Le Moniteur du Commerce international* [2003].

[20] After two decades of hesitations on the topic, the project for a new Labour code was adopted by the Moroccan Parliament in July 2003, and has entered into force on June 2004 [Réau, 2004].

[21] This statement derives from interviews held at the European Delegation and the French Mission Economique et Financière in Rabat.

[22] Data taken from an unpublished document from the European Commission, 2003.

[23] The trade-off is conceivable only to the extent that national sovereignty itself is somewhat considered as a good that can be potentially exchanged for a reward. In the case of Turkey, the prospect of joining the EU is significant enough to trigger a painful re-directioning even of internal political priorities.

[24] As Dillman states, 'Incumbent elites can forestall democratization by a selective engagement that maintains distributional coalitions and co-opts largely dependant domestic private sector' [Dillman, 2002: 200].

References

Akkaya, Y. (2002): 'The Working Class and Unionism in Turkey under the Shackles of the System and Developmentalism', in N. Balkan and S. Sungur (eds.), *The Ravages of Neoliberalism: Economy, Society and Gender in Turkey*, New York: Huntington/Nova Science.

Arin, T. (2002): 'The Poverty of Social Security: The Welfare Regime in Turkey', in N. Balkan and S. Sungur (eds.), *The Ravages of Neoliberalism: Economy, Society and Gender in Turkey*, New York: Huntington/Nova Science.

Balkan, N. and S. Sungur (eds.) (2002): *The Ravages of Neoliberalism: Economy, Society and Gender in Turkey*, New York: Huntington/Nova Science.

Carothers, T. (2002): 'The End of the Transition Paradigm', *Journal of Democracy* 13/1, pp.1–21.

Crawford, G. (1997): 'Foreign Aid and Political Conditionality: Issues of Effectiveness and Inconsistency', *Democratization* 4/3, pp.69–108.

Dillman, B. (2001): 'Facing the Market in North Africa', *Middle East Journal* 55/2, pp.198–215.

Dillman, B. (2002): 'International Markets and Partial Economic Reforms in North Africa: What Impact on Democratization?', *Democratization* 9/1, pp.63–86.

Dreher, A. (2002): *The Development and Implementation of IMF and World Bank Conditionality*, Hamburgisches Welt-Wirtschafts-Archiv (HWWA) Discussion Paper #165, Hamburg Institute For International Economics.

Eder, M. (2003): 'Implementing the Economic Criteria of EU Membership: How Difficult is it for Turkey', *Turkish Studies* 4/1, pp.219–44.

Emerson, M. (2004): 'Has Turkey fulfilled the Copanhagen Political Criteria?', *CEPS Policy Brief* 48.

European Commission (2003a): *A First Assessment of MEDA Economic Cooperation*, Euromed Special Feature 36.

European Commission (2003b): *2003 Regular Report on Turkey's Progress Towards Accession*, available at ‹http://www.europa.eu.int/comm/enlargement/report_2003/pdf/ rr_tk_final.pdf›.

European Commission (2003c): *Communication from the Commission to the Council and the European Parliament: Wider Europe – Neighbourhood: A New Framework for Relations with our Eastern and Southern Neighbours*, 11.3.2003, COM (2003) 104 final.

Fergany, N. (ed.) (2001): *Human Development and the Acquisition of Advanced Knowledge in Arab Countries: The Role of Higher Education, Research and Technological Development*, New York: United Nations Development Programme (Human Development Series).

Fierro, E. (2001): 'Legal Basis and Scope of the Human Rights Clauses in EC Bilateral Agreements: Any Room for Positive Interpretation?', *European Law Journal* 7/1, pp.41–68.

Flauss, J.F. (2002): 'Le droit international des droits de l'Homme face à la globalisation économique', *Petites Affiches* 104, pp.4–20.

Hale, W. (2003): 'Human Rights, The European Union and the Turkish Accession Process', *Turkish Studies* 4/1, pp.107–26.

IKV (İktisadisi Kalkınma Vakfı) (2004): 'Enhanced political dialogue and political criteria (Short and medium term priorities fulfilled by Turkey)', available at ‹http://www.ikv.org.tr/ikv-eng/evaluation/ evaluation.html#›.

Kapstein, E.B. and B. Milanovic (2001): 'Responding to Globalization: Social Policies in Emerging Market Economies', *Global Social Policy* 1/2, pp.173–210.

Lannon, E., Inglis, K. and T. Haenelbacke (2001): 'The Many Faces of EU Conditionality in Pan-Euro Mediterranean Relations', in M. Maresceau and E. Lannon (eds.), *The EU's Enlargement and Mediterranean Strategies*, London: Macmillan.

Martin, I. (2004): *L'impact du libre-eéhange sur les droits sociaux dans la zone euro-méditerranéenne*, contribution to the Ifri conference, L'interaction entre les trois volets du Partenariat euro-méditerranéen, January, Paris.

Masson, J.R. (2003): 'De MEDA I à MEDA II: les cooperátions europeanes dan le domaine social', *Actualités sociales Maroc* 14, pp.1–4.

Mekaoui, A. (2000): *Le Partenariat économique euro-marocain: une intégration régionale stratégique*, Paris: L'Harmattan.

Menendez, A.J. (2002): 'Chartering Europe: Legal Status and Policy Implications of the Charter of Fundamental Rights of the European Union', *Journal of Common Market Studies* 40/3, pp.471–90.

Le Moniteur du Commerce international (2003): 'Maroc: priorité au social', July, pp.14–40.

Müftüler-Bac, M. and L.M. MacLaren (2003): 'Enlargement Preferences and Policy-Making in the European Union: Impacts on Turkey', *Revue d'intégration européenne* 25/1, pp.17–30.

Nelson, J. and S. Eglington (1993): *Global Goals, Contentious Means: Issues of Multiple Conditionality,* *ODC Policy Essay* #10, Washington, DC.

Önis, Z. and U. Turem (2002): 'Entrepreneurs, Democracy and Citizenship in Turkey', *Comparative Politics* 34/4, pp.439–56.

Réau, P. (2004): 'Le Maroc réglemente son marché du travail', available at ‹http://www.cfdt.fr/actualite/inter/actualite/afrique/2004/afrique_2004_01.html›

Revue Nouvelle (1999): Special Issue on 'FMI? les droits de l'Homme ajustés', 7/8, pp. 28–89.

Santiso, C. (2000): 'International Co-operation for Democracy and Good Governance: Moving Towards a Second Generation?', *The European Journal of Development Research* 13/1, pp.154–80.

Schmid, D. (2002): *Optimiser le Processus de Barcelone*, Occasional Paper 36, Paris: Institut d'études de sécurité de l'Union européenne.

Schmid, D. (2003): 'Linking Economic, Institutional and Political Reform/Conditionality Within the Euro-Mediterranean Partnership', EuroMeSCo Paper 27.

Smith, K.E. (1998): 'The Use of Political Conditionality in the EU's Relations with Third Countries: How Effective?', *European Foreign Affairs Review* 1998/2, pp.253–74.

Stokke, O. (1995): 'Aid and Political Conditionality: Core Issues and State of the Art', in O. Stokke (ed.), *Aid and Political Conditionality*, London: Frank Cass.

Uvin, P. and I. Biagiotti (1996): 'Global Governance and the "New" Political Conditionality', *Global Governance* 1996/2, pp.377–400.

Van Westering, J. (2000): 'Conditionality and EU Membership: The Cases of Turkey and Cyprus', *European Foreign Affairs Review* 2000/5, pp.95–118.

Wai, R. (2003): 'Countering, Branding, Dealing: Using Economic and Social Rights In and Around the International Trade Regime', *European Journal of International Law* 14/1, pp.35–84.

Youngs, R. (2001): 'Democracy Promotion: The Case of European Union Strategy', CEPS Working Document 167.

Youngs, R. (2002): 'The European Union and Democracy Promotion in the Mediterranean: A New or Disingenuous Strategy?', *Democratization* 9/1, pp.40–62.

Imagining Co-presence in Euro-Mediterranean Relations: The Role of 'Dialogue'

MICHELLE PACE

European Research Institute, University of Birmingham, UK

ABSTRACT   *This article attempts to draw upon the work of a key thinker on dialogue, Mikhail Bakhtin, to shed light on dialogue in the Euro-Mediterranean Partnership. It also draws upon the work of Bruce Tuckman's 1965 forming, storming, norming and performing group development model. By applying these theoretical frameworks to the specific case of Euro-Mediterranean relations, the article aims to uncover the challenges facing EU-Mediterranean partners in developing mutual relations through dialogue. It also suggests ways in which obstacles to improved Euro-Mediterranean dialogic ties could be overcome.*

Introduction

A key external relations priority for the European Union (EU) is the creation of an area of dialogue, co-operation and exchange in the South and East Mediterranean and the Middle East – an area of vital strategic importance for the EU. With the Euro-Mediterranean Partnership (EMP), the EU created an innovative policy basket, in that, through the Barcelona declaration, the 27 signatories recognized that for the Euro-Mediterranean relationship to work, dialogue between people (not just the elite) was essential. Activities under the third (social, cultural and human affairs) basket of the EMP have since flourished (MEDA-Democracy, Euro-Mediterranean Heritage, Euro-Mediterranean Audiovisual, Euro-Mediterranean Youth Action Programme, etc). These have been complemented (since 1995) by the Forum Civil Euro-Mediterranean (FCE) through civil society conferences that run alongside all Euro-Mediterranean Ministerial Conferences. One of the main functions of the FCE is to encourage and enhance intercultural dialogue between the Mediterranean partners and the EU member states. Other turning-points in Euro-Mediterranean relations were the launching of the Euro-Mediterranean Parliamentary Assembly, the Euro-Mediterranean Non-Governmental Platform and the setting up of the 'Anna Lindh Euro-Mediterranean Foundation for the Dialogue between Cultures'. Despite these various activities, there has been no systematic analysis of what the Euro-Mediterranean dialogue actually implies and how it increasingly shapes EU-Mediterranean agendas. At a time when the perception of the irreconcilable nature of cultures is growing it is important to take seriously the concept of dialogue between European and Mediterranean cultures. This essay aims to fill this gap in the literature by critically examining the role of dialogue in Euro-Mediterranean relations. It first establishes the nature of dialogue and its significance for Euro-Mediterranean relations. For this purpose, it draws upon the work of a key thinker on dialogue, Mikhail Bakhtin. The theoretical section also draws upon the work of Bruce Tuckman's 1965 forming, storming, norming and performing group development model and adapts these theoretical frameworks to the EMP. The empirical section, which follows, sketches out what Euro-Mediterranean dialogue actually entails, analyses what dialogue seeks to attain, and finally concludes with some implications for the future of Euro-Mediterranean dialogic relations.

Nature of Dialogue and Significance for Euro-Mediterranean Relations

The nature and utility of dialogue in international politics and in the Euro-Mediterranean process in particular cannot be underestimated. Indeed, nowhere is the need for, and the difficulty of, achieving dialogue more evident than in the Euro-Mediterranean space. Emanating from the cleavages in this area – the cultural confrontations and the economic gap between the North and the South (to mention just a few) – are the central securitization discourses of our time: radical fundamentalism, proliferation of weapons of mass destruction, international terrorism, migration, the drug trade, and interstate conflicts. The task of bridging the cleavages that give rise to these securitized practices is both urgent and long overdue. The EMP represents a radical departure from past EU efforts to achieve security through alliances, economic interdependence and other conventional practices. The thrust of the Barcelona Declaration is one of community and region-building and the creation of a security partnership, eventually leading to a security community through, among other instruments, a dialogue in the sense of the progressive development of shared understandings (Habermas, 1984 and Malmvig in this volume). Certainly, the Euro-Mediterranean process has the potential to develop into a 'dialogue of partners' that could replace or at least weaken discourses on the 'clash of civilizations' in this challenging area (Huntington, 1993). But, in practice, could dialogue instead lead to a 'convergence of differences' between the factions participating in the dialogue? Do participants really engage in processes that allow them to put themselves in the shoes of the 'other'? How can the participants create the needed sense of equality so necessary for dialogue when the economic gap between the Mediterranean and European partners is so glaring? Some of the participants in the Barcelona process are states that are weak. Can their representatives be partners in the dialogue? These are just a few of the questions which shed light on the importance of a better understanding of the nature of successful dialogue which, in turn, is crucial to our understanding of the success or failure of the EMP itself. In fact, the Barcelona process is a laboratory where one of the most ambitious experiments in international relations may have started to take place.

The need for increased dialogue arose following the end of the Cold War, the EU's shift Eastward and the new post-Cold War securitization discourses of the region that motivated the EU to look to enter into dialogue with the Mediterranean in the early 1990s. During 1992 and 1993 the Commission proposed that future relations with Mediterranean Non-Member Countries (MNCs) should go beyond the financial sector and economic sphere to include a dialogue between the parties, the creation of a Euro-Mediterranean free-trade area and social, economic and cultural cooperation. These recommendations, initially looking just to a Euro-Maghrebi partnership, were approved at the Lisbon summit in June 1992 and confirmed at the Corfu summit in June 1994 (these summits are in fact European Council meetings). In the meantime, negotiations got underway with Tunisia, Morocco and Israel on the basis of mandates specifying these four basic elements. With the launching of the EMP in November 1995 and the European Neighbourhood Policy (ENP) in 2003, it has become commonly accepted that the EU's 'dialogue' with Mediterranean partners is one of the main instruments as well as achievements in EU-Mediterranean cooperation. However, although the term appears in virtually all EMP/ENP documentation, there seems to be no coherent understanding of what dialogue actually means. Its meaning is therefore in need of clarification (Monar, 1997).

Understanding 'Dialogue'

In our day-to-day interpretation of the term 'dialogue', we usually refer to dialogue as communication or discussion between people or groups of people such as governments or political parties (Collins, 1987). By means of the EMP, the EU aims to promote dialogue across the Euro-Mediterranean area on political, economic and social themes. The EMP marked a move from Euro-Mediterranean contacts, of an ad hoc and formal nature, to somewhat regular and institutionalized contacts. According to one author, three conditions have to be met for the effective use of the term dialogue:

- A formal decision of the (Euro-Mediterranean) Committee and/or the ministers to engage in a 'dialogue';
- A formal agreement with the (Mediterranean) partners concerned;
- In addition to normal diplomatic relations, regular political contacts have to be provided for at one or various levels.[1]

In Euro-Mediterranean affairs, relations are governed broadly by the EMP, of which the Euro-Mediterranean Association Agreements (EMAA) are a vital feature. The Partnership provides for a comprehensive framework for Euro-Mediterranean relations structured along three pillars: a political and security partnership, an economic and financial partnership and a partnership in social, cultural and human affairs. The three pillars or baskets offer different forms of dialogue: political/security, economic and social.

In its most recent initiative, the Neighbourhood Policy, the EU aims to deepen its relations with Mediterranean partners through 'a more intensive political dialogue' (Council of the European Union, 2002; European Commission, 2003 and 2004). The main instruments for the deepening of this dialogue are Action Plans which aim at enhancing the Barcelona Process.

Theorizing Euro-Mediterranean Dialogic Relations

Euro-Mediterranean politics have few resources to assess the quality of Euro-Mediterranean cultural interactions that shape and are shaped by the changing structures and processes of the EU system, as well as the wider international system. One way of arriving at a potential framework for critically thinking about Euro-Mediterranean dialogic relations is to draw upon the work of the critical thinker, Mikhail Bakhtin.

Despite Bakhtin's acknowledged relevance to the social sciences, Euro-Mediterranean politics have been relatively unreceptive towards his thinking. Drawing upon literary theory, Bakhtin's theories focus primarily on the concept of dialogue, and on the notion that language (that is, any form of speech or writing) is always a dialogue. Acknowledged as the philosopher of dialogue, he evolved a view of dialogue (from his earliest writings in pre-revolutionary Russia through his last unfinished manuscript in the mid-1970s), as a human condition, as an ethical imperative, and even as a prerequisite for thinking.[2] Thus, his notion of dialogue focuses on the idea of the social nature of dialogue, and the idea of struggle inherent in it. For Bakhtin, dialogue consists of three elements:

- a speaker,
- a listener/respondent, and
- a relation between the two.

Language and the outcome of language (or what language says; ideas, characters, forms of truth) are always thus the product of the interactions between (at least) two people or two groups.

Bakhtin contrasts the notion of dialogue with what it is not, that is, the idea of monologue, or what he terms as the *monologic*, which refers to utterances by a single person or entity. For Bakhtin, ideas about language have always postulated a unitary speaker, a speaker who has an unmediated relation to 'his unitary and singular "own" language.' Like Derrida's 'engineer', this speaker claims to 'produce unique meaning in [my] own speech; [my] speech comes from [me] alone.' Hence, according to Bakhtin, this way of thinking about language focuses on two pillars: language as a system, and the individual who speaks it. For Bakhtin, both pillars, however, produce monologic language: a language that seems to come from a single, unified source (Bakhtin, 1981: 666).

Bakhtin develops his work on dialogue further by arguing that there are two principal forces in operation whenever language is used: a centripetal force and a centrifugal force (ibid.: 667–8). Drawing upon physics, Bakhtin argues that, on the one hand, a centripetal force tends to push things toward a central point; on the other hand, a centrifugal force tends to push things away from a central point and out in all directions (see Figure 1).

According to Bakhtin, monologic language (monologia) operates according to centripetal forces: the speaker of monologic language attempts to push all the elements of language and all its various rhetorical modes (the journalistic, the

Centri*petal*	Centri*fugal*
Monologia/Monologue	Heteroglossa/dialogue
Assimilation of differences	Integration of multiple languages

→→→→→→→→→→→→→→→→→→o→→→→→→→ →→ →→→→→→→→→→→→→→

Central point

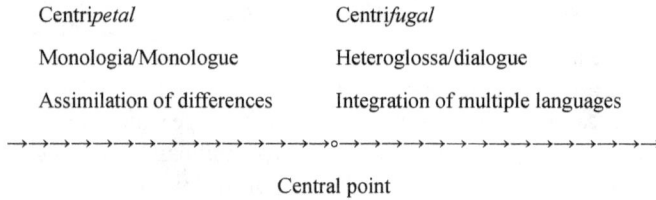

Figure 1. Bakhtin's chosen site for intercultural dialogue.

religious, the political, the economic, the academic, the personal) into one single form or utterance, converging into one central point. The centripetal force of monologia tries to get rid of differences between languages (or rhetorical modes) in order to present one unified language. Monologia is a system of norms, of one standard language, or an 'official' language, a standard language that everyone would have to speak (and which would then be enforced by various mechanisms).

An alternative form of dialogue is *heteroglossia,* which attempts to encompass a multiplicity of languages, that is by including a wide variety of different ways of speaking, different rhetorical strategies and vocabularies. In Bakhtinian terms, dialogue is therefore not understood in terms of multiple meanings for individual words or phrases, by disconnecting the signifier and the signified. Thus, instead of racing towards consensus, we may pause for reflection on the meanings conveyed by the Other.

Bakhtin argues that in any utterance, both monologia and heteroglossia, both the centripetal and the centrifugal forces of language are at work. 'Every concrete utterance of a speaking subject serves as a point where centrifugal as well as centripetal forces are brought to bear' (ibid.: 668). Language, in this sense, is always both anonymous and social, something formed beyond any individual, but also concrete, filled with specific content which is shaped by the speaking subject. Thus, for Bakhtin,

> the idea *lives* not in one person's *isolated* individual consciousness; if it remains there only, it degenerates and dies. The idea begins to live, that is, to take shape, to develop, to find and renew its verbal expression, to give birth to new ideas, only when it enters into genuine dialogic relationships with other ideas, with the ideas of *others*. Human thought becomes genuine thought, that is, an idea, only under conditions of living contact with another and alien thought, a thought embodied in someone else's voice, that is, in someone else's consciousness expressed in discourse (Todorov, 1984: 87–8).[3]

A heteroglossic view of dialogue points to a conceptualization of politics and the social focusing on the crucial importance of language for politics. Language is a creative force rather than an empty vehicle for consensus-building. Moreover, such a conception of dialogue emphasizes the inter-subjective and perpetual cognition and meaning formation inherent in this process. It also stresses that *everybody*, every member of the polity, has a voice, not only the decision makers and those who have their ear (Neumann, 2003).

This brings us to the discussion of the Self and the Other through the dialogic interaction of the two. In this context, dialogue plays itself out at various degrees. The first degree of dialogue requires the unity of the Self (Hanafi, cited in Pace and Schumacher, 2004). The dialogic process thus requires reconciliation with the Self before interaction with an Other. At the second level of dialogue, an acceptance of the Other in dialogue has to be in place. To come back to Bakhtin's work, critics interested in seeing the heteroglossia in Euro-Mediterranean relations would seek to encourage a dialogic relation embedded in social relations, which can be described as a relation with a distinct social purpose. As Neumann argues, it is precisely because dialogue plays itself out at different levels that social practices become crucial. Dialogue places subjects along a process of inter-action with others that constitute the Self (Neumann, cited in Pace and Schumacher, 2004). As the colonizer defined the colonized, so too, the colonized defined the colonizer. This mirror-image of the Self through the Other, à la Lacan, sheds light on societal codes and the way in which these are shaped, reshaped and lived out. Dialogue therefore involves a dynamic interplay of cultures between discourse (being) and practice (becoming) (ibid.: 123). Cultures are distinctive in the sense that there cannot be a one-to-one relationship between the respective phenomena that comprise them, but if a person is grounded in one culture, they can begin to grasp another by melding its phenomena into their own cultural horizon. Communication then becomes a possibility (ibid.: 123) and postulates a 'fusion of horizons' which signifies the growing 'convergence of our *and* their perspectives through a process of reciprocal learning' (Dallmayr, 2001: 341).

In aiming to understand the mythical aspect of the Other's (social) personality, a dialogical dialogue thus seeks a *common* horizon. Hence, dialogue, of necessity, must be never ending (Neumann, cited in Pace and Schumacher, 2004: 123). The process of a dialogical dialogue itself aims to bring about *a* horizon, defined as a new, emerging understanding through the exploration by imagination of new modes of human possibilities. Bakhtin argues that all utterances are directed toward an answer, a response. (In everyday speech, words are understood by being taken into the listener's own conceptual system, filled with specific objects and emotional expressions, and being related to these); the understanding of an utterance is thus inseparable from the listener's response to it. All speech is thus oriented toward what Bakhtin calls the 'conceptual horizon' of the listener; this horizon is comprised of the various social languages the listener inhabits/uses. This is why Bakhtin argues that 'discourse lives on the boundary between its own context and another, alien, context' (Bakhtin, 1981: 672–3).

A good model for what a heteroglossic Euro-Mediterranean dialogue could look like is the language of democracy. As argued by one author:

> We also need to be modest about our ability to find the answers for other socie-
> ties. Liberal democracy is the best form of government yet discovered. But if you
> rush to a multi-party election without first developing the underpinnings of liberal
> democracy – the rule of law, civil society, private property, independent media –
> you can end up with what Fareed Zakaria has called 'illiberal democracy'. We can,
> and should, offer a toolbox of experiences in all aspects of transition, from how

to write a constitution to how to deal with a difficult past. But then it's up to them (Garton Ash, 2004a and 2004b).

Thus, there is no single, unified language of democracy but many languages of democracy. In using all these languages, the aim is to increase the potential options for Mediterranean partners, as the democratic norm probably contains some kind of language which every Mediterranean partner has as part of their existing vocabulary or 'horizon'. In recognizing its post-colonial role, Europe has to bring together the best of Europe as well as the best of the Mediterranean. It is therefore helpful for analytical, as well as practical purposes, to interpret dialogue not just as conversation but also as process (Guillaume, 2002; Inayatullah and Blaney, 2004). To avoid criticisms of Eurocentrism or elitism, inter-cultural dialogue must therefore, of necessity, be the product of an *inter-action* between the parties concerned: a process of self-criticism and self-reflection through imagining the Other. A dialogic dialogue opens up the possibility for learning, so that different languages may be reconfigured through the process and may be modified (no one language emerges as triumphant). The logic of a dialogic encounter is, then, an integrationist logic. Rather than claiming to have a dialogue on Mediterranean issues, Euro-Mediterranean relations should aim for that to which the dialogue converges.

As noted earlier, another way of arriving at this conclusion is to look at 'dialogue' in a Habermasian way. A main theme running through Habermas' critical theoretical works is that valid knowledge can only emerge from a situation of open, free and uninterrupted dialogue. His chosen site for intercultural imagination is the public sphere. He argues that the idea of a neutral apolitical science, based on a rigid separation of facts and values, is untenable since questions of truth are inextricably bound up with the political problems of freedom to communicate and to exchange ideas (Habermas, 1971 and 1974). Thus, 'dialogue' is not a neutral concept; many preconditions have to be met in order to have a conversation appropriately called a dialogue. One of these is the equality of the participants. Habermas is also critical of Western social theory for its failure to avoid reductionism and to develop a valid theory of communication and rationality (Habermas, 1984 and 1987). Thus, the nature of social science, being inherently a 'Western' *praxis*, is a means to the end of an intercultural dialogue. With such frameworks for thinking about dialogue it is difficult to find the terms through which one seeks to explore Others through interactions, without falling in the trap of ethnocentrism. In order to ensure an equitable climate for dialogue, there need to be some ground 'rules for practical discourse' that demand objectification, justification and non-contradiction in order to structure dialogue as debate. If dialogue with Mediterranean partners is to inform the EU's democratic decision-making, EU-Mediterranean actors themselves have to contribute to establishing the conditions for dialogue, particularly in those cases where such conditions are not already present. A prerequisite for dialogue is that a lot of common ground already exists. Dialogue should aim at freedom, that is, to 'call something into being which did not exist before, which was not given, not even as an object of cognition or imagination' (Arendt, 1961: 151). Theorizing Euro-Mediterranean politics is not only about ordering a set of already existing signs but also about creating new ones. A dialogic dialogue requires enlightenment beyond preconceived ideas of the Other. Different and mutually exclusive universalisms have to be reconciled in order to enter into a dialogue. Every worldview, whether European or Mediterranean, can construct its own reasons to enter into dialogue, with its own historically defined meanings attached to it. Thus we will be rid of the paradoxical task of being 'objective' in defining the terms of the dialogue (Griffioen, 2002).

As Bakhtin argues, the alternative to dialogue is monologue. In this context, the appeal of dialogue as a mode for being-in-the-world is particularly strong. In the complex reality of Euro-Mediterranean relations, however, the question remains: to what degree does this choice really exist? The conceptualization of dialogue, as developed by Bakhtin, is an ethically stimulating one but tells us little by way of the role of power in politics. Likewise, Habermas's ideal speech situation falls short of the reality of such a situation. This is particularly pertinent in Euro-Mediterranean relations where the EU's hegemony adds challenges to the development of real dialogue between the partners.

In theorizing Euro-Mediterranean politics, particularly the role of dialogue in Euro-Mediterranean relations, it is the task of social scientists to embrace the role of empirical studies on how dialogue actually ensues. We need to observe how Euro-Mediterranean dialogic practices interact with other practices and how power relations (specifically the EU's hegemony) are immersed within these practices. If we are to celebrate differences and to offer a space for alternative voices to be heard, dialogue has a crucial role to play both in our intellectual conceptualizations and even more so in policy-making circles which impact on people's social lives. Keeping in mind Bakhtin's conception of dialogue as a description of the human condition, we recognize that meaning formation is an intersubjective phenomenon and therefore does not exclude the possibility of monologue. For this reason, it is even more pertinent to engage in dialogue and open up to alternative 'languages'. Rather than losing ourselves in translation, let us lose ourselves in a truly dialogic relationship with others.

Bruce Tuckman's 1965 Forming Storming Norming Performing Development Model

Before moving on to analyse aspects of existing dialogic efforts in Euro-Mediterranean relations and examining whether dialogue is really taking place in the Barcelona process, a synthesis of the theoretical arguments, developed above, into a workable model is called for. The key to ongoing dialogue processes is equal access to participation under conditions of mutual recognition and the possibility for contestation, allowing possibilities to agree to disagree (Tully, 1995 and 2004). Bruce Tuckman developed a stage-model for group development through his Forming, Storming, Norming and Performing model (Tuckman, 1965). Most analysts assume that groups go through a number of phases or stages if they exist for an extended period. Tuckman's influential model exposes four stages going from (1) orientation/ testing/dependence (forming) to (2) conflict (storming) to (3) group cohesion (norming) and to (4) functional role-relatedness (performing). We can apply this model to European-Mediterranean group development but before that the next section will briefly expand Tuckman's model.

In the forming phase, groups orient themselves through testing to identify the boundaries of their behaviour. Through this process, one group establishes a dependency relationship with other group members. This phase can be linked to Bakhtin's inter-action stage in which language and the outcome of language is understood as the product of these inter-actions. The second phase is characterized by polarization and conflict around issues with behaviours serving as resistance to group influence and task requirements. If we link this to the dialogic process, it includes contestation which, as Antje Wiener argues, involves the possibility of (1) dialogue and deliberation and subsequent agreement (logic of arguing); (2) dialogue and disagreement; (3) disagreement and conflict among negotiating elites, and (4) contentious action in the respective elite negotiators' root cultural spheres (Tarrow, 1998: 12–13 in Wiener, 2005). In Bakhtinian terms this phase would include centripetal as well as centrifugal forces. The third phase is one where resistance is overcome and in which in-group feeling and cohesiveness develops, new standards evolve, and new roles are adopted. Groups are now better able to express opinions. Thus, in dialogic terms:

> genuine dialogue or consensus requires a reciprocity of understanding, in the sense that it is not up to others ('them') to understand 'our' perspective, but it is equally up to 'us' to grasp things from 'their' perspective' (Dallmayr, 2001: 341). This phase would eventually lead to Bakhtin's heteroglossia in which diversity of voices becomes the fundamental characteristic of group dynamics.

In the final phase, the groups work towards achieving task activities. Functional and flexible roles are in place, and group energies are channelled towards targeted objectives. The resolution of structural issues is in place and the structures become supportive of group performance. In Bakhtin's terminology, this would be the phase where groups seek a 'common' horizon and group inter-actions reach a level of maturity.

Having examined the various stages that group development experiences à la Tuckman and how these phases are linked to Bakhtin's work on dialogue, it is important to highlight that occasionally groups may revert to an earlier phase, particularly if the context is unfavourable to dialogic relations. With this dual conceptual framework in mind, we now turn to the empirical sites of dialogue in Euro-Mediterranean relations.

Theory and Practice: A Review of Ten Years of Euro-Mediterranean Dialogue

This section attempts an examination of how the partners in the Barcelona process feel about dialogue and an exploration of what kind of relationship both parties want and how the dialogue that exists reflects these objectives. It brings to the fore views of existing governments and organizations involved in the process of Euro-Mediterranean dialogue. Through an application of the conceptual frameworks on dialogue presented above, this section seeks to uncover the real meaning of dialogue in Euro-Mediterranean relations and the ensuing experience of the participants involved in this process.

The Forming Phase/Bakhtin's Inter-action Stage of Euro-Mediterranean Relations

Euro-Mediterranean affairs stretch back to the Treaty of Rome in 1957 when a series of policy initiatives were designed to regulate relations between Europe and its southern periphery (Joffé, 2005). When applying the stages of dialogue to Euro-Mediterranean relations, a pertinent question to ask is how far is the dialogue, in this context, shaped by Europe's colonial past in the Mediterranean area, and how extensive is the legacy of this historical period on the struggles Mediterranean partners have had to undergo through decolonization? In conventional theoretical frameworks, Euro-Mediterranean politics seem to miss the legacy of colonial rule which formed competitive cultures and which sanctified inequality and subjugated those outside the European centre. If Euro-Mediterranean relations are to engage in a truly dialogic dialogue, our theoretical frameworks must seriously and critically confront the role of colonialism, various responses to colonialism, neocolonialism and its legacies (Inayatullah and Blaney, 2004). As Joffé claims:

> In some respects, these (EU) initiatives represented a continuation of the experiences of the colonial era, especially the French relationship with its former colonies in North Africa. In reality, however, they reflected the inevitable and vital need for collaboration in view of European dependence on migrant labour from the Southern Mediterranean region, European dominance in the economic relationship across the Mediterranean and European involvement in regional security (Joffé, 2005).

The EU (previously EC) has thus held a hegemonic position in the Mediterranean area for a long time, and EU-superiority and Mediterranean-inferiority and dependency has been the order of their relations (Pace, 2005a). Moreover, although the EU member states and the Mediterranean partners share to some extent a common or at least a closely interrelated history – a shared language à la Bakhtin – as far as economic and social development is concerned, the Mediterranean countries, particularly the Arab partners, do not constitute a homogenous group (ibid.). One of the reasons for the hegemony of the European Union, vis-à-vis the Mediterranean area, is related to the levels of economic development between North and South. With Europe being so well integrated and the South so divided, the gap in degrees of regional integration between the two areas is evident (Moré, 2004). The EU is the largest provider of financial aid to some Mediterranean partners including Jordan and the Palestinian Territories (West Bank and Gaza Strip), while the other Mediterranean partners are also beneficiaries of financial aid from the EU. Morocco has been the leading recipient among the Mediterranean partners in terms of total funds received from the MEDA programme.

Moreover, while EU member states have a high Gross Domestic Product (GDP) per capita, attaining a maximum of $53,780 in the case of Luxembourg, this is not the case for Arab countries; for example, Morocco's GDP per capita is approximately 1/15th of Luxembourg's and 1/9th of Ireland's (Pace, 2005a). This disparity is also reflected in the Human Development Index (HDI) established by the United Nations Development Programme (UNDP, 2003).

To sum up, the forming phase of EU-Mediterranean dialogic relations is very much characterized by the EU taking the lead, while Mediterranean partners have been attempting to adapt to this new context in their relations with the EU. The gaps and discrepancies in the two groups' relations often lead to the next stage of group development (see below). The forming stage is also a process through which Euro-Mediterranean partners test the grounds and boundaries of their behaviour. In Bakhtinian terms, this is a stage at which European and Mediterranean partners formulate ideas about the other group, through inter-action.

The Storming Phase: Bakhtin's Stage of Centripetal Forces in Euro-Mediterranean Relations

The declared objectives of the third basket of the EMP raised high expectations with regards to the creation of closer links between peoples in the region through a social, cultural and human partnership designed to encourage mutual understanding and cooperation between civil societies in the Euro-Mediterranean space.

It is still, however, often argued that civil society is underdeveloped in the Mediterranean partner countries (see Feliu in this volume). Arab voices acknowledge, for example, that Arab civil societies have so far played a weak role during the course of the EMP's third basket implementation process (Ammor and Shalaby, cited in Pace and Schumacher, 2004). Although several programmes have been launched under the third basket umbrella, the mobility of human beings from the South to the North remains a major obstacle and bone of contention. To make human exchange opportunities viable, certain constraints have to be addressed. To take one example, the key to lively and significant international cultural (culture defined in a narrow sense) and educational exchanges and cross-fertilization is mobility. The current visa regulations to enter the Schengen zone provide huge bureaucratic hurdles to the free flow of ideas and intellectual and artistic stimulation. The actual process of acquiring a visa is not just cumbersome and time-demanding but also very discouraging not just for an artist but also for an inviting institution. The latter is faced with some considerable challenges: an invitation letter to an artist from a neighbouring Mediterranean country has to include a written guarantee of being solely responsible for the invitee's personal and medical needs during the stay in the Schengen zone, and also for their return journey after the expiry of the visa. These stipulations can have a deterring effect particularly for smaller cultural institutions within the EU that have no prior experience in inviting guests from non-EU Mediterranean countries: such procedures thus prevent cultural exchange and intellectual mobility (Pace, 2006).

Storming relations between EU and Mediterranean partners have also related to the EMP's first basket objectives. Barcelona's first-pillar initial aims addressed issues of political governance, seeking to encourage democratic governance and respect for human rights throughout the Mediterranean, which are in turn linked to the objectives of the second and third baskets of the EMP.

But, regular references to shaky and/or undemocratic political systems, 'poor' governance, bad human rights records, regional conflicts and political violence as the order of the day in Mediterranean countries are not lacking in international media discourses, international reports and everyday political speeches. For example, although Lebanon signed up to several international agreements on human and civil rights including in 1997 the International Covenant on the rights of women, it refrained from signing the Agreement against torture. Following the arrest of anti-Syrian demonstrators in Beirut in August 2001, the EU expressed concern on human rights issues, passing of death sentences and lengthy prison sentences on journalists in Lebanon. Closure of MTV in the second half of 2002 was the subject of an EU démarche in Beirut. In its Resolution adopted on 16 January 2003, the European Parliament drew attention to the situation regarding human rights and democracy in Lebanon (Pace, 2005a). In 1997, the Islamic Action Front in Jordan boycotted that year's parliamentary elections. In August 2002, King Abdullah once again post-poned the parliamentary elections (due in November 2001) to Spring 2003, without giving any new reasons (other than the instability in the 'region') to explain the new postponement. There have been several government reshuffles since the election of Ali Abul Ragheb's government from June 2000. In fact the average life span of Jordanian governments has been less than one year (since the country's existence) making this a destabilizing factor (although key ministers do keep their portfolios). Hence, a major constraint to political and economic reforms in Jordan has been the lack of continuity in governments. Algeria continues to be threatened by internal strife both from Islamic militants who have conducted a terror campaign since 1992, the Berber minority in eastern Algeria that has resorted to violence in search of greater autonomy, and the military who continue to exert considerable power. In July 2004, all 25 member states of the EU, in spite of intensive lobbying by Israel, supported a UN General Assembly Resolution, condemning Israel for its construction of the separation fence in the West Bank and demanding its immediate dismantlement. These are instances which created storming relations in EU and Mediterranean relations.

In terms of the second basket more specifically, this aims at promoting economic development through economic cooperation, based on the principle of free trade on a bilateral basis, mainly through association agreements with some partners having privileged arrangements such as a free trade area (Israel) and a customs union (Turkey). Here, once again, storming relations have prevailed in Euro-Mediterranean dialogic encounters. Despite almost ten years of the Barcelona process, Mediterranean countries are still struggling with economic challenges including: state-controlled economies, underdeveloped infrastructures, small Foreign Direct Investment, low competitiveness, falling percentage of EU imports, deficit of the balance of payments, weak economic growth, high dependence on the EU market, low incomes, highly unequal distribution of incomes within the Mediterranean, high population growth, deficit in basic social services, high (youth) unemployment, high (illegal) emigration and environmental problems. Since 1995, only Lebanon experienced a fall in its

population figure. The population of the majority of Mediterranean countries is relatively young. Young people are in turn most affected by unemployment. Egypt is by
far the most populous country in the Arab world, and the rate at which the country's
population is increasing remains quite high, at around 1.7 per cent annually. With an
official unemployment rate of 9.5 per cent in 2002, the country faces a great challenge in providing sufficient employment for large groups of young people entering
the workforce each year. Unemployment is fairly high in most of the MPCs. Although
unemployment rates have fallen slowly in the Maghreb countries, since 2000, they
are still among the highest in the region. In fact, from 1995, the rate of unemployment in the Mediterranean has been generally increasing – only Lebanon, Morocco
and Tunisia experienced a slight decrease in unemployment since 1995. With a
young population and an estimated 27.5 per cent unemployment rate, Algeria, like
Egypt, urgently requires economic opportunities for its young. In Turkey, the government is facing a challenging test of its commitment to the reform programme of the
agricultural sector that employs nearly 50 per cent of the workforce. With more than
a quarter of the population already living below the poverty line, Turkey has yet to
organize large-scale corporate farming to compete with the world's agricultural
powers (Pace, 2005a).

Moreover, most Mediterranean partners have a trade deficit with the EU. Syria
and Algeria are the only Mediterranean partners that regularly record a trade surplus
with the EU. Algeria's resource base, its geographic location close to Europe, and
the latter's endeavours to reduce the environmental impact of burning heavy hydrocarbons for heating and power generation, make pipeline deliveries of gas to the
European energy market a feasible and highly demanded project. However, though
the country possesses some of the larger proven natural gas reserves in the world, it
is still considered as relatively under-explored. Its natural gas reserves of 160–200
trillion cubic feet put it in the world's top 10 gas resource holders (Economist
Intelligence Unit, 2003). Hence, Algeria should theoretically have a positive future
in terms of its potential as a growing supplier of gas to European markets for many
years to come. Yet, the danger lies in its dependence on the agricultural and petroleum sectors, particularly in the context of the EU's protective Common Agricultural
Policy. Although the EU is Israel's main trading partner in terms of overall trade
(imports and exports), since 1997 Israel's deficit vis-à-vis the EU has been larger
than its overall deficit (Israel imports far more than it exports to the EU). In Jordan,
this trade deficit is partially offset by a surplus in services, mostly through tourism
and remittances from Jordanians working abroad (Pace, 2005a).

Critics further argue that there is a lack of intra-Arab commercial trade. According
to the Egyptian Businessmen's Association, there are a number of reasons contributing to limited intra-Arab trade including the instability of political relations between
Arab countries, the high trade costs, with regard to trade financing, transport and
communications, the big differences in individual incomes between Arab countries,
the differences between consumption and buying behaviour in Arab countries, the
competitive commercial structures, the differences in monetary and commercial policies and the fact that Arab producers are unable to compete with international
producers in terms of price and quality, which makes it more attractive to import from

non-Arab countries (Egyptian Businessmen Association, 2000). Hence, political differences between Arab leaders also affect Arab economic relations. In the political context, apart from the periodic crises the Arab world continues to suffer, leaders frequently undermine the mutual confidence between Arab countries and, as a result, a turbulent political atmosphere prevails (Pace and Schumacher, 2004).

Also uneven is the level of integration of the Mediterranean, mainly Arab, partners in the world economy (Escribano and Jordán, 1998). Besides the differences in natural resources and potential, this gap reflects the disparities between the economic policies of European and Arab governments and within Arab states. Up until the 1980s (even the 1990s in some cases), import substitution was the norm in the Arab partner states. The high tariffs applied converted import duties into a source of revenue that constituted a barrier to international trade. New export-oriented policies had to face up to the challenge of poorly diversified economies that relied heavily on oil exports. Morocco, Tunisia and to some extent Egypt were the exceptions while other Arab countries, like Jordan and Lebanon, made progress in services. Arab econ-omies also encountered political difficulties, besides the economic ones. This led to a low inter-Arab economic integration. In 2002, Tunisia, Morocco, Egypt and Jordan decided to speed up the liberalization of trade between them through what was then the Agadir Initiative (Pace, 2005a). The Agadir Agreement provides for free trade between these four countries by 2006, and with the Commission of the European Union's provision of technical support for its implementation, there are some hopes that this initiative could move Euro-Mediterranean dialogue to a new phase. In Bakhtinian terms, although centripetal forces are at play in Euro-Mediterranean rela-tions – where contestation is the language of their inter-action – centrifugal forces may also eventually emerge through these inter-changes between the two groups.

The above is but a glimpse of the ways in which Mediterranean and European partners often communicate with each other. While on the one hand, the EU talks of democracy, free trade areas and the creation of closer links between Euro-Mediterranean peoples, Mediterranean partners talk of their own domestic chal-lenges including diverse political systems and structures, economic disparities, barriers to their peoples' mobility, explosive population growth rates, illiteracy. The storming phase in Euro-Mediterranean dialogic encounters is thus characterized by Mediterranean partners attempting to have their voices heard. At times, EU-Mediterranean relations in fact seem to be stuck in the storming phase albeit with short, brief episodes of norming and performing. What Euro-Mediterranean dialogism, à la Bakhtin, should aim for is therefore an orientation toward the interac-tion between the various languages of a speaker and the languages of a listener which may bring partners to the norming phase in their dialogic encounters.

The Norming Phase: Bakhtin's Heteroglossia in Euro-Mediterranean Relations

The solution to the Mediterranean partners' problems has been put forward in the Arab Human Development Report (HDR) of 2003. This complements the HDR 2003 in that it underlines the importance to Arab countries of education and knowledge as a powerful driver of economic growth through higher productivity. The said report asserts that an Arab educated society can achieve improved economic development (and thus the objectives of justice, human freedoms and dignity and good governance) through appropriate training of its youthful, albeit large, labour pool. This is an instance of true dialogue where, in Bakhtinian terms, Arab language coincides with the language of Europeans. In fact, this is the language of the UK's Presidency (from July 2005) whose vision of the EMP puts great emphasis on the importance of education at all levels in the South (UK Presidency, 2005). The remaining obstructions to development relate to defective structures, in particular political ones, but economic and social too (UNDP, 2003).

Although gaps persist, since 1970 many aspects of human development in the Mediterranean have improved thanks to higher incomes. Gender gaps in enrolment have been narrowing: in terms of gender equality in primary and secondary education, Mauritania led the group of poor countries through an increase in the ratio of girls to boys from 67 per cent to 93 per cent between 1990 and 1996. In Jordan, while not perfect, the democratization process has been regarded as one of the most advanced in the region. According to the UN's Human Development Report of 2003, during the 1990s, despite general economic stagnation, Lebanon and Tunisia grew by more than 3 per cent per year while Egypt realized the largest reduction in under-five mortality rates – from 10 per cent to 4 per cent (ibid.). It is not so easy to identify these positive developments as direct consequences of Euro-Mediterranean dialogic inter-actions but we could suggest that through heteroglossic interactions in which the diversity of voices in Euro-Mediterranean relations are allowed to flourish, group dynamics experience a socialization and learning process which impacts on their peoples' daily lives. Through such a process, all group members adopt new roles and one specific example of this outcome is the EMPA. At its first plenary session, 12–15 March 2005 in Cairo, the Euro-Mediterranean Parliamentary Assembly (inaugurated in Athens 22–23 March 2004) adopted various resolutions and Arab partners circulated a paper with their views in an attempt to exercise and reinforce the sense of joint ownership (European Commission, 2005). The Anna Lindh Foundation similarly creates a window of opportunity for Euro-Mediterranean relations to ensure an equitable climate for dialogue and a forum for debate.

Similar progress towards a truly Euro-Mediterranean dialogic encounter has also been made in addressing the challenge of joint ownership of the EMP process through co-chairmanship of sectoral ministerial meetings, closer consultations on the outcome of ministerial meetings and co-development of the Neighbourhood policy. The ENP's action plans are a step in the right direction if taken as a form of dialogue between the EU and Mediterranean partners on a bilateral basis. The dialogue envisioned in these action plans aims at a 'common' horizon where both groups make commitments and which, in practical terms, encourages Mediterranean partner governments to facilitate the activities of NGOs, such as to allow greater media freedom, while the European partners open up certain of their own policies and programmes to Mediterranean participation, including the internal market, police and judicial cooperation, border management, efforts to stem organized crime, money laundering and trafficking, energy and transport networks, exchange programmes and education, science and research initiatives (Leigh, 2005). One specific example of how a truly dialogic encounter between European and Mediterranean partners can develop was the international conference on the ENP organized by the Association for International Affairs and the Friedrich Ebert Stiftung in Prague, 20–21 May 2005. Participants included representatives from the Commission, the Council and the European Parliament, as well as southern and eastern representatives from civil society (including journalists, academics), political parties and opposition groups, and representatives from the Euro-Mediterranean Human Rights Network. Issues discussed included reform in the southern and eastern neighbouring countries, the EU's conditionality policies, EU's funding mechanisms, education, security and economic liberalization. Representatives of the EU took note of the suggestions made by southern and eastern partners for increasing the involvement of non-state actors and the necessity of co-ordination of all EU policies which address neighbouring states. In the context of the ENP, at the end of 2003, institutionalized or informal human rights dialogues have been initiated with several partners (European Commission, 2005). This is a good example of how European and Mediterranean partners are entering into a genuine dialogic relation with the others' ideas. Whereas, on the one hand, European representatives attempt to encompass their southern neighbours' multiplicity of languages (à la Bakhtin) and to include Mediterranean partners' ways of speaking, on the other hand, Mediterranean partners are also attempting to take in European ideas: at the same time, both groups are going through processes of reflection on the meanings conveyed by the other group. For instance, the commitments made between the EU and Mediterranean partners differ from one Mediterranean country to another, according to the particular needs and capacities and the respective country's relations with the EU (Leigh, 2005). Following the Arab Summit in Tunis in 2004 and the Algiers Summit in 2005, Arab partners reiterated 'The Drive for Development and Modernization in the Region' which will generate reforms from within their societies. The window of opportunity for a true dialogic encounter between European and Mediterranean partners seems to be opening towards a norming phase. This form of dialogue in Euro-Mediterranean relations can be enhanced if consultations with regards to action plans are also taken at the 'people' level.

The norming phase in Euro-Mediterranean relations has been further attempted, as mentioned briefly above, through the setting up of the Anna Lindh Euro-Mediterranean Foundation for the Dialogue between Cultures. This is, significantly, the first *common* institution of the EMP financed with contributions from all the Partner countries as well as the Commission. The partners established 35 national networks, enhancing the role that civil society can play in the Euro-Mediterranean space. This initiative has been further supported by the setting up of a non-governmental Euro-Mediterranean Platform following the Civil Forum in Luxembourg early in 2005. The election of a representative board and the adoption of a charter help structure inter-actions of independent civil society actors. This also provides a connection with official EMP activities. Networking among civil societies both South–South and North–South has increased exchanges of people, particularly young people. The Euro-Mediterranean Youth Action Programme I has been particularly successful in this regard. Adopted at the end of 1998 and set up with the understanding that 'youth exchanges should be the means to prepare future genera-tions for a closer cooperation between the Euro-Mediterranean partners' (European Commission, 1995), the first phase of the programme promoted mobility and non-formal educational activities for young people through youth exchanges, voluntary services and support measures. Since its launch, the programme has facilitated the participation and exchange of ideas between 20,000 young people across the Mediterranean. Following the conclusion of EuroMed Youth II, the Commission is now aiming at a new design for Euro-Med Youth III with a new decentralized management (Pace and Schumacher, 2004; European Commission, 2001). Cooperation between groups such as NGOs, trade unions, business organizations, and Social and Economic Councils has also improved Euro-Mediterranean dialogic encounters in diverse areas such as human rights, the environment, sustainable development, cultural heritage and women's empowerment (Pace, 2005b).

These recent initiatives, especially the Euro-Mediterranean Parliamentary Assembly and the Anna Lindh Foundation, are newly created sites building on already existing signs for dialogue. They are workable instruments which have the potential for dialogic encounters between European and Mediterranean partners to flourish through equal participation under conditions of mutual recognition. Such initiatives offer the groundwork for Euro-Mediterranean group development to move towards the implementation of the objectives of the EMP, that is, the performing phase.

The Performing Phase: Bakhtin's Common Horizon of Euro-Mediterranean Relations

This stage in Euro-Mediterranean relations can only be attained when there is a move from EU rhetorical modes (monologia) to the integration of the concerns of the Mediterranean partner countries. The norming phase in Euro-Mediterranean relations has already kicked off some hope in this regard. Moreover, if the Agadir process takes effect, there is a prospect that most North African countries, possibly including Libya eventually, will progressively become more open. There is also another prospect that the third basket of the EMP gets off the ground and slowly works towards greater cross-cultural knowledge and mutual understanding and appreciation (heteroglossia), through the existing instruments of the Euro-Mediterranean Foundation and the Euro-Mediterranean Parliamentary Assembly. The former promises to build networks in spheres including archives, museums, libraries, school textbooks, book translations, comparative religion, migration studies, the press and the media, film-making and the performing arts (Frendo, 2005). The latter offers a context for dialogic inter-actions among parliamentarians – in particular among those from around the shores of the Mediterranean. It also offers an environment for the sharing of experiences that will encourage the integra-tion of learning processes from each group (European as well as Mediterranean). European and Mediterranean partners need to be sensitive to the sense of bounded-ness, historicity and social determination inherent in dialogic notions of each other's languages. To enter into dialogue with each other, Europeans as well as Mediterranean partners need to attune to their own, as well as the Others', languages. Through dialogue, it is possible for Euro-Mediterranean partners to direct their speech acts towards possible responses of the Other. Through these dialogic processes both partners find more things to say, more ways to express things, so that the Other can understand the message(s). This diversity of voices in a truly dialogic relationship is the fundamental characteristic of heteroglossia. The recent Euro-Mediterranean initiatives have the potential to fulfil this imagined co-presence in Euro-Mediterranean dialogic relations. As Bakhtin reminds us, this stage of the dialogic process in Euro-Mediterranean relations is a long one and requires both partner groups to aim at achieving a 'common' horizon.

Conclusion: Is co-existence/co-presence of differences possible? Implications for Future Euro-Mediterranean Dialogic Relations

This analysis has outlined the theoretical and practical aspects of Euro-Mediterranean dialogue. It has sought to shed some new light on the process of dialogue in EU-Mediterranean relations and to apply the thinking of Bakhtin and Tuckman's stage model of group development to the practical reality that the EU and the Mediterranean partners find themselves in as they slowly attempt to move closer through dialogue.

It has argued that for a true dialogic encounter, Euro-Mediterranean partners need to find the space for critical self-reflection. Moving away from relations of domination, dialogue entails an overlap of the Self and the Other. Self-identity always owes a debt to alterity, and the Other always exists within as a source of internal difference. It is in the interest of both European and Mediterranean partners for the practice of dialogue to involve adapting to the language of the Other. Mediterranean partners need to acknowledge that the EU is going through some challenging times – the Constitutional debates, the next enlargement – while the EU partners need to adhere more to the concerns of their southern neighbours. The effectiveness of the EMP depends on the partners' capacity to 'read' each other's worlds. The more the effort at reading the Other's world, the less likely the unintended consequences of this special relationship (Inayatullah and Blaney, 2004). If we understand the Other, we are more likely to share with our partners local or global visions and to anticipate the behaviour and reactions of our partners. The opening up of spaces, in dialogic encounters, to the voices of the Other enables us to act effectively. This means some hard realities: Europeans have to face their own hegemonic practices while Mediterranean partners have to engage in more self-criticisms. The recognition of one's own participation in another's 'language' can create a bridge and a common horizon for dialogic interactions, or as Fabian describes a co-presence with the Other (Fabian, 1983). In so doing, each party to a dialogue has to move away from the idea that the Self and the values and norms it upholds are exclusive. For true dialogue and participation, recognition of one's particularities is one step toward the realization of the particularities of Others. Euro-Mediterranean dialogic relations must work towards establishing this overlap.

The artificial division between the three baskets of the EMP has thus far led to an excessive institutional complexity with a simultaneous gap in terms of involvement of social actors. As Iván Martín argued elsewhere, the biggest contradiction of the EMP is that it intends to promote democracy, bring about development and enhance mutual knowledge among the peoples of the Mediterranean by purely intergovern-mental methods, without giving any say to the people affected. Thus, 'social consul-tation' with civil society, now confined to the third basket, should be extended to the *high politics* of economic and political issues currently handled in the first and second baskets. It follows that one of the major challenges for the future of the EMP will be establishing the procedures to make consultation with all the social actors involved, central to and part and parcel of the Barcelona process (Pace, 2005b and 2005c). The setting up of a Euro-Mediterranean Academy for Best Practices could potentially empower and activate wider civil society groups within the southern Mediterranean partners without creating conflict with their governments. Existing obstacles to increased mobility across the new EU boundaries, namely rigid visa regulations, should be ultimately removed or at least eased in the short to medium term.

While the EU's enlargement of May 2004 has added new challenges to the Partnership, the EMP remains, in Bakhtin's terminology, a creative force, a systematic and structured dialogic framework – not an empty vehicle for consensus building. It is a process which has the potential to develop into an inter-subjective, meaning formation and perpetual cognition mechanism for both partners – European as well as Mediterranean. As long as every partner has a voice, and as long as each party accepts the Other along this dialogic process, the integrationist logic of the EMP can provide for a truly dialogic encounter. What remains as a major challenge is the unity of the Self – both in Europe as well as in the Mediterranean areas: for true dialogue to come about, this is an urgent call. Euro-Mediterranean dialogic relations should aim at converging towards co-presence. The EMP should move away from being an inherently 'Western' praxis towards a EuroMed praxis paving the way for a true dialogic process. This dialogue mission therefore involves a dynamic interplay of Euro-Mediterranean cultures and communities between discourse (being) and practice (becoming).

Acknowledgements

I would like to thank participants at: the Roundtable on the Third Basket of the Euro-Mediterranean Partnership on Culture and Community in the EMP which took place in Alexandria, Egypt, 5–7 October 2003; the panel on the European Union and the Mediterranean: Theoretical Reflections, ECPR conference, University of Bologna, Bologna, 24–26 June, 2004; the International workshop on 'The Impact of European Union Involvement in Civil Society Structures in the Southern Mediterranean', Friedrich Ebert Stiftung, FES Maroc, Rabat, 4–5 December, 2004; and the Policy Brief discussion workshop on Bringing the Euro-Mediterranean Partnership Closer to the People: 35 Proposals to Engage Civil Society in the Barcelona Process, Friedrich Ebert Stiftung, FES Maroc, Rabat, 18–19 March, 2005 for thought-provoking debates on this topic as well as Tobias Schumacher, Sharon Pardo, Iván Martín, Nicola Smith and two anonymous referees for their constructive feedback.

Notes

[1] Adapted from Monar (1997).
[2] Communication between the author and Iver B. Neumann, September/October 2003. See Neumann (2003).
[3] See also Bakhtin (1984) and Clark (1984).

References

Arendt, H. (1961) *Between Past and Future: Six Exercises in Political Thought* (London: Faber).

Bakhtin, M. (1981) in: M. Holquist (Ed.) *The Dialogic Imagination: Four Essays*, trans. by C. Emerson and M. Holquist (Austin/London: University of Texas Press).

Bakhtin, M. (1984) in: C. Emerson (Ed.) *Problems of Dostoevsky's Poetics* (Manchester: Manchester University Press).

Clark, K. (1984) *Mikhail Bakhtin* (The Belknap Press of Harvard University Press: Cambridge, MA/ London).

Collins (1987) *Cobuild English Language Dictionary* (London: Collins/The University of Birmingham).

Council of the European Union (2002) *New Neighbours Initiative*, Brussels, 14078/02, 12.11.2002.

Dallmayr, F. (2001) Conversation Across Boundaries: Political Theory and Global Diversity, *Millennium: Journal of International Studies*, 30(2), pp. 331–347.

Economist Intelligence Unit, Algeria Review (2003). Available at: http://www.eiu.com.

Egyptian Businessmen Association (2000) The World Trade Organisation and the Arab Countries. Communication to the 4th Forum of Arab Businessmen Society, Kuwait, May 2000, p. 6.

Escribano, G. & Jordán, J. M. (1998) Subregional Integration in the Southern Shore of the Mediterranean and the Euro-Mediterranean Free Trade Area, paper presented at the Valencia Forum on the Euro-Mediterranean Free Trade Area, organized by the Centro Español de Relaciones Internacionales, 20–21 November.

European Commission (1995) *Barcelona Declaration*. Adopted at the Euro-Mediterranean Conference, 27–28 November 1995. Barcelona.

European Commission (2001) Mid-term Evaluation of the Euromed-Youth programme, MEI/B7-4100/1B/0418, 24.08.2001.

European Commission (2003) Communication from the Commission to the Council and the European Parliament, Wider Europe-Neighbourhood: A New Framework for Relations with our Eastern and Southern Neighbours, Brussels, COM(2003) 104 final, 11.03.2003.

European Commission (2004) Communication from the Commission European Neighbourhood Policy, Strategy Paper, Brussels, COM(2004) 373 final, 12.05.2004.

European Commission (2005) Conclusions for the VIIth Euro-Mediterranean Conference of Ministers of Foreign Affairs, Luxembourg, 30–31 May, 2005. EuroMed Report (90), 1 June.

Frendo, H. (2005) Coexistence in Modernity: A Euromed Perspective, *The European Legacy*, 10(3), pp. 161–177.

Garton Ash, T. (2004a) Beyond the west, *The Guardian*, 10 June, 2004, available at: http://www.guardian. co.uk/print/0,3858,4943687-103677,00.html.

Garton Ash, T. (2004b) *Free World: Why a Crisis of the West Reveals the Opportunity of Our Time* (London: Penguin).

Guillaume, X. (2002) Foreign Policy and the Politics of Alterity: A Dialogical Understanding of International Relations, *Millennium: Journal of International Studies*, 31(1), pp. 1–26.

Habermas, J. (1971) *Towards a Rational Society: Student Protest, Science and Politics*, trans. by Jeremy J. Shapiro (London: Heinemann Educational).

Habermas, J. (1974) *Theory and Practice*, trans. (from German) by John Viertel (London: Heinemann).

Habermas, J. (1984) *Theory of Communicative Action*, trans. by Thomas McCarthy, Volume 1: Reason and the Rationalization of Society (Boston: Beacon Press).

Habermas, J. (1987) *Theory of Communicative Action*, trans. by Thomas McCarthy, Volume 2: Lifeworld and System: A Critique of Functionalist Reason (Cambridge: Polity).

Henk, G. (2002) Is the Notion of Intercultural Dialogue a Western Concept? (The Netherlands: University of Leiden). Article available at: http://sos-net.eu.org/red&s/dhdi/recherches/theoriedroit/articles/griffioen.htm (accessed on 20 May 2004).

Huntington, S. (1993) The Clash of Civilizations?, *Foreign Affairs*, 72(3), pp. 22–49.

Inayatullah, N. & Blaney, D. L. (2004) *International Relations and the Problem of Difference* (Routledge: London).

Joffé, G. (2005) The Status of The Euro-Mediterranean Partnership, EuroMeSCo working paper. Available at: http://www.euromesco.net/euromesco/artigo.asp?cod_artigo=117802.

Johannes, F. (1983) *Time and the Other: How Anthropology Makes Its Object* (New York: Columbia University Press).

Leigh, M. (2005) The EU's Neighbourhood Policy, in: E. Brimmer & S. Frohlich (Eds) *The Strategic Implications of EU Enlargement* (Washington DC: Center for Transatlantic Relations, Johns Hopkins University).

Martín, I. (Ed.) (2005) *Bringing the Euro-Mediterranean Partnership Closer to the People: 35 Proposals to Engage Civil Society in the Barcelona Process* (Rabat, Morocco: FES).

Monar, J. et al. (1997) Political Dialogue with Third Countries and Regional Political Groupings: The Fifteen as an Attractive Interlocutor, in: E. Regelsberger (Ed.) *Foreign Policy of the European Union: From EPC to CFSP and Beyond*, pp. 263–274 (London: Lynne Reinner).

Moré, I. (2004) The Economic Step Between Neighbours: The Case of Spain-Morocco, *Mediterranean Politics*, 9(2), pp. 165–200.

Neumann, I. (2003) International Relations as Emergent Bakhtinian Dialogue, in G. Hellmann (Ed.) Forum: Are Dialogue and Synthesis Possible in International Relations? *International Studies Review*, 5(1), pp. 137–140.

Pace, M. & Schumacher, T. (2004) Report: Culture and Community in the Euro-Mediterranean Partnership: A Roundtable on the Third Basket, Alexandria 5–7 October 2003, *Mediterranean Politics*, 9(1), pp. 122–126.

Pace, M. (2005a) *The Politics of Regional Identity: Meddling with the Mediterranean* (Oxford: Routledge, New IR Series).

Pace, M. (2005b) EMP cultural initiatives: what political relevance?, in: R. Youngs & H. A. Fernández (Eds) *The Barcelona Process Revisited* (Madrid: FRIDE and Real Instituto Elcano).

Pace, M. (2005c) Report: the impact of European Union involvement in civil society structures in the southern Mediterranean, *Mediterranean Politics*, 10(2), pp. 235–240.

Pace, M. (2006, forthcoming) People-to-people: education and culture, in: K. Weber, M. E. Smith & M. Baun (Eds) *Partners or Periphery? The European Union and the Governance of Wider Europe* (Cambridge: Cambridge University Press).

Todorov, T. (1984) *Mikhaïl Bakhtin: The Dialogical Principle* trans. by W. Godzich (Manchester: Manchester University Press).

Tuckman, B. W. (1965) Development sequence in small groups, *Psychological Bulletin*, 63(6), pp. 384–399.

Tully, J. (1995) *Strange Multiplicity: Constitutionalism in an Age of Diversity* (Cambridge/New York: Cambridge University Press).

Tully, J. (2004) Recognition and dialogue: the emergence of a new field, *Critical Review of International Social and Political Philosophy*, 7(3), pp. 84–106.

UK Presidency. *Achieving a Common Vision: A UK Contribution to the Future of the Barcelona Process*, position paper on British ideas on the EMP (2005).

UNDP Report (2003). Available at: http://www.undp.org/rbas/ahdr/english2003.html. Building a Knowledge Society (UN Publications: New York).

Wiener, A. (2005) The Dual Quality of Norms, paper presented at the workshop on Intersubjectivity and International Politics: Incentives from Jürgen Habermas's Work on International Relations and Political Theory, Johann Wolfgang Goethe-University Frankfurt, Campus Westend, 16–18 June 2005, R. 1.801.

Talking Tough or Talking Together? European Security Discourses towards the Mediterranean

FEDERICA BICCHI* & MARY MARTIN**

*Department of International Relations, London School of Economics and Political Science, London, UK,
**Centre of International Studies, University of Cambridge, Cambridge, UK.

ABSTRACT   *The tense security environment produced by 9/11 and subsequent terrorist bombings in Madrid, London as well as in Arab states from Morocco to Jordan had an impact on the understanding of various actors about political Islam, but this did not automatically entail a convergence of views or solutions to existing dilemmas. This article examines examples of security discourse towards Islam at three levels: at the level of the national member state (in the case of the United Kingdom), at the level of the European Union (EU) and at the level of the Euro-Mediterranean Partnership (EMP.) It highlights that while there has been a progressive securitization of political Islam at the national level within the UK, there is an absence of a coherent agenda on the part of the EU, and between the EU and the Arab Euro-Mediterranean partners there is increasing divergence towards security issues.*

After 9/11 (2001), 3/11 (2004), and 7/7 (2005), what is the relationship between Europe and Islam, and more particularly towards groups representing radical Islam? Since the end of the 1990s, the 'western' part of the world has been a privileged (though definitely not unique) target for terrorist attacks justified with a radical interpretation of Islam.

The military response of the USA in Afghanistan and in Iraq, carried out with the support of some European countries, has further sharpened the perception that there is an opening chasm between 'the West' and 'Islam'. This article will engage critically with this debate by looking at a specific case of relations between 'western' and 'Muslim' countries. It will focus on the approaches to this relationship adopted by the UK, the EU and the Euro-Mediterranean Partnership (EMP) in the area of security. The recent history of the UK shows how a country that for long did not have any specific perspective on political Islam has come to securitize the matter as a consequence of consecutive terrorist attacks. In the case of the EU, discourses about Islam reveal the extent to which the EU strives to maintain parallel though diverging approaches to a similar range of issues and people. The EMP is the place in which to look for the potential convergence of security discourses mentioned by Volpi in his introduction to this collection.

Reference to Islam can be taken to group together several issues, which tend to intermingle in any analysis of the subject. There is the issue of Islam as a religion shared by millions of people across the world. At the national level, religious Islam (as distinct from its political manifestation) impacts public discourse in terms of social and cultural mores. In the case of the EU, religious dialogue is a component often called for, but not exactly at the centre of its daily politics. The EMP, for its part, addresses the aspect in a largely apolitical manner. A second issue is connected with Muslim communities in Europe and thus with migration. Here, member states have managed through the EU to press on their southern neighbours their concerns for migration (and illegal migration in particular), as the increasing number of readmission agreements shows. The issue within the EMP discourse, however, is much more related to the economics of migration and to the readmission of illegal migrants than to the integration of Muslim migrants. Furthermore, reference to Islam is linked to the role that Islam can potentially play in the politics of Muslim countries. While the EU and the EMP have been vocal in advocating for democracy promotion, they have made virtually no reference to Islam.

Yet another aspect refers to Islam as a (distorted) ideology justifying violence and terrorism. In the UK, the linkage between religious ideology and violence, and the politicization of radical Islam has dominated public attention culminating in legislation currently before Parliament. The EU also has shown a substantial capacity for action (Den Boer and Monar, 2002), whereas agreement in the EMP has recently crumbled, with the adoption of a lukewarm code of conduct against terrorism, as this article will discuss. Therefore, we will explore here how various actors have or have not devoted attention to some of these aspects, with the intention to capture the overall dynamics of relations between Europe and radical Islamist groups. But we remain aware that the levels of our analysis are irredeemably shifting and unstable, and the very juxtaposition of Europe and Islam requires a stretch of conventional analytical categories.

In tackling this complex mix of topics we rely on the contributions offered by the 'Copenhagen school' that security issues do not exist as such, but they have to be 'securitized', that is, they need to be presented by public authorities as 'an existential threat, requiring emergency measures and justifying actions outside the normal bounds of political procedure' (Buzan et al., 1998: 24). We will examine securitization processes, by looking at security discourse, that is, what is said in official texts and what is practised in relation to security (Fairclough, 1989; Habermas, 1996).

As the Copenhagen school put it, the utterance of the term is constitutive of security, as it presents a claim to use special rights to counter the threat (Wæver, 1995; Buzan et al., 1998). Therefore, an issue is securitized (that is, becomes a security issue) when an argument is formulated about it in the name of which not only are rules broken, but the audience of citizens tolerates such action. Moreover, as argued by Huysmans (2006), securitization can occur as security 'experts' or bureaucrats with administrative responsibilities enact a security discourse without that discourse having been discussed in the public arena. Therefore, we will also look at authoritative decisions which translate an explicit or implicit security discourse in the form of new laws, directives or administrative measures.

The thesis that we will put forward suggests that there is a securitization process involving Islam, but it is predominantly at the national level. The coherence, and with it the intensity of the securitization process, gets lost as we shift from the national to the EU level and to the EMP level. The UK shows a clear process of securitization of its relations with radical Islamist groups, a process which has intensified since the London bombings of July 2005, by means of new legislation and security measures which frame radical Islam as the existential threat facing national survival. The EU, on the contrary, displays a securitization process in relation to its internal strategy and to some parts of its external security strategy. At the same time, it has traditionally had some long-standing problems in deciding the role of Islamist activists in democratization processes. While preaching for more participation of civil societies, the EU has shied away from engaging with more moderate elements of Islamist participative forms. Within the EMP, 9/11 has upset the fragile balance about terrorism that was captured by the Barcelona Declaration of 1995. After an initial moment of deep convergence in the aftermath of 9/11, profound splits are beginning to emerge between the Europeans and all of its Mediterranean partners. The impossibility to find an agreed definition and prescription on terrorism ten years after the Barcelona Declaration underlines how a commonality of views is increasingly out of the question, despite substantial cooperation on the ground.

The article analyses the three levels in turn. It starts off by examining the UK as an example of a member state within the EU where national discourse, by dint of events on the ground, presents a strong case of securitization of political Islam. It continues by focusing on the EU and its diverse and fragmented discourses about Islam. It then moves on to the EMP, with a special attention to the fiasco of the Code of Conduct against terrorism.

National Security Discourse in the UK: An Amber State of Alert

National discourses form an important part of the European response to the threat of international terrorism. The EU counter-terrorism strategy emphasizes the principle that the prime responsibility for combating terrorism lies with member states (European Commission, 2004a; European Union, 2005a). Given the importance of the counter-terrorism initiatives at national level to European responses this section examines the security discourse in the UK in the aftermath of the Madrid and London bombs to gauge the influence and impact of Islam. We conduct this examination through the following aspects of discourse: policy responses in the shape of anti-terror legislation and executive initiatives, in particular the 2005 Terrorism Bill; the policing response; and military preparedness. These genres of discourse have been chosen because they represent the key areas of practice and public policy in combating the perceived terrorist threat, while they also echo the principal themes of the counter- terrorism strategy as articulated at EU level, defined as *prevent, protect, pursue* and *respond* (European Union, 2005a), and as such represent an identifiable link between the national and supranational European security discourse.

What emerges from the national discourse is a wariness in official texts in pinpointing Islam, particularly Muslim culture, as a security challenge. This restraint is ascribed in part to the concern that community relations should not suffer by over-emphatic articulation of the Islamic nature of terrorism and reflects the reaction of civil society, particularly community and faith groups and civil liberties activists to proposed counter-terrorism measures and their impact on Muslim communities. Events since the July 2005 bombings, such as the global row over cartoons of the Prophet Mohammed and the conviction of a radical cleric Abu Hamza on charges of incitement to murder have hardened public attitudes towards radical Islam, and served to increase support for more repressive government measures towards militants. This has been accompanied by criticism of the government's previous handling of Islamic militants as too tolerant, and a popular questioning of the discourse of multiculturalism, tolerance and identity-less politics (Jones and Smith, 2005).[1]

However it was the London bombs of 7 July and the second failed attempt two weeks later which served to rethink official reticence and sharpen the targeting of radical Islam as a security threat. The 2005 UK Prevention of Terrorism Bill shows clearly how the role of faith had become progressively articulated in counter-terrorism legislation in the last five years. The bill was described by the UK government as 'not a direct response' to 7 July, but intended to reflect law enforcement and intelligence advice arising from the London bombings.[2] New offences such as the glorification of terrorism and increased powers of detention, are intended to supplement the Terrorism Act of 2000 which itself replaced temporary legislation, largely targeted at Northern Ireland terrorism. In contrast to the 2000 Act, the new legislation emphasized terms such as 'extremism' and 'radicalization' to justify its additional powers, and the deployment of a rhetoric of difference in which terrorism is contrasted with the security threat posed in the past by the Irish Republican Army (IRA).

The 12-point plan set out by Prime Minister Tony Blair on 5 August 2005, one month after the London bombs, offered further evidence of how violent Islam provided a framework for the new security discourse. Declaring that 'the rules of the game are changing', Blair spoke of public acceptance of the need to tighten legislative powers, beyond the levels agreed after 9/11.

This is not in any way whatever aimed at the decent law-abiding Muslim community of Great Britain... We know British Muslims, in general abhor the actions of the extremists... Those... that try to incite hatred or engage in violence against our country and its people have no place here (Blair, 2005).

Among the measures which reflect this new 'security game', were the proscription of two Islamist organizations, Hizb-ut-Tahir and Al Mujahiroun (its successor). The home secretary admitted that the government's decision to single out the two Islamist organizations represented a complete reversal of its position a year previously when it had warned against such an initiative, and attributed this change to public opinion as a result of the July bombings. In his words: 'the events of 7 July illuminated a certain set of issues about the kind of threat that we were under and the kinds of people who might bring those threats to pass' (House of Commons, 2005: question 32). Other initiatives included the closures of places of worship suspected of fomenting extremism, refining immigration and citizenship rules to improve integration of Muslims, and new grounds for deportation and exclusion.

With public opinion mobilized in favour of combating terrorists after 7 July, the government has used the attacks to develop a tougher and more explicit approach to counter-terrorism, drawing on measures which had been used previously in other European countries, notably the French ban on Islamic organizations after the 1995 bombing of the Paris metro. Indicative of this trend has been a change in the balance between security, civil liberties and compliance with international obligations, such as the European Convention on Human Rights. The home secretary, questioned about this shift, replied that any doubters of the new policy should consider the human rights of individuals charged with offences alongside the human rights of those who have been blown up on tube trains (House of Commons, 2005: question 36). Civil society groups opposed to the government's initiatives on detention without trial, deportation and control orders, have attacked the provisions on the basis that they are religiously and racially discriminatory and evidence of a policy which is overtly ideological and designed to fit within the US-led global War on Terror. While the government has tried to reject the invasion of Iraq as a cause of the terrorist attacks, civil society discourse in the media particularly has associated the surge in religious fundamentalism with the security threat via the concept of 'bleedback' as those trained in or inspired by the Iraqi insurgency, and in Afghanistan pose new danger within the UK (Burnett, 2005).[3]

In addition to internal security measures (and as a by-product of them) the new approach to Islamist threats has generated a foreign policy dialogue with North African states over individual terror suspects. Notwithstanding the existence of the EMP and the role of the EU as a framework for UK external relations with the Middle East and North Africa, the July attacks led the UK government to propose bilateral agreements with these states in order to facilitate the deportation of foreign terrorist suspects. The first of what is envisaged as a series of Memoranda of Understanding (MOUs) was signed between the UK and Jordan in August 2005 to ensure that tighter legislative controls on terrorist suspects would be backed up by the willingness of the country concerned to accept deportees.[4] The Jordan MOU was followed by a similar agreement with Libya in October and with Lebanon at the end of December. The Foreign Secretary has also propelled Algeria to the top of his foreign policy agenda in an attempt to sign an MOU which would enable the UK to deport ten detainees described as a 'credible threat' to British security, but who cannot be detained further in the UK without trial, which the government has insufficient evidence to pursue.[5] Caught between the appeals of civil liberties groups against prolonged detention on the one hand and the lack of guarantees against ill-treatment of deportees by their home state on the other, the government has sought a way out via the MOUs, describing the bilateral agreements with Middle Eastern and North African states as 'a truly effective international response' towards dealing with 'foreign nationals who threaten national security' (Foreign and Commonwealth Office, 2005).

The police response to the London bombs, reveals different terms of discourse: while the threat is defined as coming from Islamist 'extremism' and 'radicalization', the demands of multiculturalism are more evident. Although the police assume a dual threat from both externally based terrorists and domestic cells, the shock effect of the July bombs was to concentrate attention on the possibility of home-grown violence, requiring a counter-terrorism strategy which would prevent as well as detect terror groups, while still preserving community relations in migrant areas.

Yet, the connection to Islamization is evident in terms of the operational rules of engagement such as the controversial 'shoot to kill' policy, designed to foil 'suicide bombers' and 'jihadis', in stop and search powers which could potentially single out Asian suspects.[6] It is also evident in prevention measures such as tackling radicalization within prisons as well as places of worship.[7]

Despite the well-publicized remarks of assistant commissioner Brian Paddick in the aftermath of 7 July that 'Islam and terrorism don't go together', police practice has concentrated on the threat from radicalization of predominantly Pakistani groups, influenced by the alienation and poverty associated with migrant communities, and by the potential for ideological incitement from both the local mosque and links with Pakistan[8] Thus to the police, terrorism is seen in a broad social context, which emphasizes the particularly British nature of radical Islam, and this has become the predominant characterization of the threat after 7/7 as compared to the niche activity involving North African jihadis.

Counter-terrorism is the responsibility of the Metropolitan Police which covers the London area, although plans to regionalize the operations have also been given fresh impetus by the discovery of the Leeds cell behind the 7 July attacks. 'The Met' was given £60m of additional funding to meet the costs of investigating the July bombings, while at the same time there has been a 33 per cent increase in the number of officers working on counter-terrorism, and an internal reorganization of how terrorism is investigated. The additional resources reflect the demands of a complex murder investigation, and also the requirement for resources to detect the emergence of extremists while still maintaining a 'community partnership' with immigrant communities.

This delicate balancing act produces an ambiguous effect on the police's security discourse in relation to Islam, which highlights the religious element as a security threat, while also seeking not to overemphasize it in ways which demonize Muslims as a cultural community. While far from being culturally neutral (in contrast to what we shall show below in the case of the EMP dialogue), it seeks to downplay the ideological/religious component in the security challenge: the 7 July and 21 July investigations are, in this context, treated as large scale murder investigations.[9]

The third area we have examined for evidence of the securitization of Islam in UK discourse is the military, and its treatment of radical Islam as a defence issue. Here the picture is less clear-cut in presenting Islam as a military threat/challenge, yet it appears that a combination of threat assessment generated by the rise in transnational terrorism and the influence of US military thinking towards Islamist terrorism are influencing this aspect of the national discourse.

UK military preparedness in counter-terrorism arises from a long-term planning cycle which began with the Strategic Defence Review (SDR) of 1997, which was updated with an additional chapter added after the 9/11 attacks. The SDR approach recognizes global terrorism as a 'new' security threat requiring a comprehensive response covering prevention, armed response overseas and assistance to civilian authorities domestically. The new chapter of July 2002 outlines strategies to cover so-called 'trouble spots' which are defined as the Middle East, south-east Asia and Afghanistan without specifying an Islamist focus (Ministry of Defence, 2002). Current thinking as articulated in the Joint Doctrine Concepts Centre's *Strategic Trends* is more specific in defining Islamic terrorism as a growing 'threat to international peace and stability', although it notes that attacks on western targets will reflect the fact that the Islamic movement is not widespread and unified (Joint Doctrine Concepts Centre, 2002).

One Ministry of Defence planner describes radical Islam as 'the elephant in the room' in counter-terrorism strategy: it is a dominating presence, but one which official discourse declines to talk about. Public discourse generalizes risk assessments and avoids targeting Muslim communities either abroad or at home as a specific threat. Partly, this reflects the long shelf-life of official planning documents which are designed to situate military capabilities in a timeframe stretching out to the middle of the century, and which will outlive short-term political dramas. Partly, it is 'because ways of dealing with the elephant are outside our remit', in contrast to the approach adopted towards Irish terrorism which entailed a more limited range of political, cultural and religious sensitivities.

In practice and in private, however, the focus on Islamization of the military contribution to counter-terrorism is more entrenched than this would suggest with the greatest influence stemming from the traditional proximity of the UK armed forces to the US defence community and its intense focus on Muslims as part of the 'War on Terror'. The American agendas of retaliation for the 9/11 attacks and democratization of the Middle East have contributed to pressure on the UK armed forces, both independently and within NATO, to direct their capabilities and defence doctrine towards the security threat posed by religious radicalism. The US influence has not only been a factor in the way the UK military perceives global and domestic security threats, it has also led to the creation of joint structures and staff appointments to counter security threats with the aim of unifying the global counter-terrorism strategy.[10] An example of this kind of common approach with the USA is the participation of US officials in EU counter-terrorism discussions, and increased intelligence sharing involving not only the UK but other EU member states, which has institutionalized the US influence on counter-terrorism initiatives across a broad range of activities from internal security to military intelligence (Bunyan, 2002).[11]

The European Union and Islam: Parallel Voices, not Singing the Same Tune

At the EU level, there is no unity of discourse towards political Islam. On the one hand, the EU internal strategy to fight against terrorism, as well as the European Security Strategy (ESS) approved in December 2003, point in the direction of securitizing relations with political Islam. On the other hand, other trends pull the EU in opposite directions. Most notably, the EU's call for more democracy and human rights in the Arab world clashes with the EU's attempt to avoid any position in relation to parties and non-governmental organizations (NGOs) proposing an agenda construed in Islamic terms. This contradiction goes back to the early days of the Euro-Mediterranean Partnership and it has not been particularly affected by the events of 9/11. As we shall see, activities aimed at democracy and human rights in the Mediterranean have not included representatives of political Islam, whose presence would have been highly problematic for Brussels. But time for this strategy of avoidance seems to be running out. Legislative elections in January 2006 in Palestine, which brought a victory for Hamas, are making the internal contradictions of the EU approach to political Islam untenable, to the point that a reversal of the policy might be in sight. Whereas the EU 'domestic' debate and its general security discourse thus tend to depict political Islam as a problem, some components of its foreign policy discourse have ignored the issue, while others are now forced to face it. The overall picture is thus of confusion and parallel voices. We will first analyse the securitizing part of it. We will then move on to the exclusion of representatives of political Islam from democracy promotion activities, concluding the section with a comment about the situation created by Palestinian legislative elections.

A main component of the EU internal strategy to fight against terrorism has been the adoption of a list of terrorist organizations and of terrorists, which has displayed a tendency to expand. The list is regularly updated, and it leads to a series of possible common action. In its original version of December 2001, the list included the 'terrorist wing' of Hamas and the Palestinian Islamic Jihad, as well as a number individuals of of Arab origin, some of whom were connected with the Hizballah (Official Journal of the European Communities, 2001). Since then, the number of terrorist organizations connected to Islam and the Middle East has increased. In its October 2002 version, the list came to encompass Gama'a al-Islamiyya, from Egypt, and the Holy Land Foundation for Relief and Development, based in the USA (Official Journal of the European Communities, 2002). Most importantly, in September 2003, the EU finally gave in to US pressures and included the whole of Hamas in the list (Official Journal of the European Communities, 2003). Bit by bit, the interpretation of who is a terrorist according to the EU thus has come to include organizations which are regarded by some outside western countries as resistance movements, or doing forms of social and political work rather than simply focusing on violence and terror. The report by the EU's counter-terrorism co-ordinator Gijs van de Vries to the Council on implementation of the counter-terrorism Action Plan also specifically mentioned Islamist terrorism, highlighting Europol's contribution in 'supporting 21 national investigations into islamist [*sic*] terrorism', in addition to emphasizing the role of a strategy against 'radicalisation and recruitment into terrorism' as part of key counter terrorist initiatives taken by the EU (European Union, 2005b: paragraph 18).

Similarly, on the external front, the European Security Strategy explicitly named Islamic fundamentalist groups as among the key threats to the European Union: 'The most recent wave of terrorism is global in its scope and is linked to violent religious extremism... European countries are targets and have been attacked. Logistical bases for Al Qa'ida cells have been uncovered in the UK, Italy, Germany, Spain and Belgium' (European Union, 2003: 3). It thus introduced a substantial religious element, indirectly linked to Islam, in the debate about European security. Other key concepts which feature in the succession of EU strategy papers on counter-terrorism are the distortion of moderate Islam and the recruitment of terrorists. One recurrent phrase is 'violent radicalisation' and the need to disrupt 'the conditions facilitating the recruitment of terrorists' and both themes feature in communications among the EU's institutions after the Madrid bombs of 2003 (European Commission, 2004a: paragraph 2.1). The Presidency's report to the Council shortly before the Barcelona summit in November 2005, set out clearly that, although religious extremism was a generic issue, the current challenge to security lay in the actions of Islamic fundamentalists: 'The terrorism perpetrated by Al-Qa'ida and extremists inspired by Al Qa'ida has become the main terrorist threat to the Union' (European Union, 2005b: paragraph 3).

At the same time, there is uneasiness across the EU for a straightforward securitization of political Islam. The October 2004 Commission proposal on the prevention, preparedness and response to terrorism which prepared the ground for the subsequent 2005 EU action plan and strategy, expressed the wish for the EU's external activities to develop a cultural dialogue with the Islamic world 'addressing the underlying factors of terrorism' (European Commission, 2004a: paragraph 3.2). Similarly, the European Parliament's resolution on the Barcelona Process counted among its conclusions the need for a religious dialogue, and research into the reasons for radicalization:

> The Euro-Mediterranean partnership should promote religious dialogue... as part of the fight against terrorism. [The Parliament] recommends joint implementation of academic activities by experts and technicians into the role of Islam in democratic and open societies and consideration of the reasons that can sometimes induce members of a... religious community to take violent action (European Parliament, 2005).

While these indications point in the direction of a potential securitization of the EU's relations with Islam, the picture is further complicated by the EU's approach to democracy promotion. A fundamental component in discordance with the securitization trend is represented by the decade of the EU's efforts at democratizing the Mediterranean non-member countries, which have never managed to engage positively Islamic-minded actors. There have been no attempts to exclude officially Islamic-leaning organizations from activities promoted by the EU, but at the same time funds deriving from Brussels have not reached them. The rhetorics on democratization and civil society have come to permeate every discourse about the Mediterranean, especially since the Commission's Communication in 2003 but the practice remains the opposite. Islamist NGOs have been left out in the cold, as we will show in the case of Morocco (European Commission, 2003).

The legislative framework for EU aid is complex and tends to take its cue from the European Commission. Most of the funds disbursed by the EU to Mediterranean non-members are conveyed through the bilateral channel of MEDA, until the end of 2006.[12] As foreseen in MEDA II, priorities for the allocation of funds are decided in Brussels and expressed through Country Strategy Papers (valid for four years), National Indicative Programmes (valid for two years) and Annual Financial Plans. In the drafting process, Mediterranean partners are consulted, though their opinion is not binding. The power of member states too, with the MEDA II regulation, are curtailed once the Annual Financial Plan has been prepared by the Commission. These documents thus reflect very much the approach of the Commission and are implemented mostly by the Commission's Delegations in Mediterranean partner countries.

MEDA is heavily biased in favour of public actors and most notably in favour of governments of Mediterranean partners, in spite of attempts to broaden the range of actors involved (Philippart, 2001). The legislative basis for bilateral funds, which make up 90 per cent of the overall MEDA amount, consists of a Financing Framework Convention signed up between the Commission (EuropeAid) and the relevant Ministry(ies) in Mediterranean partners. Therefore, the inclusion of NGOs within the scope of EU aid is filtered through the preferences of national governments of Mediterranean non-members, thus leaving to them the choice between inclusion and exclusion.

For instance, in the case of Morocco, the National Indicative Programme for 2005–06 has an opening for NGOs, but the basis for the relationship is still the government. Human rights and democratization are among the priorities set and are allocated €5m (or 1.8 per cent) out of €275m that compose the MEDA budget for Morocco for 2005–06. They are split into two activities. The first activity is in support of the national plan for democracy and human rights. It is granted €2million and it aims at establishing a national programme on the matter, as called for by the Commission's Communication in 2003. The beneficiary is the Centre for Documentation, Information and Training on Human Rights (CDIFDH), a national institution established by Morocco and the UN High Commissioner for Human Rights, to which the United Nations Development Programmes (UNDP) also contributes. Although the Delegation in Morocco has insisted on a wide inclusion of Moroccan NGOs, the final decision remains with Moroccan public authorities. The second activity, funded with €3m, is more vaguely defined in the National Indicative Programme for 2005–6 ('Strengthening of Moroccan civil society organisations working for democracy and human rights') and misleadingly indicates Moroccan NGOs as among the beneficiary institutions. The truth is, however, that the 'parallel' beneficiary institution, the Ministry for Employment and Social Affairs, is in charge of selecting and funding activities. Once again, the choice for participation or exclusion of Islamic-leaning NGOs is left with the Moroccan monarchy.

If we draw the lesson from the experience of Morocco, the bilateral channel of MEDA is thus designed and managed by the Commission in such a way as to privilege the established regime, rather than to reach out for representatives of political Islam, who might express opposition to the regime. Through MEDA, the EU has left the selection of NGOs to central public authorities, which in most cases well before 9/11 have made a choice against forms of Islamist participation.

The EU also disburses money directly to NGOs, but there too Islamic-leaning NGOs are de facto not included, if not outrightly excluded. The main channel for this form of decentralized co-operation was, for the period 1996–2000, MEDA Democracy, under the umbrella of European Initiative for Democracy and Human Rights (EIDHR). Since 2001, geographical distinctions of the EIDHR have been abolished and Mediterranean countries receive funds allocated according to sectoral priorities. The rationale for establishing this direct form of support for NGOs is grounded in the idea that NGOs offer a crucial contribution to the 'development of a democracy that upholds political, civil, economic, social and cultural rights' (European Commission, 2004b). In practice, however, while it is specified that these actors should not be effectively controlled by the state or by governmental institutions, the allocation of funds once again is stacked against Islamic-minded NGOs, as we are going to show for the case of Morocco.

MEDA Democracy, marred by a host of EU internal problems, was not in a position to make an impact (Youngs, 2001, 2004). Moreover, it tended to privilege partnerships between European NGOs and local NGOs, the idea being to encourage the exchange of experience of NGOs in the participating countries. This however in practice entailed that European NGOs created 'chapters' on the ground or organized activities to address human rights and democracy in Morocco, and by doing so received the biggest share of funds.

Until recently, Morocco was not considered a 'focus country' under the EIDHR and thus received a limited amount of funds.[13] In 2001, Morocco received *c.* €550,000 for a project on 'Strengthening Civil Society in Rural Zones', although it is not clear who administered the funds.[14] It also participated in a project about the safety of journalists and a Masters programme organized by the University of Malta (European Parliament, 2002). Between June 2002 and May 2003, no specific project took place, although the EU sent monitors for elections (Council of the European Union, 2003; European Union, 2003). Between June 2003 and May 2004, Morocco benefited from a regional project on the role of women targeted to the Maghreb countries, on top of the well-established Masters programme in Malta.

In 2004, for the first time the Commission opened up the possibility of funds targeted to local NGOs, thus excluding external actors who would generally be favoured in the allocation of resources. It specified that €1m was earmarked to Moroccan NGOs, for microprojects targeted at strengthening the capacities of NGOs working on human rights, freedom of expression and advocacy for rights of women, children and prisoners. As a consequence of this expression of interest, the Delegation issued a call in 2005 for microprojects, which selected 11 Moroccan NGOs.[15] None of them was linked to pro-Islamic movements. A similar call has been issued in early 2006.

The meaning of this string of figures is that, despite a lot of talk about civil society, the case of Morocco shows the way in which the EU tends not to include pro-Islamic representatives in the activities it funds for human rights and democracy promotion. In Brussels, officials do admit to a problem existing in the implicit tension between a call for more inclusion, but a desire to limit participation on the ground. As one of them candidly said, 'the problem with allocating aid to local NGOs is that some of them are linked to Islamist movements'.[16] The Delegation in Morocco, while cautious in its doings, emphasizes the practical limitations that all local NGOs encounter when preparing an application for macroprojects or more generally for managing projects according to complex EU criteria. All local NGOs need support and also a degree of prodding by the Delegation's officials to draft an application, and Islamist NGOs have never applied for funds in Morocco. At the same time, officials in the Delegation are aware that Islamist NGOs are well rooted on the ground and carry out a broad variety of tasks, thus qualifying for any possible definition of civil society. According to one official, 'it is a matter of time' before the EU has to engage with pro-Islamic NGOs.[17] The kernel of the matter is the fact that the EU—in its democracy promotion profile—has not yet decided how to address pro-Islamic representatives of civil society, and is trying to avoid the issue for as long as possible (Grünert, 2004; Stetter, 2004).

Time might be running out, though, and putting the first securitizing trend in direct collision with this second trend towards avoidance. The election in January 2006 of a Hamas-dominated 'Parliament' in the Palestinian Authority represents a true test for the Europeans. On the one hand, according to the EU terrorist list, Hamas is a terrorist organization. On the other hand, it has been elected in a relatively free and fair process, as rarely seen in the region. The US position has been to reject outright the possibility to negotiate with Hamas as long as it does not recognize Israel and renounce violence. The EU position, while echoing the US and Israeli concerns, has been more nuanced. As the main donor of the Palestinian Authority, the EU is well aware of the consequences of an interruption of funds. Therefore, its first answer has been to put pressure on Hamas to recognize Israel and renounce terrorism, but without any specific deadline attached to it (Council of the European Union, 2006). Once again, the EU is buying time to avoid reconciling its different voices into a single framework.

The Euro-Mediterranean Partnership: Convergence of Views across the Mediterranean or Opening Chasm?

There have been three main stages in Euro-Mediterranean relations regarding how to address terrorism and, in particular, terrorist expressions of radical Islam. The first, which underpinned the Barcelona Declaration in 1995, marked a difficult but real convergence on a set of common views. The second, which came as a reaction to 9/11, expressed a unanimity of concerns. But deep differences have come to the fore and the third and current stage shows instead an opening chasm between EU member states, Israel and the Arab Mediterranean countries. This trend was highlighted by the poor result of negotiations on the Code of Conduct on Countering Terrorism, 'adopted' at the Barcelona summit in November 2005.

The issue of terrorism was present at the creation of the Euro-Mediterranean Partnership, and it held the success of the Barcelona Declaration on a knife-edge until the eleventh hour. The key issue consisted in finding a formula that would reconcile the opposite views of the Syrians and of the Israelis. As background information suggests and draft documents portray,[18] the Syrians were adamant in inserting in the relevant paragraph the formula: 'without prejudice to the legitimate right of people to resist foreign occupation', while the Israelis were equally determined to resist any definition, and thus limitation, of the concept of terrorism (Barbé, 1996). Moreover, the Israelis advanced the proposal to insert the text: 'The partners urge the Syrian government to desist from providing support and shelter to an array of terrorist groups operating within its national territory in accordance with its national law.' The proposal was flatly rejected. The agreement was reached as the Spanish presidency forced the Syrians to drop their formula in favour of a more general 'right to fully exercise sovereignty by legitimate means', thus paving the way also to the Israeli acceptance of other points, among which reference to 'relevant' UN resolutions and regional 'and/or' international arrangements, 'such as' the Non Proliferation Treaty and the Biological Weapons Convention and the Chemical Weapons Convention.

As in 1995 the main source of tension came from diverging Arab and Israeli interpretations of these thorny issues, while the big success was the fact that the Europeans were able to act as honest brokers, thus reaching a satisfactory compromise for all participants. After 9/11, the Europeans became, on the contrary, fully part of the 'interpreting game' in the EMP about who is a terrorist and why.

At first this brought an unprecedented degree of apparent cohesion among Euro-Mediterranean partners. Grand (but vague) declarations about shared security concerns were made in the wake of 9/11. EMP declarations in November 2001 'attach special emphasis... on co-operation in the fight against terrorism' and promised to refine the Barcelona Process in order to combat the terrorist threat and to address 'the structural causes of extremism' (European Union, 2001). Moreover, the agenda of the EMP shifted towards what in EU parlance is defined as 'justice and home affairs', thus abandoning the previous 'hard security' approach of the EU, represented by negotiations on the Charter for Peace and Stability. The impetus given by 9/11 to a more 'soft security' approach seemed instead to represent a more profitable ground for discussions. EMP partners chose to address the fight against terrorism mainly as a matter of judicial cooperation, and a fight against money laundering, and so on. In Valencia, in April 2002, EMP partners approved a Framework Document which codified the shift to a more 'soft' interpretation of security challenges.[19]

The negotiations prior to the Barcelona summit of November 2005 seemed to point to a similar degree of cooperation. The mere perspective of a meeting at the level of heads of state and government was extremely positive. The idea had been around for a very long time, the French presidency in 2000 having been particularly keen on organizing such an event. However, the darkest moment of the second intifada had put a brake on any progress in that direction. Thanks to the concerted attempt to create new momentum in the EMP and the symbolic occurrence of ten years of EMP cooperation, it was eventually possible to plan the summit during the British presidency and with the active involvement of the Spanish government. Thus the meeting seemed the right answer to criticisms the EMP had drawn for its lack of real achievement (Johansson-Nagues, 2002; Holden, 2005).

It was in this context, that the idea for a joint initiative codifying an anti-terrorism position within the EMP arose a year before the Barcelona summit and was proposed by Tunisia. At the Hague meeting of EMP foreign ministers in November 2004, which agreed an agenda to prepare for the tenth anniversary of the Barcelona Process (including a comprehensive review of activities), Egypt and Tunisia had both proposed initiatives to raise the profile of anti-terrorism cooperation within the EMP. The move followed increasing dialogue between the EU and a group of Arab states, comprising Morocco, Algeria and Tunisia about cooperation against terrorism, within the framework of the Justice, Freedom and Security agenda. The proposal for a more comprehensive approach and more concrete forms of cooperation focused on attacking the financing of terrorism and a dialogue about the factors relating to the recruitment of terrorists. It was followed by a meeting in which ministers acknowledged that despite terrorist attacks affecting both sides of the Mediterranean, 'regional dialogue is too often beset by disagreements on definitions' and urging consensus on a text for a 'comprehensive Convention on Combating Terrorism' (European Union, 2004).

Whereas these prior signs were positive, the actual meeting in Barcelona, in November 2005, was a fiasco on a scale unprecedented in the EMP. Of the Mediterranean partners, only the Palestinian Leader Mahmud Abbas and the Turkish Prime Minister Recep Erdogan attended, whereas all heads of state and government of the 25 EU member states were present, albeit briefly.[20] Moreover, the discussion on the Code of Conduct on Countering Terrorism displayed the usual differences between Israel and the Arab states. The key difference was that the Europeans, this time, did not effectively mediate between the two, and tried instead to force their own agenda onto their partners. As a consequence, the final outcome was a Presidency Declaration, instead of a common statement, and a 'Euro-Mediterranean Code of Conduct on Countering Terrorism' that was notable for the little it said. The Code, which stretches to barely two pages, pledges the EMP to exchange information, cooperate in disrupting terrorist networks and pursuing terrorists, and work to combat the factors which contribute to the terrorist threat. It affirms the principles of respect for human rights and international law as set out in the UN Counter-Terrorism Conventions and UN Security Council Resolutions. However, it fails to address a common definition of terrorism. Moreover, it expressly avoids any mention of the role of radical Islam within the Arab Euromed states as constituting a terrorist threat to EMP members.

The reasons for the public split in Barcelona among Euro-Mediterranean participants are several. Years of renewed Arab–Israeli tensions have taken a toll, with both sides radicalizing their views. Moreover, the war in Iraq has further soured relations between western and Muslim countries. Most important of all, the successive waves of terrorist attacks in the USA, Spain and the UK which at first prompted the Europeans to converge on their southern neighbours' views, have also radicalized the Europeans into a more intransigent approach to terrorism. A bone of contention in Barcelona was that Arab countries wanted (as usual) to differentiate between terrorism and what they call the 'right to resistance to occupation'. Contrary to 1995, not only Israel, but also European member states opposed the move, afraid that it would have consequences in Iraq.[21] The Code thus declares that 'terrorism is never justified'.[22] More generally, European countries, Israel and Arab states diverge about how to address terrorism. While Arab countries would opt for a mix of authoritarian responses and economic development, the Europeans would rather promote transgovernmental cooperation and reforms within Arab countries. Thus, one of the prevailing interpretations for the absence of the Arab heads of state and government was that they were disinclined to listen to European lectures on democracy backed by some extra funds to support reforms.[23] Therefore (and paradoxically), the Europeans faced a situation in which disenchanted Arab representatives let Israel obstruct a deal on the common declaration, as it rejected reference to the peace process.[24]

At the Barcelona summit, it became clear that as a result of terrorist attacks in the USA, Spain and the UK, it is now possible that southern Mediterranean partners (both Arab countries *and* Israel) unite in opposing the EU. While progress was achieved on illegal immigration, the opening gap that came to the light in Barcelona suggests little hope for a common future understanding on how to deal with radical Islam and with terrorism.

Thus the failure both to define the terrorist threat and devise measures to combat it, which the Code was meant to represent, masks quite separate discourses about the nature of the problem which has produced it. For the EU member states, despite their concern to avoid blaming or inciting a cultural clash, religious extremism and the subversion of moderate Islam to radicalism represent the pre-eminent threat to security around the Mediterranean. For the Arab states, the cornerstone of the security problem remains the unresolved conflict in the Middle East and the need for economic development. Meanwhile, Israel remains disinclined to compromises. While all sides acknowledge the importance and relevance of the others' concern, the Barcelona summit showed that the fear of privileging one 'cause' over another strangled the dialogue. If the Code was intended to put flesh on the bones of a regional security analysis and presage a security community across the Mediterranean, the flaws at its centre suggest this is a fraught, possibly even doomed, enterprise.

Conclusion

Discourses and practices within Europe and in the Euro-Mediterranean area have thus shown that there is no unified approach to radical Islamist groups, or even towards the concept of contemporary transnational terrorism. The impact of 9/11 has not been the straight forward securitization of relations between European and Islamist actors. There are several processes taking place at the same time.

At the national level, as shown in the case of the UK, there has indeed been a process of securitization of Islam. The discourse has increasingly stressed the need for emergency measures and powers to counter the threat from religious radicals, even at the risk of civil liberties, especially so after 7/7. However the security discourse is split between foreign based security threats such as North African or wider Arab imported terrorism and the perceived threat from radicalized indigenous populations, stemming largely from a Pakistani dominated local migrant community.

Within the EU, there is a plurality of discourses. The internal EU strategy for countering terrorism has indeed shown signs of securitization. The lists of terrorist organizations have progressively included not only a number of 'jihadists', but also a few Islamist organizations that not everybody in the world regards as just terrorist. Hamas is a case in point. The European Security Strategy has also mentioned religious fundamentalism as a key threat. At the same time, trends towards a securitization of the relationship between the EU and radical Islamist organizations are to be cast against the EU approach to democracy promotion in the Mediterranean. The rhetoric of democratization has permeated the EU political agenda, but at the same time the practice of fund allocation through MEDA and through the EIDHR shows a clear reluctance of the EU in deciding what to do with Islamic-leaning NGOs. The EU seems unable to choose where to draw the line whenever reference to Islam is made, and thus hesitates between its desire for new powers to fight radical Islamist groups and the reluctance to acknowledge the social and political role that Islamist parties play in Muslim societies.

The situation within the EMP is equally complex, and increasingly fraught with problems. The initial fragile compromise embodied by the Barcelona Declaration has not withstood the test of the terrorist attacks in the USA, Spain and the UK. The EU's role as an honest broker has become untenable. After a period of apparent convergence of understandings about how to fight terrorism, this has produced the fiasco of the Barcelona summit in 2005. The de facto boycott of Arab and Israeli governments has underscored the diminished authority that the EU now commands in the area. While the trend might be reversed in the future, it would take a substantial investment of resources on the part of the EU to do so. More generally, the time might have come for the EU to choose among conflicting discourses, as the result of Palestinian legislative elections has emphasized.

The overall picture is thus of a lack of convergence on a securitizing agenda between Europe and its Mediterranean partners if only because of the variety of EU discourses about Islam, radical Islam and 'jihadism'. While there are several indications that point in the direction of a community of understanding based on securitization, at the same time the plurality of discourses and practices depict a necessarily more complex picture. This situation highlights not merely the evident fragmentation of pro-Islamic movements, and the nature of the terrorist threat facing western countries, but crucially, the deep seated problems that the EU has in finding a single voice in its external relations, even when faced with an overwhelming issue of concern. At the same time this weakness may become a source of strength, as it leaves the road open to a very wide array of potential outcomes in Euro-Mediterranean relations.

Notes

[1] The passage of the 'glorification of terrorism' clause in the Terrorism Bill in February 2006, despite a threatened challenge to it, is one example of this new harder line.

[2] See the UK's Home Office website, available at www.homeoffice.gov.uk/security/terrorism-and-the-law

[3] See F. Gardner, evidence to Foreign Affairs Select Committee, 2 November 2005. Available at www.parliament.uk/pa/cm/cmfaff.htm#.

[4] A programme of 'deportation with assurances' was undertaken in 2005 before the London bombs, but following Madrid, as part of the strengthening of the 2001 Terrorism Act. This led in August 2005 to the first of the MOUs with Arab states. See C. Clarke, statement to House of Commons, *Hansard*, 26 January 2005, column 305.

[5] J. Doward, 'Race to prevent Algerian terror suspect release', *The Observer*, 19 February 2006.

[6] The Metropolitan Police has issued guidance to officers to avoid targeting any particular ethnic group, although the British Transport Police suggested the powers would affect Asian suspects. See N. Morris, 'Hundreds of British terror suspects are under surveillance', *The Independent*, 13 September 2005.

[7] Metropolitan Police Commissioner Sir Ian Blair and Assistant Commissioner Andy Hayman (House of Commons, 2005).

[8] C. Moore, 'Where is the Gandhi of Islam?', *Daily Telegraph*, 9 July 2005.

[9] Telephone interview, Metropolitan Police, 10 January 2005.

[10] See, for example, Evidence of Joint Chiefs of Staff to House of Commons Defence Select committee, 20 April 2004, particularly General Sir Michael Walker (Q256) on command structures and strategic and tactical cooperation with US counter-terrorism operations in Iraq. Also Martin Howard, Director General Operational Policy, Ministry of Defence on the relationship of UK and US military structures within NATO operations in Afghanistan, Uncorrected evidence to Defence Select Committee (HC558), 17 January 2006. Available at www.publications.parliament.uk/pa/cm/cmdefence.htm

[11] See The emergence of a global infrastructure for registration and surveillance, *International Campaign against Mass Surveillance*, 20 April 2005. Available at www.statewatch.org.uk/news/2005

[12] MEDA is an acronym of 'MEsures D'Accompangement financières et techniques à la réforme des structures économiques et sociales dans le cadre du partenariat euro-méditerranéen'. The regulation in place until 2006 is the so-called MEDA II, approved in 2000 (Council Regulation (EC) n.2698/2000), amending the MEDA Council Regulation (EC) 1488/96. After 2006, the financial instrument connected to the European Neighbourhood Policy (ENP) will enter into force.

[13] 'Focus countries' in the Mediterranean and the Middle East were Algeria, Gaza and the West Bank, Iraq and Tunisia.

[14] Given the emphasis put on the participation of women in local politics, it is unlikely to have included pro-Islamic NGOs, though. General Secretariat, Council of the European Union, *Annual Report on Human Rights*, Brussels, 2002.

[15] They are Amicale Marocaine des Handicapés, Association Atlas-Sais, Association démoratique des Femmes du Maroc, Association Horizon de Femme et Enfant, Association Tanmia Maroc, Fondation Zakora, Forum DES ONG du Nord du Maroc, Organisation Marocaine des Droits Humains, Réseau des association de la réserve de Biosphère Arganeraie, Union de l'Action Féminine Tétouan, Union des associations et des amicale humanitaires de Fès Médina.

[16] Telephone interviews, DG Relex, January–February 2006.

[17] Telephone interview, Delegation of the European Commission, Rabat, February 2006.

[18] The following quotations have been taken from unofficial drafts of the Barcelona Declaration, as amended by national delegations.

[19] See the Presidency Conclusions, Valence, 23 April 2002, about the 'Regional co-operation programme in the field of justice, in combating drugs, organised crime and terrorism as well as co-operation in the treatment of issues relating to the social integration of migrants, migration and movement of people.'

[20] The EU did not encourage the participation of the Syrian and Lebanese presidents, though, because of the tension with Syria. See Ewen MacAskill, 'Leaders put brave face on summit absentees', *The Guardian*, 28 November 2005; Euromed: les dirigeants arabes absents, les Européens pessimists, *Le Monde*, 27 November 2005.

[21] *Agence France Press*, 28 November 2005.

[22] Euro-Mediterranean Code of Conduct on Countering Terrorism, 27–28 November 2005, p. 3.

[23] (*Agence France Press*, 29 November 2005).

[24] Sommet Euromed: accord sur un 'code de conduite' contre le terrorism, *Le Monde*, 28 November 2005; Barcelona summit fails to agree on "shared vision", *European Report*, 30 November 2005.

References

Barbé, E. (1996) The Barcelona conference: launching pad of a process', *Mediterranean Politics*, 1(1), pp. 25–42.

Blair, T. (2005) PM's press conference, 5 August 2005. Available at http://www.pm.gov.uk/output/Page8041.asp

Bunyan, T. (2002) The war on freedom and democracy, *Statewatch analysis*, 13. Available at www.statewatch.org.uk

Burnett, J. (2005) Hearts and minds in the domestic "war on terror", *Campaign against Racism and Fascism*, 18 October. Available at www.carf.demon.co.uk/feature.html

Buzan, B., Wæver, O. & deWilde, J. (1998) *Security: A New Framework For Analysis* (Boulder, CO and London: Lynne Rienner).

Council of the European Union (2002) *Annual Report on Human Rights*, General Secretariat.

Council of the European Union (2003) *A Secure Europe in a better world*, European Security Strategy.

Council of the European Union (2006) Press release, 2706th Council Meeting, External Relations, 30–31. I. 2006.

Den Boer, M. & Monar, J. (2002) 11 September and the challenge of global terrorism to the EU as a Security Actor, *Journal of Common Market Studies*, 40(1 Supplement), pp. 11–28.

European Commission (2003) *Communication from the Commission to the Council and the European Parliament, reinvigorating EU actions on Human Rights and democratisation with Mediterranean partners*, Strategic guidelines, COM (2003)294 final.

European Commission (2004a) *Prevention, preparedness and response to terrorist attacks*, COM (2004) 698, 20 October 2004.

European Commission (2004b) *About the EIDHR*.

European Parliament (2002) *Annual Report on Human Rights in the World in 2002*.

European Parliament (2005) *European Parliament resolution on the Barcelona Process revisited*, 2005/2058 INI.

European Union (2001) *Presidency conclusions*, meeting of Foreign Ministers, Brussels, 5–6 November.

European Union (2003) *European Union's human rights policy*, A5–0274/2003 Final.

European Union (2004) *Presidency conclusions*, Euro-Mediterranean meeting of Ministers of Foreign Affairs, The Hague, 30 November, DOC 14869/04.

European Union (2005a) *The European Union counter terrorism strategy*, 30 November, DOC14469/4/05.

European Union (2005b) *The European Union strategy for combating radicalisation and recruitment to terrorism*, 24 November, DOC 14781/1/05.

Fairclough, N. (1989) *Language and Power* (London: Longman).

Foreign and Commonwealth Office (2005) Press release, 18 October.

Grünert, A. (2004) Loss of guiding values and support: September 11 and the isolation of human rights organizations in Egypt, in: A. Jünemann (Ed.) *Euro-Mediterranean Relations After September 11: International, Regional and Domestic Dynamics* (London and Portland, OR: Frank Cass), pp. 133–52.

Habermas, J. (1996) *Between Facts and Norms: Contributions to a Discourse Theory of Law and Democracy* (Oxford: Oxford Polity Press).

Holden, P. (2005) Partnership lost?: the EU's Mediterranean aid programmes, *Mediterranean Politics*, 10(1), pp. 19–37.

House of Commons (2005) Oral evidence taken before the Home Affairs Committee, Tuesday 13 September.

Huysmans, J. (2006) *The Politics of Insecurity: Fear, Migration, and Asylum in the EU* (Milton Park: Routledge).

Joint Doctrine Concepts Centre (2002) *Strategic Trends*. Available at http://www.jdcc-strategictrends. org/1st_Edition_frames.html

Jones, D. M. & Smith, M. L. R. (2005) Greetings from the cybercaliphate: some notes on homeland insecurity, *International Affairs*, 81(5), pp. 925–950.

Johansson-Nagues, E. (2002) The distant neighbors—EU, the Middle East, North Africa and the Euro-Mediterranean Partnership, *Working Paper* 37, Observatory of European Foreign Policy, Barcelona.

Ministry of Defence (2002) *SDR: a new chapter*, CM5566.

Official Journal of the European Communities (2001) *Common Council position*, 2001/931/CFSP, 27.XII.2001.

Official Journal of the European Communities (2002) *Council decision*, 2002/848/EC, 28.X.2002.

Official Journal of the European Communities (2003) *Council decision*, 2003/646/EC, 12.IX.2003.

Philippart, E. (2001) The MEDA programme: analysis of the new design of EU assistance to the Mediterranean, in: F. Attinà & S. Stavridis (Eds) *The Barcelona Process and Euro-Mediterranean Issues From Stuttgart to Marseille* (Milano: Giuffrè).

Stetter, S. (2004) Democratization without democracy?: the assistance of the European Union for democratization processes in Palestine, in: A. Jünemann (Ed.) *Euro-Mediterranean Relations After September 11*, pp. 153–173 (London and Portland, OR: Frank Cass).

Wæver, O. (1995) Securitisation and desecuritisation, in: R. D. Lipschutz (Ed.) *On Security* (New York: Columbia University Press).

Youngs, S. (2001) *The European Union and the Promotion of Democracy* (Oxford: Oxford University Press).

Youngs, R. (2004) Normative dynamics and strategic Interests in the EU's External Identity, *Journal of Common Market Studies*, 42(2), pp. 415–435.

Converging, Diverging and Instrumentalizing European Security and Defence Policy in the Mediterranean

EDUARD SOLER I LECHA

Coordinator of the Mediterranean and Middle East Programme CIDOB, Barcelona Centre for International Affairs

ABSTRACT *This article addresses the degree of convergence, divergence and in some cases indifference of Southern and Eastern Mediterranean Countries towards the European Security and Defence Policy. Focusing on two cases, Morocco and Turkey, but also referring to other Mediterranean partners, this contribution analyses the dynamics of this specific issue area, arguing that policy convergence in the field of security and defence has reflected process-oriented goals rather than a substantive convergence of strategic interests. The article concludes by exploring how the EU's differentiated geographical approach in security and defence cooperation in the Mediterranean impacts on the broader region-building endeavour.*

Mediterranean, Security and Cooperation are three terms that do not necessarily come together. Too often, insecurity and conflict have prevailed in the Euro-Mediterranean area. Nevertheless, this article will look at different Southern and Eastern Mediterranean Countries (SEMC) with the aim of identifying which are the factors and the expected outcomes that push particular SEMC to opt for convergence with the EU on security and defence issues. Thus, in accordance with the goals of this volume, this contribution studies geographical differentiation and policy-convergence dynamics and their impact on the region-building efforts within the Euro-Mediterranean space.

The article contemplates broader security and defence cooperation but focuses on the dynamics of a specific issue area: European Security and Defence Policy (ESDP).[1] The ESDP is a relatively new policy raising interest both in the European Union and among its closest neighbours. The EU's attempts (and previously the EEC's) to create a common policy in the security and defence domain have been faced with various challenges: internal divisions, dependence on NATO's military facilities, reluctance of external actors, etc. Nevertheless, since 1999 this policy has been gradually developed, benefiting from strong support from public opinion in EU, deploying ESDP missions in different continents, cooperating with several international organizations and welcoming the participation of third country personnel.

Although all the SEMC participate in the ESDP's so-called Mediterranean dimension, that is, regular exchange of information on ESDP issues with Mediterranean partners, geographical differentiation has also taken place. Two countries have been particularly active in ESDP cooperation: Morocco and Turkey. Consequently, they deserve special attention in this article. Nevertheless, we will also refer to countries that have been more reluctant or have preferred to cooperate with EU members outside of ESDP mechanisms. This is, for instance, the case of Algeria's involvement in NATO's Mediterranean Dialogue instead of the ESDP's Mediterranean Dimension.

Whenever the article highlights these dynamics of geographical differentiation, it must be emphasized that this is not the only differentiation vector taking place. Normative and sectoral differentiation are also important, as cooperation addresses slightly different topics and adopts various normative benchmarks depending on the country/ies involved in every particular setting of cooperation. Therefore, in the terms used in the introduction to this volume, the region-building model developing in the issue area of security and defence is rather mixed: on the one hand, a scheme of differentiated integration in the framework of the ESDP seems to be developing steadily with specific partner countries; but on the other hand, these dynamics coexist with a plethora of bilateral, sub-regional and regional frameworks, which makes à la carte cooperation a most appropriate term to capture the development and challenges of Euro-Mediterranean relations in the domain of security and defence.

The article starts by presenting a general overview of the main elements shaping regional cooperation attempts in the area of security and defence, as well as the evolution of this cooperation in the last two decades. It then moves to the analysis of differentiated dynamics in the area of ESDP, stressing that cooperation or even policy convergence is not solely motivated by common interests or shared approaches on security and defence issues. Indeed, convergence or divergence can relate to a more comprehensive approach of getting close to the EU or to the expression of discontent with the nature of bilateral relations with the EU. Finally, the article assesses the outcomes of these differentiated processes in terms of region-building, presenting bilateralism and sub-regionalism (both forms of geographical differentiation) as a second best option when the regional track is deadlocked.

Security Cooperation in the Mediterranean: Regional, Sub-regional and Bilateral Strategies

There has been a substantive debate among scholars as to how to describe the Mediterranean in terms of security. One axis of debate has been whether the

Mediterranean is a security complex or is a space containing different security complexes.[2] Niklas Bremberg (2007: 2) for instance depicts the Mediterranean not as a 'regional security complex', but rather as a geographical space where at least two different regional complexes meet (the EU, on the one hand, and the Middle Eastern and North Africa complex, on the other). Sven Biscop (2003: 191) refers to the Mediterranean as a single security complex, arguing that 'though the Mediterranean partners are a very diverse set of countries, from the EU's viewpoint they are involved in an interrelated set of security issues: unresolved disputes and conflicts across the region, militarization and proliferation, and violent Islamism, to name just the major 'hard' security factors'. Some scholars also point to the existence of differentiated security cultures in the Euro-Mediterranean space (Attinà, 2006; Bilgin, 2004; Ruacan, 2007). From that perspective, the existence not only of different strategic interests but also different security cultures has impeded the countries of the Euro-Mediterranean space from moving towards a 'security community' understood as a region or group of countries for which war has ceased to be conceivable as a means to resolve their disputes.[3] Other scholars (e.g. Volpi, 2006: 120–21) argue, however, that a Mediterranean security community could be built on a set of insecurities shared by states and populations of both shores of the Mediterranean.

Has the EMP contributed somehow to build this security community? The EMP could be labelled as a project of 'regional security partnership'. According to Fulvio Attinà (2006: 249–50) this differs from the aforementioned security community as the countries forming this partnership 'may have different security cultures, but they are not so distant from one another as to prevent the formation of consensus on cooperation in security problems'. The evolution of this project proves that it has failed to reach its goals, at least in the security domain. The Barcelona declaration, foundation stone of Euro-Mediterranean cooperation, stated that one of its main goals was to progress towards the establishment of an area of peace and stability. Fifteen years after the launch of the Barcelona Process and two years since its transformation into the Union for the Mediterranean, it is quite evident that the EMP has been unable to create neither a safer and more stable Euro-Mediterranean space, nor a common narrative for Mediterranean security. The overall picture is, according to Bicchi and Martin (2006: 204) of a lack of convergence on a securitizing agenda between Europe and its Mediterranean partners.

It is essential to understand the elements that shaped security cooperation attempts in the Mediterranean during the 1990s and how this context has evolved since then. It is well known that the whole Barcelona Process, and specifically the partners' willingness to cooperate in security issues, was only feasible due to the changes in the Arab–Israeli conflict, mainly after the Madrid conference in 1991 and the Oslo agreements in 1993. It is also well known that before the Barcelona conference, Spanish and Italian diplomats failed to convene a Conference for Security and Cooperation in the Mediterranean (replicating the Helsinki Process) but the design of this unborn initiative was very influential in the launch of the Barcelona Process.

Next to these two key facts, is worth recalling that the Barcelona Process was initiated in a context characterized by the proliferation of Mediterranean cooperation initiatives in the security field. In 1992 the Western European Union (WEU) started a Mediterranean Dialogue mainly focused on the Maghreb (Biscop, 2002: 93) which suffered from the mistrust felt by Maghribian partners regarding the creation, in 1994, of the European Maritime Force (EUROMARFOR) and the European Operational Rapid Force (EUROFOR). The Maghreb countries perceived these two forces as serving eventual interventions of their northern neighbours on their shores, particularly in the context of the Algerian crisis. Next to the WEU Mediterranean Dialogue, NATO also launched its own Mediterranean Dialogue with the aim being to strengthen political dialogue, fight terrorism, modernize the armed forces and improve the interoperability between the forces of different countries (Bin, 2002). However, this dialogue did not cover the whole Mediterranean basin but involved a limited number of southern Mediterranean countries: Egypt, Israel, Mauritania, Morocco and Tunisia in a first stage and, since 2000, also Algeria.[4]

The Barcelona Process was created in an environment that offered a better ground for cooperation on security and defence issues, but where some Mediterranean partners had been unhappy over the development of security cooperation initiatives that excluded or only partially included them. Thus, even if the Barcelona Process was not designed to focus on conflict resolution and explicitly discarded the possibility of substituting or interfering with the Middle East Peace Process, it did have a security agenda that intended to create conditions for dialogue and cooperation among all the countries of the Euro-Mediterranean area.

In this spirit, the Barcelona Process started working on disarmament, confidence-building measures and even attempted to agree on a Charter for Peace and Stability in the Mediterranean (Aliboni, 1999; Biad, 2001). Nevertheless, in the late 1990s, the deterioration of the situation in the Middle East watered down the initial expectations and, following the Second Intifada, Euro-Mediterranean countries proved unable to agree on the aforementioned charter. This led the security basket of the Barcelona Process to considerable paralysis and obliged the members of this process to explore new possibilities for cooperation in the security field (Aliboni, 2005).

Since 2002, that is since Valencia's Euro-Mediterranean conference, this adaptation has taken place in four different and complementary directions. Firstly, Euro-Mediterranean countries have put more emphasis on 'inter-mestic' issues, such as cooperation against terrorism (culminating with the adoption of a lukewarm Euro-Mediterranean Code of Conduct on Countering Terrorism in 2005) and also cooperation against clandestine migration flows (Justice and Home Affairs becoming a separate chapter since Barcelona's 2005 summit). Secondly, they have invested in issues politically less sensitive, such as civil protection which has been the object of cooperation projects since 1997 with the Italian–Egyptian initiative and has gained importance in recent years (Bremberg et al., 2009; Courela, 2004). Thirdly, sub-regional cooperation (mainly in the western Mediterranean) has become a means to escape the blockages at the broader regional level as illustrated by the launch of a 5 + 5 Dialogue of Ministers of Defence in 2004 (Coustillière, 2007). And, fourthly, and this is particularly relevant to this article, the EU has proposed that southern Mediterranean partners explore cooperation within the ESDP on bilateral, voluntary and gradualist bases.

This evolution coincided with the ESDP's early stages. In 2002 the EU reached an agreement with NATO on permanent arrangements, which allowed the EU to launch in 2003 the first ESDP missions in the Balkans which were open to the participation of third countries. The first, and for the moment the only missions in the southern rim of the Mediterranean were approved two years later and both took place in the Palestinian Territories. EUBAM-Rafah, launched in 2005, focused on border control between Gaza and Egypt and EUPOL COPPS has dealt since 2006 with the reform of the Palestinian police. The future of these two Mediterranean ESDP missions is not particularly promising as the evolution of the Arab–Israeli conflict, as well as the internal struggles in Palestine, have hindered the development of both missions.[5] However, the EU seems willing to keep this commitment and perhaps could explore new missions in the Euro-Mediterranean area if such demand exists.

Next to these missions, the EU has also developed the so-called 'ESDP's Mediterranean dimension' which is continuing the work of the previous WEU Mediterranean Dialogue. This Mediterranean dimension started in 2002, with Valencia's Action Plan when the members of the EMP agreed to develop an 'effective dialogue on political and security matters, including on the ESDP'.[6] Following that statement, the EU approved a document which defined the aims and the mechanisms of this dialogue. More specifically, this document foresaw the following possibilities: (a) meetings between the Political and Security Committee (PSC) Troika and the Heads of Mission of the Mediterranean Partners once per Presidency; (b) the establishment by the Mediterranean partners of contacts with the Secretariat General of the Council and the Commission, with a view to exchanging information on respective crisis management procedures, as well as other issues related to crisis management; (c) holding regular meetings (every six months) by the Presidency and the Secretariat, including the European Union Military Staff on specific subjects of crisis management; and (d) an invitation to the EU Institute for Security Studies to examine possible activities in support of the dialogue with Mediterranean partners (seminars and other such activities). Moreover, this document foresaw, in the mid-term and on a case-by-case basis, offering the possibility to observe or take part in ESDP missions, to appoint an officer as point of contact accredited to the EU Military Staff and to participate in EU training courses within ESDP (Council of the European Union, 2003).

The Mediterranean dimension of the ESDP combines, then, a multilateral and a bilateral track. In the multilateral one, it has attempted to create confidence among the SEMC by a continuous effort to inform and familiarize them about the developments and possibilities of this policy. Nonetheless, following the tendency observed in the case of the Barcelona Process, the multilateral track of the ESDP's Mediterranean Dimension has suffered from the existence of regional conflicts. The main success was the uninterrupted meetings between the EU and its Mediterranean partners. However, in 2009 no meetings were convened owing to the consequences of the Gaza crisis and the multilateral dialogue was only supposed to restart in 2010.[7]

In contrast, the bilateral dimension has been less exposed to the ups and downs of the regional context and has satisfied the demands of some of these partners to deepen their cooperation. This trend has also been reflected in the development, since 2004, of the European Neighbourhood Policy (ENP), which envisage the possibility to involve partner countries in aspects of CFSP and ESDP, conflict prevention, crisis management, the exchange of information, joint training and exercises (European Commission, 2004a).

The participation of third countries (and this includes the EU neighbours, and among them the SEMC) in ESDP has not triggered a substantive scholarly debate. Most probably, this is due to the fact that the main challenge remains the consolidation of the ESDP itself (Helmerich, 2007). However, we agree with Esther Barbé et al. (2009: 848) that there is no reason to exclude these issues from analyses of external governance in the neighbourhood even if the ENP has not been able, at least in the Mediterranean, to offer enough incentives to produce a structural, rather than punctual, convergence in ESDP matters.

Finally, the launch in 2008 of the Union for the Mediterranean is not altering this situation even if it represents a significant transformation of Euro-Mediterranean relations at large.[8] The Union for the Mediterranean still refers to Barcelona's classic wording on disarmament, vaguely includes the issue of the fight against terrorism in the agenda and civil protection is the only project dealing with security approved in the Paris 2008 summit and the Marseilles ministerial meeting of November 2008 (Soler i Lecha and García, 2009: 3f.). More significant, the Union for the Mediterranean does not alter bilateral relations with Mediterranean partners, be they current or potential candidate countries to accession (the Balkans and Turkey) or countries benefiting from the ENP.

Convergence, Divergence and Indifference

The SEMC have had very different reactions regarding the broadly defined offer to deepen dialogue and increase cooperation on ESDP issues. Their attitudes range from active involvement in ESDP cooperation to passive indifference or even episodes of confrontation. The following intends to identify which SEMC, in which circumstances, have been more or less inclined to cooperate in the framework of the ESDP.

Converging Dynamics

Two SEMC have been the most active on ESDP issues: Turkey and Morocco. Although in both cases we can refer to a strategic choice in their respective foreign policies towards the EU, the nature of their relations with the Union differs greatly. While Turkey has been a NATO member since 1952 and a candidate country for EU accession since 1999, Morocco is a partner of NATO's Mediterranean dialogue, has an association agreement with the EU which aims to upgrade via the so-called 'Advanced Status'. The different starting points of these two countries in their relations with the EU are determining their approach on ESDP issues.

Turkey is a unique case. Turkey's convergence with ESDP consists, on the one hand, of the adoption of EU norms, principles, methods and actions. On the other hand, its role as a key NATO member allows Ankara to favour or obstruct the development of a stronger and autonomous European defence policy. ESDP, which is a relatively young policy, still depends on EU–NATO cooperation (Ojanen, 2006: 69ff.). Thus, Turkey's agreement is needed to make any substantial step towards a deeper NATO–EU cooperation.

Turkey's convergence with EU norms, principles, methods and actions is supposed to take place within the framework of the ongoing accession negotiations. However, these elements have either been left to the end of the accession negotiation process or have been partially blocked by the resistance of some EU members (France and Cyprus).[9] This environment has not favoured a smooth adoption of the EU *acquis* and has not favoured an automatic alignment with the EU policies in this field, particularly if these measures could compromise national interests which, according to the EU, correspond to issues 'regarding its geographical neighbourhood (Iraq, Caucasus, etc.), human rights and developments in Muslim countries, where it [Turkey] insists on a distinct national position' (European Commission, 2004b: 9). However, it is worth pointing out that recent studies show that in many issues there has been convergence with the EU, also in the field of security (Luif *et al.*, 2009: 38)

Actually, Turkey has also accepted to participate in several ESDP missions. In Bosnia-Herzegovina, Turkey contributes to the EU military operation in Bosnia and Herzegovina (EUFOR Althea) and it is supporting the EU police mission (EUPM) in the same country. Turkey is one of the five non-EU countries contributing to the EU Rule of Law Mission (EULEX) in Kosovo. It has also participated in the ESDP mission in Congo and it has provided both this and other missions with the necessary transport facilities.[10] By all this, Turkey has been one of the most active non-EU members in the implementation of this policy.

In addition, Turkey is willing to be further involved in ESDP structures. Turkey is regularly associated, in its double status of candidate country and European NATO member, in the PSC and other ESDP organs.[11] However, Turkey has continuously asked the EU to upgrade its role in the ESDP decision-making mechanisms as there is a widespread feeling that its position is weaker than in the previous WEU system (Tatli, 2008). A perfect illustration of Turkey's determination is Turkey' recurrent demand to participate in the European Defence Agency (EDA), the body set up to nurture EU-wide defence industry policy. In that respect, Turkey would like to follow the example of other NATO non-EU countries such us Norway.[12] However, Cyprus has vetoed Turkey's participation in this Agency (Ülgen, 2008: 105).

On top of it, it is worth underlining that the current level of ESDP development would not have been possible without Turkey's assent. Between 2001 and 2002, two negotiation processes (on the enlargement prospects and on a NATO–EU agreement) took place in parallel, involving Turkey and the EU and, in some circumstances, the US. The result of this double-edged negotiation was that the very same day that Turkey was given a 'date for a date' perspective to start accession negotiations,[13] the EU and Turkey were able to reach an agreement, contained in an annexed declaration to the Conclusions of the European Council, allowing the EU to effectively develop its ESDP.

That declaration stated that the 'Berlin plus' arrangements and their implementation would only apply to those EU member states which were either NATO members or parties to the Partnership for Peace, and which have consequently concluded bilateral security agreements with NATO. The declaration clarified that for the time being, Cyprus and Malta would not take part in EU military operations conducted using NATO assets once they have become members of the EU. It was also said that they could participate and vote in EU institutions and bodies, including PSC, with regard to decisions which do not concern the implementation of such operations. Finally, it recognized their right to receive EU classified information, within the limits of the EU Security Regulations, provided the EU classified information does not contain or refer to any classified NATO information (European Council, 2002). Turkey has made use of these provisions, effectively limiting EU–NATO dialogue on security and defence issues since 2005 and, consequently, has made the development of ESDP more difficult. Thus, as we shall see below, Turkey has alternated both converging and diverging dynamics regarding ESDP.

As said before, Morocco is the other example of convergence dynamics in ESDP issues. In fact, Moroccan participation in the ESDP is listed together with Galileo and the Open-sky agreement as illustrating Morocco's readiness to be fully involved in EU policies and agencies. The advanced status approved in 2008 contemplates the adoption of the *acquis communautaire*.[14] At the current stage, that is, in a relationship based on the Association Agreement and complemented by non-binding Action Plans, alignment only takes place on a voluntary basis. As stated in the 2008 ENP's progress report, Morocco had agreed to give its support to CFSP declarations on a case by case basis but the EU and Morocco have not yet approved the procedures to implement it. In other words, on this point, Morocco and the EU are still at a declaratory level. Moving towards a more sophisticated cooperation would require, according to Larbi Jaidi (2007), a phase of cooperation leading to a common understanding and, even, a common language on security and defence issues. In a similar direction, Lannon *et al.* (2007: 11) consider that institutionalization should take place after a strengthened association.

Generally, convergence is taking place not in terms of systematic alignment but in terms of participation in ESDP missions and structures. Morocco has actively participated since 2004 in the EUFOR ALTHEA mission in Bosnia and Herzegovina and this case is also brought to the attention of the EU, so as to show Morocco's commitment not only to the ESDP but also to European security. In fact, this participation already took place under the NATO umbrella as 1,300 Moroccan forces were previously involved in the Implementation Force (IFOR) and in the Stabilization Force (SFOR). When the EU and NATO agreed that SFOR should be replaced by a ESDP mission in accordance with the Berlin Plus mechanisms, the EU requested the Moroccan forces to be placed under European control and Morocco agreed (Marsou, 2007: 50). As a contributor to the mission, Morocco has co-decision-making powers on an operative level of the ESDP missions. However, strategic direction remains in the hands of the PSC and the EU Military Committee (EUMC). Morocco has already expressed its willingness to be more involved in the PSC's works and discussions and the Moroccan ambassador to the EU has been invited to participate in some of its meetings.[15]

Other Mediterranean partners are far from Turkey's and Morocco's level of participation in ESDP. Action Plans such as those of Tunisia, Lebanon and Jordan contain only vague references to the need to establish points of contact and conduct open exchanges of information on ESDP with the Council Secretariat and the Commission; however, this has not yet been translated into concrete action. In the cases of Israel, the Palestinian territories and Egypt, references to ESDP in their Action Plans and progress reports relate specifically to the two missions EUBAM-Rafah and EUPOL-COPSS, which have been blocked due the deterioration of the conflict in the area.

Divergence and/or Indifference

Compared to the mid-1990s mistrust towards the EUROMARFOR and EUROFOR expressed by Maghribian officials, the development of ESDP has had considerable acceptance on the part of the SEMC (EuroMeSCo, 2002). The EU's willingness to develop its own security and defence policy is seen in many Arab capitals as a way to reinforce and build the EU's civilian power and endorse multilateralism, thus counterbalancing the US presence in the region (Jünemann, 2003: 45). Therefore, even those partners that have been more reluctant to move towards greater cooperation in this field have had an indifferent rather than defensive attitude regarding ESDP development. Interestingly, the only two episodes of confrontation correspond to a country, Turkey, which in different situations, has been far more cooperative.

The first of these episodes was the blockage from 1999 to 2002 of the adoption of EU–NATO arrangements ('Berlin Plus') as a protest against their insufficient participation in the decision-making and decision-shaping mechanisms of the ESDP. The second is more recent and started in 2006, when Turkey–EU relations entered in its current *impasse* due, among other factors, to the situation in Cyprus. In this context, Turkey has opted for a less cooperative stance vis-à-vis ESDP. Turkey has vehemently opposed Cyprus attending EU–NATO meetings when Berlin Plus mechanisms were discussed, creating an embarrassing situation of asking Cyprus to leave the room. This position hardened in mid-2007 when Turkey threatened to withhold its approval of the EU's use of NATO military capacities in new ESDP missions and decided not to commit personnel to new ESDP missions. Turkey justified this attitude as a complaint against the insufficient role that it played in the EU–NATO dialogue.[16] On the other side, the EU has appealed to the 'EU solidarity principle' to claim that Cyprus can no longer be left outside the scope of this arrangement and refuses to engage in dialogue with NATO without all EU members sitting around the table. As a result, while there is an agreed mechanism to do so, this hampered a meaningful dialogue between NATO and the EU on emerging threats (Ülgen, 2008: 100) and, according to sources quoted by Miguel Ángel Medina-Abellán (2009: 8), this situation has even put at risk the lives of the civilians deployed in unsafe scenarios, rendering many allies furious and creating enemies in NATO (Valasek, 2008: 5).

With the exception of Morocco and Turkey, all the other Mediterranean countries' attitudes towards ESDP can be best characterized as indifference. In some cases, this indifference is expressed as preference to cooperate with Western countries (including with the EU member states) in other frameworks. This is the case of Algeria and Jordan, two countries that have been very active in NATO's Mediterranean Dialogue and much less in the ESDP. To some extent, this is also the trend in Israel and Egypt, although in these cases this indifference reflects their strong ties with the United States, with which both countries have a strategic partnership. Libya has cooperated with five European countries in the 5 + 5 dialogue of Ministers of Defence since 2003 but is still negotiating some kind of Association Agreement with the EU.

In the case of Syria is not the preference for an alternative framework for cooperation but the low level of relations with the EU and other Western actors which, despite some recent progress, has prevented deeper cooperation in the field of defence and security with Damascus. Finally, the case of Lebanon has some particularities as well. Many European countries have deployed troops in the United Nations Interim Force in Lebanon (UNIFIL) mission in this country but, as this is a UN mission, this has not been translated into Lebanon–EU cooperation in the ESDP domain.

Instrumentalizing ESDP Cooperation

For many SEMC, cooperating in ESDP matters is not necessarily seen as an outcome *per se* but cooperation in this area is meant to serve broader interests, mainly regarding the general nature of EU–partner bilateral relations. This is precisely what Esther Barbé *et al.* (2009: 837) have labelled 'process-driven considerations'. In other words, the dynamics of policy convergence in security and defence can be the result of a more comprehensive goal of upgrading relations with the EU rather than the expression of coinciding strategic interests or the acceptance of the ESDP as the optimal framework for cooperation on security and defence matters. Similarly, the lack of policy convergence can express dissatisfaction with the nature of these relations rather than an indication of divergence or even incompatibility between the EU and third countries on security interests.

As we shall see, the two countries that have been more active on ESDP issues are good examples of this process-driven dynamic. Turkey has linked its support to ESDP development to other considerations, such as the evolution of its accession process or the Cyprus dispute. In the case of Morocco, involvement in ESDP issues, which became very visible with its participation in ALTHEA, serves the kingdom's interest of showing a 'European strategic choice'. On a different token, Algeria's preference for NATO's Mediterranean Dialogue confirms Algiers' discontent with the asymmetrical cooperation offered, not only within the framework of ESDP but also under the ENP.

ESDP, Turkey's Accession Negotiations and Cyprus

ESDP, enlargement and Cyprus have been kept formally separated over the years, however, as noted by Antonio Missiroli (2002: 20), these dossiers proved to be hardly separable. Turkey has always used its strategic position as a NATO member to push the EU to opt for a more inclusive approach. Turkey has always sought to be more involved in the EU's security architecture since the times of the WEU (Cebeci, 1999) and has continued to do so in the framework of ESDP (Çayhan, 2003; Terzi, 2004; Turkes and Gökgöz, 2004; Yilmaz, 2007). However, the ultimate goal of these demands was to confirm the EU's commitment to Turkey's accession and confirm the irreversibility of this process.

Turkey's perception of the EU's commitment on enlargement has determined Turkey's convergence or divergence towards ESDP. As described in the previous section, when there has been a significant consensus that accession was the final goal of EU–Turkish relations, Turkey has agreed to facilitate the launch of ESDP (2002–04). This approach contrasts with the current context characterized by, on the one hand, some EU leaders' statements that a 'privileged partnership' rather than full accession should be the ultimate goal of EU–Turkish relations and, on the other, by the deadlock of Cyprus reunification talks and the maintenance of the isolation of the northern part of the island. In such circumstances, Turkey is far less cooperative and keeps the ESDP as part of its bargaining assets. This can be seen, for instance, with all the discussions regarding ESDP's missions in Afghanistan or Kosovo.[17]

As noted by Sinan Ülgen (2008: 98), 'had there been a clear political will on the EU side for supporting Turkey's full membership objective, Turkish policymakers may have been more flexible with regard to their demands [on ESDP], knowing that these arrangements would necessarily be upgraded once Turkey became a full member'. Also, if future talks between Greek and Turkish Cypriot leaders lead to reunification, one of the biggest obstacles for ESDP development would be removed. Thus, broader considerations on the EU accession process and the reunification of Cyprus are likely to prevail, determining Turkey's position in ESDP.

ESDP and Morocco's Advance Status

Morocco has traditionally asked for differentiated treatment by the EU, justifying this demand on the basis of its decades-old European vocation and shown, among other facts, by Morocco's application in the mid-1980s to join the EU. Morocco knew that this would be rejected but still decided to submit it to show the determination of its European vocation; hence Hassan II's famous sentence comparing Morocco with a tree with its roots in Africa and its branches in Europe.[18]

Rabat's positive and cooperative approach to ESDP issues is also intended to reflect the extent of Morocco's commitment to the EU. Moroccan diplomats often refer to 'Morocco's strategic choice for Europe'.[19] It is, certainly, debatable whether this choice was Morocco's only alternative in a complicated regional context (deteriorating relations with Algeria and Morocco's withdrawal from the Organization of African Unity in 1994 as a protest against the acceptance of the Western Sahara into this organization) or whether it reflects a commitment to tie up the links with Europe. Be that as it may, the EU itself builds on this idea and it is reflected in the Morocco's Action Plan. In this document it is stated that 'for Morocco, rapprochement with the Union represents a fundamental foreign policy choice' (Association between the European Union and Morocco, 2005).

This country had welcomed the ENP's philosophy, as the policy offered integration *à la carte* and allowed those partners that were ready for the necessary reforms to go faster and deeper. Nevertheless, Morocco wanted to go even further. With the early support of Spain (in 2004) and later on, with the collaboration of France, Portugal and the European Commission, Morocco asked to upgrade its relations with the EU. These upgraded relations were soon known as 'Advanced Status'. Negotiations between the EU and Morocco took place through the work of an ad hoc group and quite quickly, in Luxemburg, in October 2008, both parties agreed on a road-map and a catalogue of potential areas of increased cooperation, to be accompanied by additional funds to ensure the viability of this new phase of EU–Moroccan relations.

As far as the ESDP is concerned, Advanced Status proposes to conclude two framework agreements: one which would deal with Moroccan participation in crisis-management operations, and another on information security. The EU has also opened the European College for Security and Defence to the participation of Moroccan nationals (EU–Morocco Association Council, 2008). None of this progress explains in itself Morocco's practical and rhetorical desire to converge on ESDP issues. In fact, as noted by Iván Martín (2009: 240), Advanced Status does not introduce many novelties in terms of practical cooperation. However, agreeing to explore cooperation in ESDP, as in other areas, places Moroccan officials in a better position to demand the substantiation of this status via upgraded political dialogue, comprehensive Free Trade Areas, visa facilitation or additional funding.

Algerian Lack of Interest

Algeria has participated, as have all other members of the EMP, in the multilateral track of ESDP. Nevertheless, as noted in the previous section, Algiers has opted for a low profile in the bilateral track. Interestingly, this coincides with the country's lack of interest in the ENP and/or proposals to upgrade their bilateral relations (with the exception of the possibility to conclude in the future a so-called 'Strategic Energy Partnership').

Many have explained that this lack of interest towards ENP shows that the country has been benefiting from additional policy options. This is due to its position in the global economy as an energy supplier, which has made Algeria less dependent on EU funding (e.g. Çelenk, 2009: 182). However, a more sophisticated analysis, such as that of Hakim Darbouche (2008), argues that this element needs to be complemented by a larger interpretation in the framework of a reinvigorated Algerian foreign policy. Thus, although Algeria was receptive to advances inherent in the Association Agreement, this was not the case for the ENP. Algeria has constantly denounced the 'Eurocentrism' of the initiative causing the 'the credibility of the Neighbourhood Policy [to be] undermined by the fact that its contents and format had not been the "subject of democratic dialogue" prior to its introduction' (Darbouche, 2008: 337).

Actually, the ESDP's bilateral cooperation reproduces the Eurocentric and vertical approach of the ENP. Thus, not surprisingly, Algeria's attitude towards ESDP diverges with the strategy of policy convergence (albeit limited and instrumental) of Morocco, precisely because Algeria does not share the process-driven considerations that shape Rabat's position on ESDP. However, there are three additional factors that should also be taken into account.

The first is Algeria's traditional strategic thinking, which has emphasized its independence and its rejection of foreign intervention. As Abdennour Benantar (2006: 179) explains, Algeria 'has always held an independent national security doctrine and has not signed defence agreements with foreign powers, even during the cold war era'. Moreover, this tradition meets with a deep-rooted anti-colonial rhetoric which emphasizes the need to keep independence and rejects any foreign intervention. According to EuroMeSCo (2002), this is one of the elements that explains why Algerian officials were less enthusiastic than other SEMC regarding ESDP developments, as they were fearing European defence strategies and capabilities as entailing a real risk of intervention in the Mediterranean. This is not surprising as on many occasions, as for too many years, the Mediterranean was associated in this country with invasion and colonialism (Baghzouz, 2009: 46)

The second factor is the rapprochement between Algeria and the US since 11 September 2001 (Benantar, 2007; Driss, 2009; Zoubir, 2009). In fact, Algeria has become a fundamental US ally in various geographical areas (the Maghreb, the Sahel) with a particular emphasis on the fight against terrorism. According to Benantar (2006: 177), 'elevating Algeria to a pivotal state, the Americans have lured some Algerians into a political seduction game'; consequently, NATO's Mediterranean Dialogue has become far more attractive (and instrumental) than the ESDP's Mediterranean Dimension.

The third is that the bilateral channels for cooperation with individual member states of the EU can fulfil Algeria's needs in terms of security cooperation. In fact, in areas such as the fight against terrorism (probably the most important priority for Algeria's political and security apparatus) bilateral cooperation with European countries can bear more concrete fruit than cooperation with the EU as a whole. In other words, if Algeria is able to keep this cooperation with countries such as France or Spain, the attractiveness of policy convergence in the realm of ESDP is rather small.

Concluding Remarks: ESDP Bilateral Cooperation and Region-Building

The participation of third countries, including the Mediterranean partners, in ESDP reinforces the legitimacy of this policy as it proves that ESDP is not directed against these countries. However, this article points out that it is not only the security chapter of the Barcelona Process that has been paralysed: the multilateral track of ESDP's Mediterranean dimension has been deadlocked too and its scope has been kept to the level of regular information meetings and training activities. Therefore, policy convergence in ESDP matters has occurred through selective geographical differentiation as the EU has pushed for bilateral cooperation with a limited group of 'like-minded' countries.

Actually, few SEMC have been willing to explore the possibility of broader cooperation within ESDP, as illustrated by the fact that only Morocco and Turkey have been involved in ESDP missions. In contrast, many other countries have had a lower profile and some have preferred to focus on other security and defence initiatives such as NATO's Mediterranean Dialogue and/or the 5 + 5 in the Western Mediterranean.

To some extent, this situation could be described as an *à la carte* cooperation model. The EU and the other members are formally committed to the goal of cooperating at a multilateral level but are unable to overcome obstacles such as the interference of regional conflicts. The EU offers differentiated integration to some countries that are (or seem to be) willing to converge with EU norms, policies and practices. Finally, both those countries that are involved in this process of policy convergence and those that are reluctant or indifferent towards the possibility of increasing cooperation within ESDP, can opt to cooperate with the EU countries through other channels such as bilateral relations with specific member states, sub-regional cooperation or NATO's Mediterranean Dialogue.

Generally, process-driven considerations, rather than substantive convergence in terms of interests, values and perceptions on threats and risks, explain SEMC's preferences towards ESDP. All this has limited the depth and rapidity of policy convergence in this area. Turkey's example is very telling. Even if Turkish and EU strategic interests seem to converge in many fields, this country is not likely to lift the obstacles to ESDP development if EU–Turkish relations remain in the current *impasse*.

Taking into account these limitations, it is necessary to discuss whether bilateral cooperation in security and defence issues contributes to regional efforts to build a Euro-Mediterranean area of peace and security. The EMP and now the Union for the Mediterranean seem the optimal frameworks for regional integration in the Euro-Mediterranean area. They are comprehensive in terms of issue areas and regional scope and they constitute an attempt to build a regional security partnership, using Fulvio Attinà's wording. However, the security and defence dimension of the EMP has traditionally suffered, and was almost paralysed, due to the Middle East conflict; the multilateral track of the ESDP's Mediterranean dimension has also suffered the interference of regional conflicts and nowadays, the UfM is experiencing similar problems (Soler i Lecha and García, 2009: 4).

In this state of affairs, bilateral cooperation, complemented in specific cases with sub-regional cooperation, has become the best or even the only means to circumvent these blockages. Bilateralism becomes, then, a second-best option in terms of regional integration which, for some countries such as Morocco, stands as the best choice as differentiated relations becomes a goal in itself. Thus, policy convergence in ESDP allows a third country to express its willingness to cooperate further with the EU in other areas and, if possible, to upgrade the nature of these relations, via Advanced Status or a similar formula. In addition, differentiation strategies could also trigger a positive spill-over effect. Following Morocco's Advanced Status, other countries such as Jordan, Egypt and Tunisia have asked to establish a similar framework of upgraded relations and this could result, in the medium term, in a shift of preferences of some of these countries which have previously been indifferent towards ESDP development.

This dynamic can be contested as confirming an EU attempt to differentiate SEMC between 'smart' and 'less smart' students, which could have been damaging to region-building endeavours. Others may question the effectiveness of a policy which 'imposes discourse norms and practices rather than elaborate them with southern member states' (Volpi, 2006: 131). Indeed, the emphasis on a bilateral and vertical cooperation on security issues does not pave the way to a region-oriented multilateral cooperation in security and defence with either a strong normative component or at least a shared narrative on security issues. Nevertheless, this goal seems unachievable in the current regional environment. Consequently, bilateral or sub-regional cooperation will be stimulated. Thus, in the medium term, SEMC's policy convergence dynamics towards ESDP are most likely to (i) follow geographical self-differentiation as has been the case until now; (ii) be dependent on process-driven considerations rather that a substantive convergence on security matters; and (iii) have a limited effect in terms of building a security partnership in the Euro-Mediterranean region.

Acknowledgements

The author would like to thank Tobias Schumacher and Anna Herranz for their comments and suggestions and Fadela Hilali and Irene García for their assistance.

Notes

[1] With the entry into force of the Lisbon Treaty, ESDP is now called Common Security and Defence Policy (CSDP). However, the article will refer to ESDP as the empirical evidences and the analysis correspond to a period previous to the entry into force of the Lisbon Treaty.

[2] The concept of a 'security complex' is defined by Barry Buzan (1991: 90) as 'a group of states whose primary security concerns link together sufficiently closely that their national securities cannot realistically be considered apart from one another'.

[3] We refer, here, to the seminal work of Karl Deutsch *et al.* (1957).

[4] According to Benantar (2006: 170), when the Mediterranean Dialogue was launched there was quasi-consensus to exclude Algeria due to its internal crisis and Syria and Libya for their 'alleged support to terrorism'. It was not until 2000 that Algeria joined the Dialogue.

[5] Among the analyses of these missions see CITpax (2006), Collantes Celador *et al.* (2008) and Sabiote (2006, 2008).

[6] Vth Euro-Mediterranean Conference of Ministers for Foreign Affairs, Valencia Action Plan, 23 April 2002.

[7] Information provided by an official of a EU Member State based in Brussels (January 2010).

[8] On these transformations see, among others, Aliboni and Ammor (2008), Gillespie (2008), Barbé (2009), Khader (2009) and Balfour (2009).

[9] Interviews with Turkish diplomats in Ankara (January 2009) and Brussels (April 2009).

[10] According to Miguel Ángel Medina (2009: 5) the Turkish C130 plane and its crew help to overcome the strategic transport deficit of the Congo mission. Erdal Tatli (2008) also refers to the importance of the C130 aircrafts and adds Turkey's capacity to mobilize up to 50.000 soldiers on short notice and air refueling capacities that make Turkey able to participate in overseas operations.

[11] The Annex IV of Nice Presidency Conclusions differentiates consultation and participation mechanisms of non-EU European NATO members and other countries which are candidates for accession to the UE and foresees regular consultations with this countries on a regular basis when there is no crisis and to associate them to the greatest possible extent in EU-led military operations in times of crisis.

[12] As Didier Billion and Fabio Liberti (2009: 8) put it: 'Turkey, like Norway, was a member of the WEAG (Western European Armaments Group), the organization responsible for cooperation in the field of armaments within the framework of the WEU. Since the absorption of the WEAG functions within the EDA, Norway has been able to conclude an administrative arrangement with the EDA, which allows it to be associated with certain activities of the agency. On the contrary, Turkey has not been able to obtain such an agreement'.

[13] The Presidency Conclusions of the 2002 Copenhagen European Council promised Turkey that if the European Council in December 2004, on the basis of a report and a recommendation from the Commission, decides that Turkey fulfils the Copenhagen political criteria, the European Union will open accession negotiations with Turkey without delay.

[14] On the Advanced Status see Florensa (2008) and Martín (2008).

[15] Interview with Moroccan official, Brussels, April 2009.

[16] 'NATO declines support Turkey's veto over EU's Kosovo mission' in *Today's Zaman*, 22 June 2007.

[17] As Didier Billion and Fabio Liberti (2009) explain 'in the cases of Afghanistan and Kosovo, where the two organizations simultaneously conducted complementary missions, logic would contend that these operations be perfectly coordinated. Turkey is opposed to this type of cooperation and it has thus not been possible to introduce an agreement allowing NATO to guarantee the protection of police forces participating in the European Union EUPOL mission in Afghanistan'.

[18] This sentence can be found in his book *Le Défi*, published in 1976.

[19] See, for instance, references to the notion of choice in several Moroccan officials' statements such as those of André Azulay, Youssef Amrani, Salahedine Mezouar or Karim Ghelab, collected in Florensa (2008).

References

Aliboni, R. (1999) Building blocks for the Euro-Mediterranean Charter on Peace and Stability, *EuroMeSCo paper*, 7.

Aliboni, R. (2005) 10 ans de dialogue politique et de sécurité au sein du processus de Barcelone, *Geoeconomie*, 35, pp. 101–120.

Aliboni, R. & Ammor, F. (2008) Under the Shadow of 'Barcelona': From the EMP to the Union for the Mediterranean. *EuroMeSCo paper*, 77.

Association between the European Union and Morocco. The Association Council (2005) EU/Morocco Action Plan. UE-MA 2702/1/05, Brussels, 27 July.

Attinà, F. (2006) The building of regional security partnership and the security–culture divide in the Mediterranean region', in: E. Adler, F. Bicchi & R. del Sarto (Eds) *The Convergence of Civilizations, Constructing a Mediterranean Region* (Toronto: University of Toronto Press).

Baghzouz, A. (2009) L'Algérie face à l'Europe. Quelle place dans les dispositifs de coopération en Méditerranée, *Maghreb-Machrek*, 200, pp. 45–56.

Balfour, R. (2009) The transformation of the Union for the Mediterranean, *Mediterranean Politics*, 14(1), pp. 99–105.

Barbé, E. (2009) La Unión por el Mediterráneo: de la europeización de la política exterior a la descomunitarización de la política mediterránea, *Revista de Derecho Comunitario Europeo*, 32, pp. 9–46.

Barbé, E., Costa, O., Herranz, A. & Natroski, M. (2009) Which rules shape EU's external governance? The patterns of rule selection in foreign and security policies, *Journal of European Public Policy*, 16(6), pp. 834–862.

Benantar, A. (2006) NATO, Maghreb and Europe, *Mediterranean Politics*, 11(2), pp. 167–188.

Benantar, A. (2007) *Les États-Unis et le Maghreb, regain d'intérêt?* (Alger: CREAD).

Biad, A. (2001) La Charte Euro-Méditerranéenne: Cadre pour le Partenariat de Sécurité, in Fondation Méditerranéenne d'Études Stratégiques (Ed) *Euro-Méditerranée 1995–1999, Premier Bilan du Partenariat* (Paris: Publisud).

Bicchi, F. & Martin, M. (2006) Talking tough or talking together? European security discourses towards the Mediterranean? *Mediterranean Politics*, 11(2), pp. 189–207.

Bilgin, P. (2004) Clash of cultures? Differences between Turkey and the European Union on security, in: A. Karaosmanoglu & S. Tashan (Eds) *The Europeanization of Turkey's Security Policy: Prospects and Pitfalls* (Ankara: Foreign Policy Institute).

Billion, D. & Liberti, F. (2009) The Relationship between NATO and the European Security Defence Policy (ESDP): The Cypriot/Turkish disruption, in: J. P. Maulny (Ed.) *NATO's 60th Birthday: What Does the Future Hold for the Transatlantic Military Alliance?* (Paris: Affaires Stratégiques).

Bin, A. (2002) NATO's Mediterranean dialogue: a post-Prague perspective, *Mediterranean Politics*, 7(2), pp. 115–119.

Biscop, S. (2002) Network or labyrinth? The challenge of coordinating western security dialogues in the Mediterranean, *Mediterranean Politics*, 7(1), pp. 92–112.

Biscop, S. (2003) Opening up the ESDP to the South: a comprehensive and cooperative approach to Euro-Mediterranean security, *Security Dialogue*, 34(2), pp. 183–197.

Bremberg, N. (2007) Between a rock and a hard place: Euro-Mediterranean security revisited, *Mediterranean Politics*, 12(1), pp. 1–16.

Bremberg, N., *et al.* (2009) Flexible multilateralism: unlimited opportunities? The case of civil protection in the Mediterranean. *EuroMeSCo paper*, 80.

Buzan, B. (1991) *People, States and Fear* (Boulder, CO: Lynne Reinner).

Çayhan, E (2003) Towards a European security and defense policy: with or without Turkey, in: A. Çarkogly & B. Rubin (Eds) *Turkey and the European Union, Domestic Politics, Economic Integration and International Dynamics* (London: Frank Cass).

Cebeci, M. (1999) "A Delicate Process of Participation: The Question of Participation of WEU Associate Members in Decision-making for EU-led Petersberg Operations, with Special Reference to Turkey", *Occasional Paper*, 10 (Paris: European Union Institute for Security Studies).

Çelenk, A. (2009) Promoting democracy in Algeria: the EU factor and the preferences of the political elite, *Democratization*, 16(1), pp. 176–192.

CITpax (2006) EU civil missions in the Palestinian Territories: frustrated reform and suspended security, *Middle East Special Report*, 1.

Collantes Celador, G., *et al.* (2008) Fostering an EU strategy for security sector reform in the Mediterranean: learning from Turkish and Palestinian police reform experiences, *EuroMeSCo Paper*, 66.

Council of the European Union (2003) *Option paper on dialogue and co-operation on ESDP between the EU and Mediterranean Partners*, Brussels, 19 February.

Courela, P. (2004) Civil protection as a Euro-Mediterranean project: the case for practical co-operation, *EuroMeSCo paper*, 34.

Coustillière, J. F. (2007) The '5 + 5 security and defence' initiative, in: E. Soler i Lecha & L. Mestres (Eds) *Fifth Seminar on Security and Defence in the Mediterranean: Multi-Dimensional Security* (Barcelona: CIDOB Foundation and Ministry of Defence).

Darbouche, H. (2008) Decoding Algeria's ENP policy: differentiation by other means? *Mediterranean Politics*, 13(3), pp. 371–389.

Deutsch, K. *et al.* (1957) *Political Community and the North Atlantic Area* (Princeton, NJ: Princeton University Press).

Driss, C. (2009) L'Algérie et le Sahel: de la fin de l'isolement à la régionalisation contraignante, *Maghrek-Machrek*, 200, pp. 57–69.

EU–Morocco Association Council (2008) Document conjoint UE–Maroc sur le renforcement des relations bilatérales/Statut Avancé, 13653/08, Brussels, 13 October.

EuroMeSCo (2002) European Defence. Perceptions vs. Realities, *EuroMeSCo Working Paper*, 16.

European Commission (2004a) *European Neighbourhood Policy, Strategy Paper*, Brussels, 12 May, 2004 COM(2004) 373 final.

European Commission (2004b) *Issues Arising from Turkey's Membership Perspective*. Commission Staff Working Document, COM(2004) 656 final.

European Council (2002) Annex to Presidency Conclusions of the Copenhagen European Council, 12 and 13 December.

Florensa, S. (Ed.) (2008) *Le Maroc et l'Union Européenne, vers un statut avancé dans l'association euro-méditerranéenne* (Barcelona: IEMed).

Gillespie, R. (2008) A 'Union for the Mediterranean' or for the EU?, *Mediterranean Politics*, 13(2), pp. 277–286.

Helmerich, N. (2007) CFSP and ESDP: how to include new partners?, in: J. Varwick & K. Lang (Eds) *European Neighbourhood Policy. Challenges for the EU-Policy Towards the New Neighbours* (Opladen and Farmington Hills: Barbara-Budrich Publisher).

Jaidi, L. (2007) Estatuto avanzado Unión Europea – Marruecos: ¿un nuevo modelo de partenariado? *Afkar-ideas*, 14, pp. 20–23.

Jünemann, A. (2003) Repercussions of the emerging European security and defence policy on the civil character of the Euro-Mediterranean partnership, *Mediterranean Politics*, 8(2/3), pp. 37–53.

Khader, B. (2009) *L'Europe pour la Méditerranée. De Barcelone à Barcelone (1995–2008)* (Paris: l'Harmattan).

Lannon, E., Braga de Macedo, J. & Vasconcelos, A. (2007) Maroc-UE: Vers un Statut Avancé dans le Cadre du PEM et de la PEV. *Papers IEMed*, 2.

Luif, P., Senyüncel, S. & Ak, C. Z. (2009) *How Common is the Common Foreign and Security Policy of the European Union? Where does Turkey fit in?* (Istanbul: TESEV).

Marsou, M. (2007) The participation of the Moroccan royal armed forces in operation ALTHEA, in: E. Soler i Lecha & L. Mestres (Eds) *Fifth Seminar on Security and Defence in the Mediterranean: Multi-Dimensional Security* (Barcelona: CIDOB Foundation and Ministry of Defence).

Martín, I. (2008) El estatuto avanzado de Marruecos en la UE: ¿cuánto más que la asociación y cuánto menos que la adhesión? *ARI del Real Instituto Elcano*, 158

Martín, I. (2009) EU–Morocco relations: how advanced is the advanced status?, *Mediterranean Politics*, 14(2), pp. 239–245.

Medina-Abellán, M. A. (2009) Turkey, the European Security and Defence Policy, and accession negotiations. *SINAN Working Paper*, 1.

Missiroli, A. (2002) EU-NATO cooperation in crisis management: no Turkish delight for ESDP, *Security Dialogue*, 33(1), pp. 9–26.

Ojanen, H. (2006) The EU and Nato: two competing models for a common defence policy, *Journal of Common Market Studies*, 44(1), pp. 57–76.

Ruacan, I. (2007) A study in state socialization: Turkey's EU accession and CFSP, *Southeast European and Black Sea Studies*, 7(4), pp. 573–590.

Sabiote, M. A. (2006) EU BAM Rafah: a test for the EU's role in the Middle East?, *CFSP Forum*, 4(4), pp. 8–10.

Sabiote, M. A. (2008) EUPOL COPPS in the Palestinian Territories: Neutral Force or a Protagonist in the Shadow? *CFSP Forum*, 6(3), pp. 5–7.

Soler i Lecha, E. & García, I. (2009) The Union for the Mediterranean. What has it changed and what can be changed in the domain of security?, *INEX Policy Brief*, 4 (Brussels: CEPS).

Tatli, E. (2008) Turkey turns cold to European defense: implications for western security, *Policy Watch*, 1376 (Washington: the Washington Institute for Near East Policy).

Terzi, Ö. (2004) Evolving European security capabilities and EU–Turkish relations, *Perceptions, Journal of International Affairs*, 9(1), pp. 99–118.

Türkes, M. & Gökgöz, G. (2004) Reflections on the EU Strategy Paper 2003 – two approaches, moving conditions and a new juncture, *Perceptions, Journal of International Affairs*, 9(1), pp. 61–81.

Ülgen, S. (2008) The evolving EU, NATO, and Turkey relationship, in: F. Burwell (Ed.) *The evolution of U.S.–Turkish Relations in a Transatlantic Context*, pp. 97–109 (Carlisle: Strategic Studies Institute of the US Army War College).

Valasek, T. (2008) France, NATO and European defence, Centre for European Reform Policy Brief (London: CER).

Volpi, F. (2006) Introduction: strategies for regional cooperation in the Mediterranean: rethinking the parameters of debate, *Mediterranean Politics*, 11(2), pp. 119–135.

Yilmaz, S. (2007) Turkey and the European Union: a security perspective, in: G. Gasparini (Ed.) *Turkey and European Security, IAI–TESEV Report* (Rome: Instituto d'Affari Internazionali).

Zoubir, Y. (2009) Les États-Unis et l'Algérie: antagonisme, pragmatisme et coopération, *Maghreb-Machrek*, 200, pp. 71–90.

The Ties that do not Bind: The Union for the Mediterranean and the Future of Euro-Arab Relations

OLIVER SCHLUMBERGER

Institute of Political Science, Eberhard-Karls Universität Tübingen, Germany

ABSTRACT   *What impact does the Union for the Mediterranean (UfM) have on the future evolution of Euro-Arab relations? This contribution first reflects on Arab reactions to the UfM, and subsequently analyses what alterations the UfM brings to existing Euro-Arab relations in terms of actors, institutional arrangements, and policy contents. In sum, the UfM caters well to Arab regimes' priorities, namely the maintenance of authoritarian rule: The UfM tends to exclude societal voices and leads to a re-governmentalization of relations; the institutional set-up elevates Arab regimes to become formal veto-players, and the prioritized policy areas have – from an Arab regime perspective – the advantage of being de-politicized and stripped of any ambitious macro-political goals such as democratization. The UfM can thus be considered a triple victory for authoritarian Arab rulers in re-shaping their relations with Europe, and casts serious doubts on the hypothesis of the EU acting as a norm entrepreneur.*

Euro-Arab relations form an important part of the European Union's overall foreign policies. Over half of the Arab population, including the politically most important Arab states, is included in the Euro-Mediterranean Partnership (EMP) established by the EU in 1995 and which superseded earlier co-operation schemes under the so-called financial protocols. After the re-launching of the EMP as the Union for the Mediterranean (UfM) in 2008, one pertinent question is how the new design of this partnership will affect the future evolution of Euro-Arab relations. I argue here that despite initially hesitant Arab reactions, the shifts in actors involved, in the new institutional framework as well as in policy content, seem almost tailor-made to Arab regimes' political preferences while defying any European claims of aiming at meaningful social and political reform (let alone transformation) that could lead to enhanced regime convergence between the northern and southern shores of the

Mediterranean (as a pre-requisite of deeper integration), and to enhanced broad-based economic and human development prospects in the Arab region.

A first glance at the addressees of this policy initiative, i.e. the Arab partner countries, demonstrates some key features which characterize this group of states. First, they are all developing nations that figure within the group of middle income countries according to the World Bank's classification; they are thus not among the world's poorest states. However, a second remarkable feature is that they all face relative economic stagnation or decline when compared to other developing regions around the world (e.g. Henry and Springborg, 2001: ch. 1). As is also well established, one – if not *the* – key reason for this fact is the political stagnation that hampers social, economic and political development in this region, as is evidenced by the fact that the Arab region has been the world's most unfree region for decades (UNDP/AFESD, 2005; Heydemann, 2007; Schlumberger, 2007, 2008). Author-itarian power maintenance has been the top priority of Arab political leaders, even in the face of economic and financial crises which have repeatedly brought Arab states close to bankruptcy. This entails a range of serious consequences for neighbouring regions such as the EU. Among such consequences are primarily hard and soft security issues (such as terrorism, illegal migration, transnational organized crime, drug trafficking and trafficking of humans), but also a lack of international policy co-ordination in sectoral domains such as environmental, water, energy, or financial policies in which today transnational co-ordination gains ever greater importance. All of these aspects may have negative impacts on the Arab region's neighbours.

There are thus manifest and very tangible social, economic and political reasons why Europe should take a pro-active interest in how its Arab neighbours are governed. If Europe, then, is the 'normative power' Manners (2002) and his followers tend to see in the EU, or the 'norm entrepreneur' that Pace (2007) searches for in Europe's foreign policies, we should expect the Arab world to be *the* prime addressee of European efforts at exporting its core political norms and values (such as respect for human rights, the rule of law, or pluralistic, inclusive, transparent and accountable modes of political decision making), whether for utilitarian or idealistic reasons.

This contribution examines whether or not this is the case under the new framework of the UfM. It does so by outlining Arab reactions to the initiation of the UfM which – despite the 'Joint Declaration' (2008) signed by both the EU members and the southern Mediterranean partners in Paris – at first clearly was a European (or rather: French) endeavour at re-shaping Euro-Mediterranean relations (next section). These sceptical reactions are contextualized and discussed before I turn to the UfM proper in its core dimensions of actors, institutions and policies (section three). The analysis of these three dimensions leads to two alternative scenarios as regards the future development of EU–Arab relations (section four). This, in turn, enables me to conclude on the UfM's impact on future political, social and economic developments within the Arab countries themselves, as well as for those countries' future role within the larger fabric of Euro-Mediterranean relations (conclusions).

Arab Reactions to the UfM

Generally, Europe is seen as a reputable partner of Arab countries and a desire often heard in the streets of Cairo, Amman or Algiers is that the EU should play a more prominent role in Middle Eastern affairs of global relevance, such as the Israeli–Palestinian conflict, but in other matters as well. In its regional policies towards the Arab countries, the EU has largely been perceived on the southern shores of the Mediterranean as a welcome antidote to US Middle East policies which at times have been perceived as overly aggressive, little sensitive to the region's peculiarities, and certainly not as occupying the position of what 'the Arab side' would expect from an external power in terms of honest brokerage in regional conflicts.

But the Arab countries have also benefited individually from the EMP and the subsequently established umbrella of the European Neighbourhood Policy (ENP; since 2004) which has brought them high levels of support for national goals in development and policy reform issues that are – to a large extent – in the genuine interest of Arab regimes. Despite some EU rhetoric to the contrary that chiefly seems to address European audiences, Arab countries were given enough room for manoeuvre to engage in civil society programmes funded by the EU without having to cede control over the latter. Conveniently, they were able to effectively exclude the risk of a real empowerment of societal actors who might otherwise have turned into contestants for political power at home.

The UfM, then, rather than threatening to erode these benefits for Arab countries, offered the prospect of augmenting and deepening them, including prospects of filling new and prestigious international positions within the planned UfM Secretariat and in a range of other bodies yet to be established, while at the same time the contents that were envisaged to form the core of new UfM programmes and projects seem to be void of much of the impetus towards political reform which both the EMP framework and the ENP implicitly and explicitly carried with them.

Nevertheless, as in much of Europe, French President Sarkozy's announcement of plans to establish the UfM clearly met with less than enthusiastic reactions from the Arab countries: initial responses ranged from cautious scepticism to outright disapproval. Two issues were at the core of this Arab scepticism and criticism:

(a) Deteriorated Arab–Israeli relations and an unwillingness, on the Arab side, to enter into what might become a creeping normalization of relations with Israel, and

(b) fears about a renewal of what in the past was sometimes perceived as European paternalism.

The most important issue concerned Arab–Israeli relations which, at the time of the announcement of the UfM, were at a low point. The Israeli invasion of Lebanon (known as the 'Summer War' of 2006) had destroyed most of the latter country's infrastructure just two years earlier. Given these tense Arab–Israeli relations and with little left of a former 'peace process', Arab states were particularly 'worried that if they join' this would 'imply a normalisation of bilateral relations' with the

Jewish state (Vucheva, 2008). Nevertheless, there had been an initial willingness to co-operate and find joint solutions. In late 2008, Israel agreed that the Arab League attend all UfM meetings, while Israel was promised the post of a deputy secretary-general in return. However, with Israel's bombardment of the Gaza Strip in December 2008, relations deteriorated once again. Arab governments felt they had to make sure not to send any signals on the international stage that could be interpreted as any sort of improvement of these relations, let alone a 'normalization'.[1] In this respect, Arab countries initially tried to act as veto-players – and they still do, as is evidenced by the frequent postponements and cancellations of meetings due to reasons associated with Israel's policies in the Middle East conflict.

A second key reason for Arab hesitancy in embracing the French idea of re-framing Euro-Mediterranean relations through the UfM stemmed from a certain degree of dissatisfaction with the Barcelona Process as it had evolved since 1995, and more specifically with an at least perceived paternalism that had been inherent to the EMP/ENP from Barcelona through the European Neighbourhood Policy Instrument (ENPI). Again, it was Algeria's foreign minister Medelci who found clear words: 'Relations with the EU are unbalanced and decisions belong to those who now have money and know-how' (Vucheva, 2008). If this language appears rather undiplomatic, then Libya's Colonel Qaddafi expressed Arab concerns about European domination even more forcefully, calling the initiative 'an insult' that was 'taking us for fools'. At a 2008 summit between North African states and Syria, he pointed out that 'we do not belong to Brussels. Our Arab League is located in Cairo and the African Union is located in Addis Abbeba. If they want cooperation they have to go through Cairo and Addis Abbeba' (Reuters Africa, 2008, as quoted in Katz, 2008). Whatever the EU may think about the emanation of its norms and values, the fact that this has not translated into trust and ownership for Europe's endeavours in the South is hard to contradict. As Schwarzer (2009) put it: 'No equal partnership has been established between the northern and southern states. The Mediterranean Union is still seen in the southern region primarily as an EU project, if not as a project of French political interests.' In a similar vein, the reputable Swiss daily *Neue Zürcher Zeitung* found that

> it should have attracted Sarkozy's attention that the interest the Mediterranean countries share in the EU's multi-billion offers has flagged over the years. Rather than thinking about ways of throwing fresh millions southwards over the sea, there should be an examination of the reasons for this disinterest. (Winkler, 2008; author's translation from German)

These reactions point to two facts. First, the omnipresence of the Arab–Israeli conflict in Arab foreign affairs, which may impact negatively on external relations even if it is not the object of concrete policies. This issue can hardly be resolved by the EU as long as it entertains positions towards that conflict which appear primarily informed by transatlantic strategic considerations rather than by its own political standpoint, and for the foreseeable future the EU will have to live with this potentially disruptive element in its Mediterranean relations unless it is prepared to disrupt its relations with the US. Second, Arab reactions have made it clear that the frameworks of both the EMP and the ENP have not been perceived by the Arab side as a partnership among equals. They have not resulted in greater levels of Arab trust in European foreign policies toward the Middle East and North Africa truly aiming at progress for the benefit of the partner countries. While the first point is a fact Europe will have to accept as long as its transatlantic priorities are a given, the second demonstrates that reactions have been critical towards the new initiative regardless of its concrete contents: the UfM promised the southern partners much more of a say in the joint design of policies and programmes than the EMP/ENP framework, and thus for the Mediterranean Partners Countries (MPCs) could potentially represent a significant step forward as regards their own weight and voice in Euro-Mediterranean relations.

While Arab reactions to the French announcements and to the UfM itself during its initial phase (2008/09) leave little room for interpretation, the more analytical question to be addressed below is whether the Arab countries were well-advised in their early criticism of the UfM. *Should* the Arab states be as critical towards the UfM as they have been initially? The answer arguably hinges upon what the UfM's impact on Arab countries will look like, which in turn will shape the future of Euro-Arab relations.

Core Dimensions of the UfM: Actors, Institutions, Policies

To assess the UfM's possible impact for future Euro-Arab relations, I refer to its three core dimensions as carved out in the introduction by Bicchi. A first focus is on *actors* who are likely to be decisive driving (or blocking) forces; second, changes to the *institutional set-up* of Euro-Med relations are discussed with a view to their consequences for the Arab partners; third comes the question of politicization/de-politicization of Euro-Mediterranean relations discussed in the introduction. This (sub-)section will be labelled *policies* because it is the policy domain that demonstrates a de-politicization which is often overlooked by EU foreign policy analysts. While to some extent unclear at the time of writing (late 2010), UfM policy contents must be referred to because they are necessary in order to assess possible risks and benefits the UfM carries with it for the Arab partners as well as for overall Euro-Arab relations.

Actors: The Re-governmentalization of Euro-Arab Relations

Among the most striking features of the UfM is undeniably that the agreed upon institutional arrangement takes the form of an inter-governmental body or even an international organization (see Johansson-Nogués, this collection). With two heads of state as co-presidents, two secretary-generals and six deputy secretary-generals selected by the seconding countries' governments, a Joint Permanent Committee (JPM) drawn from the so-called 'senior officials', all new UfM bodies that have been created or are in the process of being established are of a decidedly (inter-)governmentalist character (Aliboni and Ammor, 2009). Rather than representing the *societies* of their member countries in a broader sense, the UfM's institutions almost exclusively represent their respective governments, or rather: *heads of state* in the majority of Arab cases where these do not form part of the respective governments. While this arguably poses no serious problem in the case of the (democratic) European UfM member countries, it certainly does so in the case of the (authoritarian) Arab partner countries because here, governments do not necessarily represent the will of their populations; quite the contrary, many Arab governments and heads of state are ruling over populations who are deeply disenchanted with their autocratic leaderships.

This is remarkable because it stands in contrast to the previous arrangements of the EMP/ENP framework. Back in 1995, the EMP was founded based on the idea of three baskets, one of which was explicitly devoted to co-operation on the societal and cultural levels. The 1995 Barcelona Declaration itself stated the importance of 'support for democratic institutions and for the strengthening of the rule of law and civil society', and explicitly acknowledged 'the essential contribution civil society can make in the process of development' (Euro-Mediterranean Conference, 1995). Later developments, such as the establishment of the Anna Lindh Foundation in Alexandria and some work that evolved under the Euro-Mediterranean Study Commission, added substance to this emphasis on 'decentralized' (read: non-governmental) forms of co-operation. True, even under the older EMP framework, in actual practice these more openly political issues received far less attention from both European and Arab policy makers than Arab intellectuals and European scholars would have liked to see, but rhetorically at least they clearly figured more prominently in the official discourse than they do today.[2] Even today, the Commission still assumes that the 2004 adoption of the ENP framework for the southern Mediterranean partners was based on 'a mutual commitment to common values (democracy and human rights, rule of law, good governance . . .)', and 'the level of ambition of the relationship depends on the extent to which these values are shared' (European Commission, 2010).

Under the UfM, the contradictions persist. On the one hand, the 2008 'Joint Declaration of the Paris Summit for the Mediterranean', the inaugural document of the UfM, speaks of a – then already somewhat illusionary – 'shared political will' to turn the Mediterranean region 'into an area of peace, *democracy*, cooperation and prosperity' (Union for the Mediterranean, 2008; emphasis added). On the other hand, reference to those norms and values which figure so prominently in how Europe has come to portray itself remain even more on the margins than in both the EMP and ENP frameworks. While the former frameworks saw the establishment of the Euro-Mediterranean Parliamentary Assembly, the Commission-supported Euro-Mediterranean Human Rights Network and its Foundation and the European Instrument for Democracy and Human Rights, emphasis is now placed on joint projects as opposed to larger-scale and more macro-level programmes. Mutual interests in technical co-operation seem to deliberately gain in importance in relation to political areas of dissent due to regime divergence. While the UfM does not, of course, supersede the ENP, it nevertheless supersedes the EMP. The UfM does not contain those earlier ambitions of a common regional space that would incorporate respect for basic rights and freedoms.

What does that mean for the Arab partners? In a nutshell, societal forces in the Arab world will most likely look upon the UfM as yet another instance where Europe and its governments side with the much-hated Arab regimes for strategic reasons while ignoring the Arab peoples' quest for self-determination and greater freedom from oppression, both by their own governments as well as by external powers. Of course, this latter point may cause a frown among Europeans, but the feeling of being dominated by external forces is a deep-rooted perception within Arab societies that must be taken seriously if one seeks to understand prevailing reactions and attitudes towards European (or other foreign) policy initiatives (see also Moïsy, 2009: 56ff.).[3]

By contrast, Arab decision makers increasingly realize that the practical exclusion of societal forces as autonomous actors from the UfM framework is in their best interest. Struggles with the big EU donor over how far voluntary organizations will benefit from co-operation schemes will diminish to the extent that co-operation under the umbrella of the UfM, which hardly seems to know societal actors, gradually replaces schemes agreed upon within the former EMP/ENP framework under which participation of non-governmental actors figured more prominently. It is in this light that the first Arab proposals for projects within the priority areas have been submitted, indicating a change in general roles from laggards or veto-players towards hesitant supporters. In this respect – and in contrast to their stance with regard to the Arab–Israeli conflict – at least some Arab regimes have come to adopt roles of fence-sitters or cautious supporters, albeit with virtually no investment in resources, let alone for a 'common good'.

Therefore, the overall picture that derives from the UfM in relation to the key actors is one of re-governmentalization of Euro-Mediterranean relations. One could even ask whether the UfM's exclusive focus on governmental actors might contradict the very spirit of the Barcelona Declaration which saw a much more explicit role for non-state actors than does the UfM. On the other hand, this might well have been an important trigger enabling the EU to overcome initial Arab resistance.

Institutions: The Chance for Arab Countries to become Veto-players

The focus on regime actors outlined above comes along with an effort to generate greater co-ownership by southern partners than was evident within the EMP/ENP framework.[4] Looked at from a European perspective, the key feature of this 'inter-governmentalist' institutional design and its key marker in comparison to the EMP as well as the ENP framework may be the question of the role of the European Commission and the struggles between France and the European opponents of such an inter-governmentalization of Euro-Mediterranean relations under the UfM that engaged in efforts to Europeanize it.

By contrast, from the perspective of development policies, it seems that the core principle upheld in international development co-operation is more likely to be achieved within the institutional arrangement of the UfM than it could have been before: To ensure partners' *ownership* of programmes and projects, and thereby create a higher degree of responsibility on the partners' side in the implementation and sustenance of co-operation measures (and thus move away from earlier, more paternalistic conceptions of 'aid' towards 'true' partnerships). In fact, the MPCs not only continue to be de facto able to block European-devised Mediterranean policies, but their role has been upgraded so that they become recognized veto-players on an official, i.e. institutional level.

Even though the magnitude may not be assessed with certainty, this trait of the UfM's institutional arrangement is likely to have effects on policy choices even beyond the current priority areas. Since, according to the rules of the 'UfM game', decisions have to be taken in consensus between the two co-presidents and within the Secretariat, effective policies will only be devised (and, more importantly, implemented!) in fields where political commonalities exist and views on both sides of the Mediterranean converge. Such activities will therefore be limited to issues that are considered non-sensitive to both sides.

With respect to the Arab regimes, it is the consensus today that *the* key political priority is power maintenance (Albrecht and Schlumberger, 2004; Heydemann, 2007; Schlumberger, 2007). From an Arab perspective, this means that any measure that could threaten Arab rulers' firm grip on autocratic power will certainly not find the consent of at least one co-president. De facto, then, both co-presidents are in the position of potential veto-players with respect to any suggestion of the other side. They have the power to effectively block any policy proposal by the other which may impact negatively on topics that are deemed of vital importance to either side.

Therefore, the UfM cannot become a vehicle for any sort of meaningful political reform. By contrast, institutional reform has created an instrument for Arab regimes that makes it yet easier to avoid any reform of domestic autocratic governance.

Policies: Two Dimensions of 'De-politicization'

The 'de-politiciziation' of EU foreign policies towards the Mediterranean were one of the French objectives: the UfM and its activities were meant to be more immune from the Middle Eastern context in that they were assumed to be less prone to politically induced failures originating from a deterioration in Arab–Israeli relations. This contradicts Arab preferences at least in part, namely as regards the Arab–Israeli conflict: Arab countries would have preferred conflict resolution mechanisms to remain high on the European agenda whereas the EU seemed to have searched for avenues of co-operation that were less subject to possible negative spill-overs from an unresolved Arab–Israeli conflict than the initial EMP scheme (see Hollis, this collection). In this sense, a latent dissent seems to exist between the Arab MPCs that would like to see the Euro-Mediterranean framework as a stage on which they are able to pronounce their view on the Middle East conflict regularly before high-level European counterparts whereas Europe seems to have seen some virtue in a possible de-politicization of Euro-Mediterranean relations in order to not have possible progress on other issues impeded by a stalled regional conflict.

As Asseburg and Salem (2009: 13) state, the Arab–Israeli conflict has been 'one of the main stumbling blocks to progress towards regional cooperation, stability, and economic and political reform in the Mediterranean. It has also severely impaired confidence and trust building between the two shores of the Mediterranean'. But the solution to enhanced Euro-Mediterranean relations will hardly lie in ignoring the existence of this conflict and trying to exclude it from the agenda of the UfM.

The relevance of this tricky topic, however, can ultimately be traced back to *domestic* Arab politics. It is essential for regimes that enjoy little legitimacy at home not to open up new areas of popular dissent, and given the broad public support the Palestinian cause receives in Arab public opinion, there is a strong disincentive for Arab regimes to adopt an accommodating attitude with respect to the Arab–Israeli conflict on the international scene – a disincentive deriving from the domestic Arab polity level (on legitimacy in Arab states, see Schlumberger, 2010). But there is a different, albeit related, dimension of 'de-politicization' – a dimension which also has to do with Arab domestic politics. Arguably, this is the more important dimension or understanding of 'de-politicization' which enters Euro-Arab relations with the advent of the UfM.

On the one hand, the Arab–Israeli conflict and its global dimensions impact on the general prospects of the UfM, and namely on the question of the willingness of Arab partners to engage in regional policy dialogue and projects. On the other hand, it is precisely because of the Arab–Israeli conflict's global dimensions that European options to assume a more active role, possibly one of 'honest brokerage', remain limited. By contrast, while European options as regards political reform *within* individual Arab partner countries are limited as well, they are far less prone to influences beyond Euro-Arab relations than is the case with the EU's role in the Middle East conflict. This topic neither involves that conflict directly, nor necessarily transatlantic considerations. European support for political reform in the Arab world can be self-determined in an autonomous manner by the EU to a much greater degree than can European policies towards the Arab–Israeli conflict. The question of European support to Arab political reform, in turn, is an extremely relevant policy issue because the political stagnation and lack of political development which has characterized the Arab world over recent decades is *the* key obstacle to enhanced economic and human development in the region (see, e.g., UNDP/AFESD, 2005), along with a range of ensuing political questions and challenges that impact directly on European political and security interests (see my introduction above). This has not only been unambiguously and boldly pointed out by the United Nations Development Programme's (UNDP's) regional reports on human development (the Arab Human Development Report [AHDR] series), but also by a broad consensus of scholars specialized in Middle East politics and political economy.

Let me therefore take a closer look at what impact the renovation of the overall Euro-Mediterranean framework under the UfM may have on the question of the EU as an effective supporter of processes of political reform in the Arab world. The UfM from its earliest stages has been dubbed a 'project of projects' or a 'union of projects' in which, as hinted at above, concrete projects are given priority over large and 'high' policies such as conflict resolution or democracy assistance. The six priority projects that have been identified for future UfM activities[5] display a high degree of similarity in terms of their technical (as opposed to political) nature to development schemes of the 1960s when international development co-operation was inspired by classical modernization theory's belief in the primacy of economic growth which later on would somehow trigger democracy.

What is clear from comparing the UfM's design to the EMP/ENP policy framework – apart from its institutional and actor-related specifics – is that political conditionality seems to have been given up.[6] Not only is the principle of conditionality unknown in the UfM proper, but also policy contents have been technicized to the extent that political reform no longer seems to be part of Europe's ambitions in its relations with the MPCs. In this sense, the transfer from EMP to UfM may not be all that smooth and harmonious. While struggles behind the scenes (and, in fact, also on stage) have been discussed in other contributions, certain questions as regards the compatibility of the old framework with the new can also be asked with respect to policy contents. The technicization of relations inherent in the UfM, Schwarzer (2009) holds, 'contradicts the aims of the previous Barcelona Process, which understood Europe's involvement in the region primarily as a contribution to transforming the economic and political systems in the southern Mediterranean area'. Indeed, combating pollution in the Mediterranean sea, schemes for co-operation in infrastructure, energy, and even in trade and private sector development surely have the potential to result in quicker consensus among the dual structure than in the past, but do not address the overarching issues necessary for political, human and economic development. Schwarzer (2009) even goes as far as to allude to potential risks for Europe inherent in such a de-politicized approach:

> the de-politicisation of the EU's Mediterranean policy taking place within the project-focused cooperation, coupled with an insufficiently developed involvement of civil society in the southern Mediterranean states, is unlikely to promote transformation, and may even reduce transformative potential. A policy that does not seriously support transformation processes, however, will do no favours to the EU member states' medium and long-term security interests.

Two Scenarios for Future Euro-Arab Relations within the UfM Framework

The UfM will not transform Euro-Mediterranean relations altogether. With regard to Euro-Arab relations in particular, it will certainly change some of the previously existing patterns of interaction, but it will do so to a limited extent only. This is so because, on the one hand, the institutional arrangements that are being installed under the umbrella of the UfM do not supersede and replace the previous frameworks entirely, but can rather be seen as a complement that will contribute to a re-arrangement of the previous policy frame in some respects, but not to its demise. It has been made clear in all relevant official deliberations that bilateral association agreements will remain in place and valid. This has been pointed out and explained in various contributions on the UfM and therefore need not be repeated at length (Aliboni and Ammor, 2009).

The second reason that limits the degree to which the UfM will alter Euro-Arab relations lies in the latter's geostrategic importance not only as Europe's neighbours. The Arab Mediterranean countries, of course, are part of the family of Arab nations which represent not only a relatively homogeneous group of countries as regards a joint linguistic, cultural and religious heritage, but, more importantly, which represents the world's largest reservoir of exportable fossil fuels – and these, in turn, will remain indispensable for the OECD member countries' economies despite the gradual rise of renewable energies for decades to come (Schlumberger, 2006). Moreover, with the rapid increase in new great powers' thirst for oil, the EU has no alternative but to entertain as good as possible political relations with the providers of what makes their economies run.

For all that, the UfM will alter existing patterns of Europe's relations to the Arab countries to a limited extent only. This does not mean that the UfM has no impact at all on future Euro-Arab relations. Let me therefore propose two scenarios pointing to the different directions these relations may take in the future due to the influence of the UfM. First, I sketch out the possibility of future Euro-Arab relations evolving along the officially proclaimed logic that, as the public has been told by the French administration, underlies the UfM, and which could be dubbed the 'Schuman–Sarkozy scenario'. Second, I propose an alternative scenario which might be termed the 'pessimist picture' or the 'realist scenario' in the sense that it is based less on a functionalist logic compatible with a social-constructivist understanding of EU foreign policies than on a more traditional or 'realist' understanding of the nature of international relations (see Holden, this collection).

The 'Schuman–Sarkozy Scenario'

As has been hinted at above, one of the core features of the UfM is its focus on technical projects and on the introduction of possibly more flexible possibilities of ad hoc co-operation in non-sensitive areas where consent is relatively easier to achieve. This comes along with an obvious 'lack of mention of strategic issues of politics', as Emerson (2008: 11) puts it, based on the EU's 'extreme caution over issues of desirable democratic political reforms and respect for human rights' (Emerson, 2008: 11). Presumably, however, this 'extreme caution' is not (only?) rooted in what some might call European cowardice or accommodativeness (i.e. shying away from the more complicated and conflictual issues in the partnership), but in a so-called 'functional logic'. As Balfour and Schmid (2008: 4) point out, 'according to the French, the "union of projects" approach is inspired by EU founding father Jean Monnet's functionalist method and his "solidarités de fait" (solidarity created by actually achieved facts)'.[7] In brief, this logic holds that the modest creation of functional links will over time result in deeper integration, similar, in one sense, to interdependence theory which argues that increasing levels of (economic) interaction will lead to increasingly non-violent modes of conflict regulation.

It cannot be denied that this 'functional logic' has some attractiveness to it: Translating this logic into a scenario for the future, functional co-operation in (some few) areas of truly shared interests will over time lead to increased levels of interaction, to a widening of the areas of co-operation, to deeper Euro-Mediterranean integration, and will ultimately – after the political systems north and south of the Mediterranean have converged significantly enough due to this dynamic of functional co-operation – one day even convince Arab rulers to cede power in favour of their hitherto disenfranchised populations. Normalization of relations with Israel and democratization, then, will not come about tomorrow, but they can and will come about. There is thus no need to aggressively exert pressure for quicker or more meaningful political reform on the MPCs; rather, this would be detrimental to the development of an overall positive political climate and an evolving spirit of co-operation. 'Core policies, such as conflict resolution or political reform and democratisation, are being excluded in favour of small-scale cooperation in key areas of common interest, with the aim of improving the overall political climate in the region' (Balfour and Schmid, 2008:3). What adds to the plausibility of this scenario is that while the divergence of political regimes around the Mediterranean may seem great today, levels of trust and confidence were certainly no higher between, say, France and Germany in the aftermath of World War II when Schuman delivered his declaration than those that exist today between the Arab world and the EU and its members after 15 years of the Euro-Mediterranean partnership. In this logic, then, there is not only no need to pursue active peace policies or democratization efforts, but these could even have a negative impact on the evolution of the overall UfM.

The 'Realist Scenario'

Let there be no doubt that this author would gladly welcome a future development of Euro-Arab relations along the lines of the 'Schuman–Sarkozy scenario' as outlined above. But there is an alternative scenario of future Euro-Arab relations which differs decisively from the one just presented.

This second or 'realist' scenario holds that even a power that might consider itself 'normative' by nature will eventually not run the risk of devising (let alone implementing) policies that contradict its own material interests and preferred policy outcomes in international relations. It will therefore prefer pragmatism and self-interest over a normative vision, even if that latter was grounded in a functional logic. The second scenario therefore starts from revisiting the agreed upon frame of the UfM with its three core dimensions of actors, institutions and policies as discussed above and, from there, concludes on the likelihood of major alterations the new political frame might bring about or not.

The three core dimensions of the UfM reveal clearly that the European side has largely given up on previously established larger and normatively based foreign policy goals in its relations with the Arab world. While core values such as the rule of law, respect for human rights, or participatory and inclusive modes of governance have – at least on a rhetorical level – figured prominently in the EMP framework established at Barcelona in 1995 and also in the Neighbourhood Policy pursued since 2004, these hardly appear at all in the renovation of Euro-Arab policies under the UfM. Quite the opposite is the case

1. With regard to *actors*, societal forces from the Arab world have virtually been excluded and their inconvenient voices seem less audible in the UfM. This represents a political priority which Arab regimes, through elaborate mechanisms of co-optation and repression in neopatrimonial contexts (Albrecht and Schlumberger, 2004), had already effectively implemented on national levels, but which have now been transferred to the international level of Euro-Arab relations through the UfM.

2. It is unlikely that despite this exclusion of potentially deviant voices policies will be suggested within the frame of the UfM that could be regarded as inopportune to the prime Arab political priority of authoritarian regime maintenance. The new *institutional arrangements* elevate Arab regimes to institutionalized veto-players and allow the Arab side to block any unwelcome political initiatives more effectively than before, even without Arab regimes having to agree on paper first and circumventing agreements in practice later. Under the UfM they can block any initiatives that run counter to their desire to cling to power and even prevent them from being formulated as Mediterranean policies. This can arguably be considered a second safeguard mechanism towards the maintenance and consolidation of authoritarian rule in addition to the first aspect. While co-ownership in theory is nice to have, this is only so in practice if the respective partners agree on joint political preferences.

3. *Policy contents* as reflected in the UfM's prioritized issue areas represent a near total de-politicization of co-operation. This makes it less likely that Arab regimes' political priorities of power maintenance are addressed. De facto, then, political conditionality – an instrument never used, but theoretically existing under the EMP scheme and within the ENP – has been abandoned in the new framework of the UfM.

The UfM in this sense, then, represents a triple victory of Arab political preferences – and a clear step back from earlier EU policies that not always exerted high pressure for norm-compliance or political reform, but which nevertheless made an explicit claim that there could be a long-term European policy goal related in one way or another to what are regarded in Europe as core norms and values of politics. The disappearance of these norm-based policy goals in the UfM certainly does not only represent a European naivety in foreign policy making. Rather, it seems that European decision makers have come to accept the fact that insisting on political goals (as opposed to micro- or meso-level technocratic goals) might not serve European interests best: If pursued seriously, this might in some cases even lead to ruptures in Europe's transatlantic relations (because of strategic US support to key Arab regimes), not to speak of the potentially devastating impacts systemic political transformations might have for regional stability – the latter being a necessary ingredient for European energy security, or for safeguarding markets that have been opened up not least through the Euro-Med economic co-operation schemes for the export of European industrial (and financial) products.

In other words, the UfM may not only be considered a triple victory for Arab authoritarian regimes, but may also be read as a convergence of interests by European and Arab political elites around the political status quo. As Kausch and Youngs (2009: 967) argue: 'the EU has moved further and further away from seeking a "ring of well-governed states" on its southern edge towards seeking a "ring of *firmly* governed states"'. Note, however, that this is not per se illegitimate – after all, European policy makers are supposed to pursue European political interests. However, the more norms and values are openly disregarded in both European foreign policy design and policy implementation, the less convincing it becomes to cover up real and material interests in a public political rhetoric based on such norms and democratic values vis-à-vis the European public.

The official Schuman–Sarkozy scenario, then, seems like a rather helpless effort at such public rhetoric since it neglects the key ingredient of any type of deeper integration, which is *political regime convergence*. Even during the rivalry between France and Germany after World War II, both countries were rooted in democratic constitutions and the issue was about reconciliation rather than about a clash over fundamental norms of how the political process can legitimately be conducted. The issue in the relations between a democratic Europe and authoritarian Arab regimes, by contrast, is that functional co-operation will not serve as a vehicle to regime convergence so that these differences can be overcome. This is because they are differences in kind, not in degree, and because the maintenance of these differences is made a precondition for co-operation by one side.

Realistically, then, if Europe does want co-operation – and in the absence of military options for forced regime overthrows – it seems to serve the EU's own economic and security interests best to engage in such co-operation under given political constellations. At any rate, the UfM demonstrates forcefully that efforts at altering or transforming contradictory political regime constellations between north and south of the Mediterranean are no longer on the European agenda, if ever they have been. With Seeberg (2010: 291), then, 'we can speak of cooperation between two uneven partners where the dominant part realizes that *realpolitik* is what can be pursued in the Middle East'. The only question, however, seems to be about who is the dominant part in this game of Euro-Arab relations: Bearing in mind the triple victory for Arab political priorities, Europe does not give the impression of being the dominant player in this game, even though certainly the one who invests the lion's share in terms of resources into the partnership. However, this could – from a realist perspective – relatively easily be explained by the fact that in Euro-Arab relations, the potential gains for Europe in the realms of security and the economy are much larger than those for the Arab side. I concur, then, with Peter Seeberg that the EU is to be viewed as 'a realist actor in normative clothes' (Seeberg, 2009: 81), and, to stay within the analogy, that the UfM strips off more and more of these clothes from the materialist, self-interested, and pragmatist body of European foreign relations towards its southern neighbours. The fundamentally erroneous notion of a qualitative difference of the EU's foreign policy behaviour as more norm-based in comparison to other actors on the international scene such as the USA, India or China thus becomes increasingly difficult to uphold.

Conclusions

Obviously, the scenario based on the functional logic of Europe's own integration does not take into account the qualitative differences between the European integration process among democracies on the one hand and the very heterogeneous group of democracies and autocracies around the Mediterranean on the other. Power distribution within national political systems and the resulting modes of governance, as is well established, have an enormous influence on prospects for both integration and development. The idea of replicating around the Mediterranean today what worked over past decades among European democracies is wishful thinking and contradicts not only everything we know today about the impact of European efforts at promoting democracy in its near abroad without offering full membership (cf. inter alia Schimmelfennig and Scholz, 2008). What is more, even when offering full membership, the EU's effort to promote democratic rule elsewhere has only been successful if and when political conditionality was employed. As Comelli (2009: 161) notes correctly: 'If conditionality – together with socialisation – was the most effective method through which the EU successfully transformed Central and Eastern countries, it follows that without the application of conditionality, the reforms envisaged by the ENP are doomed to fail.' The UfM threatens to eliminate political conditionality from Euro-Mediterranean relations altogether or at least to greatly reduce it. Therefore, the second scenario, which is based on the assumption that the EU has its own policy priorities (preventing terrorism, combating illegal migration and transnational organized crime, etc.), which it pursues independently of whether it spreads its own norms and values, is much more likely to unfold over the next decade.

If the purpose of the present contribution was a brief and concise prediction of the UfM's impact on the future of Euro-Arab relations, I would stress two points. First, its impact will be of an incremental rather than transformative nature, all the more so since the former rhetoric of political reform and democratization was never seriously given priority by the EU in the past and therefore the de-politicization inherent in the UfM's design will not result in *dramatic* shifts in actually implemented policies. Second, and notwithstanding the first point, the shift in the framework as regards the three dimensions under consideration in this contribution (actors, institutions and policies) carries in it an inherent tendency towards a stabilization of authoritarian modes of governance as well as towards de-development. This is so even though in the short term the UfM may benefit from renewed activism and maybe consent between the EU and its Arab neighbours may be reached somewhat more easily in the apolitical priority areas for future co-operation. But if it is correct that 'the EMP can only be reinvigorated and maintain its relevance into the future if it turns its *potential* acquis into *specific actions* designed to create a Euro-Mediterranean community of democratic states' (EuroMeSCo, 2005: 9), then the UfM does not have the potential to spur deeper integration in the long run, or to provide a substantial impetus for sustainable economic and human development within the Arab world: both depend on meaningful Arab political reform on the domestic scene.

Ironically, therefore, the UfM inherently contradicts the declared policy goals (long-term economic development; economic and political integration through functional co-operation) its designers say they wish to achieve. The UfM not only represents a European capitulation to an intractable Arab–Israeli conflict but also to the challenge of fostering greater respect for human rights and more participatory governance inside the Arab partner countries. While this will be welcomed by Arab governments, they will – as initial reactions demonstrated – nevertheless remain hesitant to enter into much closer relations with the EU than they already have because of their unwillingness to normalize relations with Israel and, second, because of the fears of getting caught in too close a political network in which Europe could be able, one day, to dictate policies that might be perceived as an infringement of national sovereignty or to impact negatively on vital questions of political power distribution within their own borders.

Having said this, the above provides more than just an assessment of the future shape of Euro-Arab relations. Rather, it can also be read as a contribution to the growing counter-evidence against the essentialist notion of a 'normative power Europe' which some scholars still tend to see in the EU and its foreign policies. True, the new institutional set-up of the UfM, especially its co-Presidency, the composition of the Secretariat and the JPC drawn from both sides of the Mediterranean as well as other monthly meetings suggest that it may not necessarily be correct to conceive of Euro-Mediterranean policies as 'the most imperialist project since World War II', as argued at a 2000 conference panel on the Euro-Mediterranean Partnership initiative.[8] Yet the EU will most likely not feel comfortable with giving up substantial policy priorities merely for the sake of achieving greater MPC co-ownership.[9]

Thus, apart from the fact that the concept of 'normative power' itself still awaits a viable operationalization, available empirical evidence suggests that – no matter how we define it – Europe in its foreign policies is no more of a 'normative power' than are the US – or even China, for that matter. Rather, it seems that Europe's Mediterranean policies continue to be one of the international factors which play a role in the durability of authoritarian rule in the Arab world. In the words of Comelli (2009: 161): 'To be questioned is not only the effectiveness of the EU in transforming the economic and political systems in the Mediterranean, but also its willingness to do so.' In this light, the present contribution may also be read as part of a newly emerging literature that focuses on international factors not in democratization but in the survival of autocracies and the 'authoritarianization' of national political regimes (Burnell and Schlumberger, 2010).

Acknowledgements

Earlier drafts of this study were discussed at LSE London, 10 May 2010, and at the World Conference of Middle East Studies, 16–20 July 2010, Barcelona. The author wishes to thank the editors of this special issue as well as Annette Jünemann and an anonymous referee. Special thanks go, again, to Federica Bicchi and Richard Gillespie for detailed and critical but very helpful comments, as well as careful edits.

Notes

1 See Bicchi's introduction as well as Hollis' contribution to this collection for details. For details on Arab fears for normalization, see especially Khatib (2010).

2 For discussions of the earlier Barcelona Process under the architecture of the EMP/ENP with a focus on its impact on the Arab countries, see Schlumberger (2000) or Kienle (1998).

3 To be sure, this rhetorical emphasis of the need for political convergence around democratic governance never translated in actual practice the way it was initially intended – and, of course, the 'Euro-Mediterranean Community of Democratic States' which 'Barcelona Plus' Euromesco Report of 2005 had in its title will not materialize any time soon. This report summarized the situation quite clearly: 'Progress towards democracy has fallen short of original expectations, and thus the degree of political convergence on which integration is predicated has failed to materialise' (EuroMeSCo, 2005: 22).

4 For details of the UfM's institutions, see Johansson-Nogués (this collection).

5 For more detailed discussions of the priority areas see Darbouche (this collection) and Hunt (this collection). The 'Business Development Initiative' (priority no. six) reads like a remnant of the failed neoliberal approach the IMF and the World Bank have pursued for over 20 years in their respective macro-economic reform and structural adjustment programmes (ERSAP), which in the Middle East and North Africa have failed to produce desired outcomes mainly because the legal and political environment for private business, above all the structural absence of the rule of law and contract security as well as impartial arbitration mechanisms and effective enforcement of anti-trust legislation, had been thoroughly ignored (Heydemann, 2004; Schlumberger, 2008).

6 While it is true that the bilateral Association Agreements which contain a political conditionality clause referring to human rights and democracy remain in place, the routine violations of this by Arab regimes have never been raised by the EU. With policy contents becoming less contentious and more technicized, the gap between actually implemented policies on the one hand and political principles the EU would like to uphold on the other is bound to widen and the likelihood of the said clause gaining practical relevance is decreasing.

7 Back in 1950, French foreign minister Robert Schuman, in a speech written together with his advisor and friend Jean Monnet, had put forth the first proposal for a 'European federation' based on a union between France and Germany (plus others) for the joint exploitation of coal and steel. However, with the symbolic issues of coal and steel (both essential for military industry) he clearly envisaged the establishment of a 'European federation' that would one day be a guarantor for peace in Europe (Schuman, 1950).

8 The quote is borrowed from a political science colleague and former president of the British Society for Middle Eastern Studies.

9 Moreover, a proposal by Arab League Secretary General Amr Mousa that was tabled at the Arab summit held in Sirte, Libya, in March 2010 (Libyaonline.com, 2010) has gained international attention lately. The Arab League recently released plans to establish a 'Union of Arab Neighbours' as a body that is to co-operate with other regional organizations such as the EU or the African Union as well as with larger neighbouring countries of the Arab world (Abu Husain, 2010). Whether this uncoordinated, but almost simultaneous announcement of two inter-governmental unions really represents an Arab effort to counterbalance potential negative impacts of the UfM for the Arab countries does not matter here; at any rate, it demonstrates that Arab countries are cautious not to rely too heavily on the promises of European policy initiatives. If Europe's normative radiance was as great as some of us assume, this would certainly not have been a necessary development – in other words, the level of trust between actors that have been Mediterranean partners for more than a decade in a 'thick institutional context', as Bicchi correctly points out in her introduction to this collection, should be assumed to be high enough for these partners to closely co-ordinate two similar policy initiatives which clearly overlap in both geographical scope and in the goals they seek to achieve.

References

Abu Husain, S. (2010) A conversation with Arab League SecGen Amr Musa, *ash-Sharq al-Awsat*. Available at http://www.aawsat.com/english/news.asp?section=3&id=20664 (accessed 26 July 2010).

Albrecht, H. & Schlumberger, O. (2004) 'Waiting for Godot': regime change without democratization in the Middle East, *International Political Science Review*, 25(4), pp. 372–391.

Aliboni, R. & Ammor, F. (2009) Under the shadow of 'Barcelona': from the EMP to the Union for the Mediterranean, *EuroMeSCo Paper*, no. 77 (January).

Asseburg, M. & Salem, P. (2009) No Euro-Mediterranean community without peace, *10 Papers for Barcelona 2010*, No. 1 (September) (Paris: European Union Institute for Security Studies).

Balfour, R. & Schmid, D. (2008) Union for the Mediterranean, disunity for the EU? *Policy Brief February 2008* (Brussels: European Policy Centre).

Burnell, P. & Schlumberger, O. (2010) Promoting democracy – promoting autocracy? International politics and national political regimes, *Contemporary Politics*, 16(1), pp. 1–15.

Comelli, M. (2009) Conclusions, in: M. Comelli, A. Eralp & Ç. Üstün (Eds) *The European Neighbourhood Policy and the Southern Mediterranean. Drawing Lessons from the Enlargement*, pp. 157–165 (Ankara: METU Press).

Emerson, M. (2008) Making sense of Sarkozy's Union for the Mediterranean, *CEPS Policy Brief No. 177* (March) (Brussels: Centre for European Policy Studies).

Euro-Mediterranean Conference (1995) *Barcelona Declaration adopted at the Euro-Mediterranean Conference 27–28 November 1995*. Available at http://trade.ec.europa.eu/doclib/docs/2005/july/tradoc_124236.pdf (accessed 20 October 2010).

EuroMeSCo (Ed.) (2005) *Barcelona Plus. Towards a Euro-Mediterranean Community of Democratic States* (Lisbon: Institute of Strategic and International Studies). Available at http://www.euromesco.net/media/barcelonaplus_en_fin.pdf (accessed 20 October 2010).

European Commission (2010) The policy: what is the European Neighbourhood policy? Available at http://ec.europa.eu/world/enp/policy_en.htm (accessed 12 October 2010).

Henry, C. M. & Springborg, R. (2001) *Globalization and the Politics of Development in the Middle East* (New York: Cambridge University Press).

Heydemann, S. (Ed.) (2004) *Networks of Privilege in the Middle East. The Politics of Economic Reform Revisited* (New York: Palgrave).

Heydemann, S. (2007) Upgrading authoritarianism in the Arab world, *Saban Center Analysis Paper*, No. 13 (October) (Washington, DC: Brookings Institution). Available at http://www.brookings.edu/papers/2007/10arabworld.aspx (accessed 20 October 2010).

Kausch, K. & Youngs, R. (2009) The end of the Euro-Mediterranean vision, *International Affairs*, 85(5), pp. 963–975.

Katz, J. (2008) Proposed Mediterranean alliance faces resistance. Available at http://www.findingdulcinea.com/news/international/May-June-08/Proposed-Mediterranean-Alliance-Faces-Resistance.html#3 (accessed 31 October 2010).

Khatib, K. (2010) The Union for the Mediterranean: views from the southern shores, *The International Spectator*, 45(3), pp. 41–50.

Kienle, E. (1998) More than a response to Islamism: the political deliberalization of Egypt in the 1990s, *Middle East Journal*, 52(2), pp. 219–235.

Libyaonline.com (2010) Arab summit twenty-second leader of the revolution headed by close of its meeting held in Sert in a public hearing [sic.]. Available at http://www.libyaonline.com/news/details.php?id=12855 (accessed 20 October 2010).

Manners, I. (2002) Normative power Europe: a contradiction in terms? *Journal of Common Market Studies*, 40(2), pp. 325–358.

Moïsy, D. (2009) *The Geopolitics of Emotion: How Cultures of Fear, Humiliation and Hope Are Re-Shaping the World* (New York: Doubleday).

Pace, M. (2007) Norm-shifting from EMP to ENP: the EU as a norm entrepreneur in the South? *a Cambridge Review of International Affairs*, 20(4), pp. 659–675.

Reuters Africa (2008) Libya and Turkey object the Union for the Mediterranean, http://af.reuters.com/news/country/?type=libyaNews (accessed 30 December 2009).

Schimmelfennig, F. & Scholz, H. (2008) EU democracy promotion in the European neighbourhood: political conditionality, economic development and transnational exchange, *European Union Politics*, 9(2), pp. 187–215.

Schlumberger, O. (2000) Arab political economy and the European Union's Mediterranean policy: what prospects for development? *New Political Economy*, 5(2), pp. 247–68.Schlumberger, O. (2006) Rents, reform and authoritarianism in the Arab Middle East, *International Politics and Society*, 2, pp. 57–72.

Schlumberger, O. (2007) *Debating Arab Authoritarianism. Dynamics and Durability in Nondemocratic Regimes* (Stanford, CA: Stanford University Press).

Schlumberger, O. (2008) Structural reform, economic order, and development: patrimonial capitalism, *Review of International Political Economy*, 15(4), pp. 622–649.

Schlumberger, O. (2010) Opening old bottles in search of new wine: on non-democratic legitimacy in the Middle East, *Middle East Critique*, 19(3), pp. 233–250.

Schuman, R. (1950) Déclaration du 9 mai 1950. Available at: http://www.robert-schuman.eu/declaration_9mai.php (accessed 25 October 2010).

Schwarzer, D. (2009) Future of the Mediterranean Union. growing challenges, lack of political will, *Qantara*. Available at http://en.qantara.de/webcom/show_article.php/_c-476/_nr-1152/i.html (accessed 20 October 2010).

Seeberg, P. (2010) Union for the Mediterranean – pragmatic multilateralism and the depoliticization of EU–Middle Eastern Relations, *Middle East Critique*, 19(3), pp. 287–302.

Seeberg, P. (2009) The EU as a realist actor in normative clothes: EU democracy promotion in Lebanon and the European Neighbourhood Policy, *Democratization*, 16(1), pp. 81–99.

Union for the Mediterranean (2008) *Joint Declaration of the Paris Summit for the Mediterranean.* Available at http://www.emuni.si/Files//Dokumenti%20PDF/Joint_declaration_of_the_Paris_summit_for_the_Mediterranean-EN.pdf (accessed 30 October 2010).

United Nations Development Program (UNDP)/Arab Fund for Economic and Social Development (AFESD) (2005) *Arab Human Development Report 2004: Towards Freedom in the Arab World* (New York: UNDP-Regional Program for the Arab States, Iran and Turkey).

Vucheva, E. (2008) Arab countries complicate Med Union plan, http://euobserver.com/9/26293 (accessed 30 October 2010).

Winkler, P. (2008) Was bringt die Mittelmeerunion, *Neue Zürcher Zeitung*, 14 March. Available at http://www.eurotopics.net/de/presseschau/archiv/article/ARTICLE25463-Was-bringt-die-Mittelmeerunion (accessed 26 July 2009).

PROFILE

The Return of Arab Politics and Europe's Chance to Engage Anew

RASMUS ALENIUS BOSERUP & FABRIZIO TASSINARI

Danish Institute for International Studies, Copenhagen, Denmark

It is not possible to predict whether the uprisings that have shaken the Arab world in 2011 will bring about a process of 'democratization'. It is just as difficult to rule out that the upheavals will eventually revert to an authoritarian political order. But it is possible, and indeed necessary, to conceptualize the changes taking place in numerous Arab countries as a multidimensional process of *politicization* in which large numbers of individuals, networks and institutions have emerged for the first time as active political participants in informal contention as well as formalized politics. The process is not linear, and varies considerably from one country to another. Yet the most immediate result in all cases has been an abrupt end to the political and social fatigue that had characterized the region in recent decades. In order to shape an adequate policy response to the momentous developments taking place in North Africa, the European Union and other international actors must first understand the nature of this change.

The return of Arab politics can be divided into at least four types of politicization. The first type consists in the return of contentious politics. During 2011, we have seen an unprecedented level of contentious political events across the Arab world. Non-violent campaigns, sit-ins, demonstrations and protest marches were observed in a number of Arab countries; millions risked their lives and thousands lost them in the course of such events. Although the region did experience similar events in previous years, as in the case of the Egyptian social and political campaigns organized on Facebook, as well as workers' protest movements, the scale of popular participation exploded during 2011– and so did its impact. In Tunisia and Egypt, such instances of social mobilization brought about divisions between military and civil actors in the old regimes. Later on, they were instrumental in causing the fall of the heads of state and keeping the transitional regimes that replaced them in check. All this amounted to a revitalization of the social base that for decades had appeared to be struck by political fatigue in the face of authoritarian repression.

The second type of politicization consists of the return of popular participation in formal electoral politics. Millions voted for the first time, thousands were listed as candidates, and hundreds of new political parties have been formed. Much of this is likely to dissipate soon, but some of these individuals and organizations will become important players in shaping the future of these countries. The revitalization of a previously inert electoral base is particularly visible in Egypt and Tunisia, but to a lesser extent also in countries where the regimes have survived intact, as in Morocco. In Tunisia, some 50 per cent of the electorate participated in electing a constitutional assembly in September and in Egypt 60 per cent of the electorate participated in the first rounds of the parliamentary elections in November and December. Compared to the estimated 10–15 per cent participation rate in previous elections, this represented a quantum leap in popular participation in formal politics.

A third type of politicization has appeared above the state and regime level – in the realm of supranational cooperation at the regional and international levels. The increasingly assertive role in regional politics played by the Arab League and the Gulf Cooperation Council features among the most significant processes of politicization in this area. Initiated with the unprecedented call for a no-fly zone over Libya, the activism of these regional groupings has overcome decades of intra-regional deadlock. The ousting of Syria from the League in late 2011 represents the most powerful example of this new dynamic.

A last type of political and social revitalization concerns the micro-level of politics in its broadest sense. During 2011, and most visibly in Egypt, a number of state and semi-state organizations and institutions have undergone processes of renegotiation and reorganization of leadership hierarchies and systems. A telling example is the struggle inside state institutions like al-Azhar and state-owned media corporations like al-Ahram, where employees and observers have pressured for increased independence from the state as well as a replacement of politically appointed leaders by elected candidates.

So far, the significance of this return of Arab politics is less visible in the concrete outcomes that it has produced in relation to the region's democratization than in the way in which it has pushed for the restructuring of the political order in North Africa. Politicization has been instrumental in breaking the nexus between authoritarian rule on the one hand, and political as well as social fatigue on the other.

Regime Collapse and Politicization

In terms of political developments, the return of Arab politics has been particularly manifest in the North African sub-region. During 2011, this part of the Arab world witnessed a series of variations to politicization and different regime responses to it, ranging from regime collapse in Tunisia, Egypt and Libya, to top-down reform in Morocco and political stand-by in Algeria.

The Egyptian and Tunisian cases followed comparable patterns. Here the civilian political elites built around Zine al-Abidine Ben Ali and Hosni Mubarak and their de facto single parties, the Rassemblement Constitutionel Démocratique (RCD) and the National Democratic Party (NDP), attempted to quell the tide of protest by, initially, unleashing broad campaigns of police repression, and subsequently by proposing top-down political reforms. As these tactics failed to halt the protests, the regimes turned to the military establishment. In both cases, the military chose to break away from the civil elite rather than engage in regime preservation through large-scale military repression. However, subsequently the armies in the two countries played very different roles.

In Tunisia, the military historically played little part in politics. During 2011, it continued to stay out of it and opted for a role of neutral watcher. This appears to have allowed, and even enabled, the civilian actors to compete for and eventually agree upon a plan for the transition of power within a strictly civilian arena. The process has had its natural ups and downs, with contentious politics and social movement campaigns: several post-Ben Ali governments resigned before a broad consensus about the process was established over the summer. This evolutionary and consensus-driven process manifested itself in the October elections for a constitutional assembly – which effectively qualified as the first successful free and fair elections in an Arab country for decades. The quick reorganization and electoral victory of the moderate Islamist political party al-Nahda represents the most significant change in Tunisian politics.

This notwithstanding, the character of the Tunisian transition provides useful lessons for the region and beyond. The process has so far been characterized by a pragmatic drive for evolutionary institutional change rather than revolutionary zeal. The electoral process, with its low levels of fraud and high levels of voter turnout, places itself as something of a paradigm for political transitions in the rest of the region. It disproves the essentialist assumptions about the incompatibility between democratic practices and 'Arab' or 'Islamic' culture, perpetuated over the decades by regional autocrats and many western observers alike. Moreover, it sets a high standard for what is possible and desirable with regard to peaceful political transition towards democratic rule in the region.

In Egypt, the direct role of the military in politics dates back to the Free Officers' military coup against the monarchy in 1952. Since then, the Egyptian army has played a key role in politics, among other things in providing candidates for the state's most important political functions: president, defence minister, as well as a number of other key policy portfolios (minster of aviation, minister of military production etc.). When Mubarak stepped down in February, the military high command in the form of the Supreme Council of Armed Forces (SCAF) assumed the executive powers there by placing itself as key player in the transition process aimed at rebuilding a civilian political system. While Tunisia's civilian actors managed to lay out a transition plan that was generally accepted by the large majority of political and social forces, the actors engaged in the Egyptian political process have failed to strike a consensus for the transition. The domination of the political field by the military contributed to this uneasy situation: the military high command's insistence on remaining a central figure in the negotiations with civilian actors, as well as its unilateral control over the state apparatus, appear to have negatively affected the stability of the Egyptian transition process.

Already in the spring of 2011 splits between the military and the core of civilian activists led to the decision by numerous key youth groups to boycott the constitutional referendum organized by the SCAF. The beginning in November of the protracted process of parliamentary elections took place shortly after large street protests in Cairo and Alexandria were organized by several of the youth networks that had mobilized against Mubarak in the early spring. Regardless of the electoral outcome, the split among civilian actors will prove a long-term challenge for the future government of Egypt. A key task of this government will be to renegotiate the power-sharing balance between military and civilian actors. In that process, it will be stronger if it proves capable of coordinating the efforts of the complete range of civilian actors – from parliament to the street. Failing to do that, the military will have an opportunity to consolidate its role in the political order by repeating the divide-and-rule tactics of the past decades.

The regime collapse in Libya was less a result of a fractioning elite and more a result of the UN-sanctioned no-fly zone. During the first months of the ensuing military campaign, Gaddafi's regime remained surprisingly resilient. It was capable of utilizing the full range of its institutions against the protestors located mainly in the eastern provinces. In that respect, it can be argued that the logic of repression witnessed in Libya has been mirrored by similar dynamics later observed in Syria, Bahrain and Yemen.

By the end of 2011, the future of politics in Libya remains highly uncertain. On the one hand, the National Transition Council (NTC) appears to act as a generally accepted power-broker and interim government. The country has, so far, avoided both of the worst case scenarios of full-scale civil war and partition of the state into two or more political units. On the other hand, reports of war crimes allegedly committed by pro-NTC militias have emerged and the central government will most probably continue to lack monopoly over the means of violence. It remains to be seen whether and how the transitional authorities will impose their authority on mobilized and armed autonomous actors that grew out of the prolonged military struggle on the ground that led to the fall of Gaddafi's regime. While the international military engagement was triggered by, and has succeeded in stopping, the impending slaughter of civilians in eastern Libya, it also prevented a 'natural selection' of political actors emerging out of the civil war. Western support decisively helped the cause of the rebels, but it also engendered a weak and dubiously legitimated central authority in Tripoli, which may not be able to prevent a descent into renewed conflict. At the same time, for the time being, all the opportunities are also there: resources to rebuild the state apparatus, mobilized population groups to staff bureaucracy and institutions, and a historical momentum to build on. In Libya, everything still seems possible.

Regime Endurance and Politicization

In the two North African countries where the politicization in 2011 did not lead to regime collapse, Morocco and Algeria, the political elites opted for different tactics for survival. In Morocco, the regime adopted a familiar strategy in the kingdom of a pre-emptive top-down political reform programme, materializing in a revision of the constitution and subsequent election of a new government. Although criticized as window-dressing, the Moroccan programme seems so far to present the most extensive political reform plan in the region; just as importantly, it appears to be the most effective approach in ensuring the survival of the regime. In other parts of the Arab world, monarchs have opted for more modest reforms. In Jordan, the government was sacked in early spring, while in Saudi Arabia King Abdullah increased state spending on welfare benefits for citizens by tens of billions of dollars during 2011. Yet political reforms have not materialized fully in these other Arab countries.

In Algeria, the government has so far shown little capacity to implement political reforms that address the distribution of power and the widening gap between the country's political elite and its youthful social base. Facing growing social protests in spring 2011, the government lifted the state of emergency and approved increased public spending in areas such as housing, salaries and basic commodity subsidies. In December the government passed a reform package that, amongst other things, included deregulation of the broadcast media sector as well as reforms of the electoral and party laws. However, the absence of deeper political reform of the distribution of power is linked both to the ongoing intra-elite struggles between government and security forces and to the inertial attitude of the country's social base: in 2011 Algerian civil society did take the initiative to formulate genuine political demands – in particular the creation of the National Council for Democratic Change (*Coordination nationale pour le changement et la démocratie*), but as in the case of other Arab countries that have experienced prolonged military strife and civil wars (such as Iraq, Palestine, Sudan and Lebanon), Algerians appear caught in continued political and social fatigue. In consequence, Algerian regime responses to the regional upheavals were marked by stand-by policies ensuring the continuation of a largely unstable political and social status quo.

The Politicization of Europe's Response

How have western actors, and the EU in particular, responded to this momentous return of politics in the Arab world? While several taxonomies have been tried and tested, an independent observer could be forgiven for lumping Europe's response under the heading of continuity and upgrading. Over the past year, the large number of policy initiatives, documents or generous shuttle-diplomacy on the part of senior officials such as EU High Representative Catherine Ashton corroborate the overall impression that European institutions and governments are aware of the scale of the challenge in North Africa and the serious implications that this will have for the security of Europe. Yet the policy responses implemented or announced so far can be variously characterized as responding to a 'much-more-of-the-same' rationale.

Policy makers in Brussels and most EU capitals do not dispute the need for an increase in democracy assistance to the region; 'deep democracy', for one, comes as the very top priority of the review on the European Neighbourhood Policy published by the European Commission in May. But while the EU's proposals are more detailed than in the past, neither their language nor their substance seem to differ fundamentally from what Brussels had been advocating before the events in Tunisia and Egypt. Several observers have roundly criticized an apparent western rush to pour money into the revolutions – a practice that seems as likely to entrench power structures of the old regimes as to accompany profound social transformations. The western financial pledges accompanied by references to a 'Marshall Plan' for the region are emblematic of Europe's orthodoxy.

The European response is not only the result of a lack of creative thinking. In the case of Morocco, Europe's recipe of close relations with the regime in return for gradual political reform can be interpreted as being successful. The European preference for technical, and largely value-neutral, assistance appears to be vindicated. Accordingly, it is not surprising that the EU's recent allocation of new development funds for North Africa directs over a third of them to Rabat, whose constitutional reform is deemed a 'clear commitment to democracy'.

Europe's own existential difficulties cannot be underestimated. The financial crisis and ensuing economic maelstrom touch on the very foundations of Europe's market-based liberal democracies, which it seeks to promote abroad. Different from previous instances of European crisis, the current introspection concerns not only the widening and deepening of the European integration process; it concerns the very future of the European construction. Such a context makes it difficult to look beyond the constraints of domestic politics. But the 'indignados' in crisis-stricken Greece and Italy or the emergence of a 'Tahrir Square' in Madrid remind us of the European neighbourhood's indispensable function as a mirror of Europe's own travails. As in previous ages, Europe's neighbours provide the much-needed impulse to look again beyond our borders.

A plethora of proposals are currently crowding the desks of European policy makers, variously advocating closer engagement in the region and institutional streamlining at European level. While these are all valid policy recommendations, our focus on politicization is aimed at a level of analysis that concentrates on the normative underpinnings of Europe's policy options. Arab politicization is giving rise to different, and at times conflicting, understandings of democratic politics. This diversity is likely to generate different outcomes in everything from constitutional arrangements to the application of the rule of law. Europe itself is characterized by hugely different political and diplomatic traditions. Not coincidentally, European political actors have been interrogating themselves for years about what exactly should comprise the EU's democracy promotion strategy. The Arab politicization represents a unique window of opportunity to substantiate the terms of this debate.

In order for Europe's response to the Arab upheavals to be credible and effective, the return of Arab politics should be mirrored by the emergence of a politicization of sorts in the making of European foreign policy. In the short to medium term, it is unlikely that EU's common foreign, security and defence policy will be any more coordinated than it is now. That as such is not necessarily a problem, as long as whatever has been achieved so far contributes to the way in which the EU presents itself in the global arena. For that to improve, EU member states ought to put more political and diplomatic weight behind the many things that EU institutions have proven capable of delivering on the ground, from crisis management to development assistance. The recent Polish EU presidency, during which foreign minister Radek Sikorski introduced himself as the 'loyal deputy' of Lady Ashton, may be a small example pointing in this direction.

EU support programmes for civil society are key to accompanying the extraordinary social mobilization in the southern Mediterranean: continuous stock-taking of these programmes, at the level of EU governments and institutions, is important to reflect the conditions on the ground in North Africa, which are likely to remain in flux for some time to come. Moreover, stock-taking should reflect the different positions and understandings on democracy promotion policies within Europe itself, as well as the consequences which this diversity carries with respect to how 'Europe' as a foreign policy actor is perceived by its Arab counterparts.

Lastly, EU policies aiming at opening up areas of the EU's internal market, as well as initiatives facilitating 'mobility' of selected categories of North African citizens, have serious implications for European citizens too. At a time of growing perception of economic and social insecurity within western Europe, a genuine politicization of Europe's international actorness entails a frank conversation between European political actors and the general public about the strategic objectives of European policies towards its southern neighbours, as well as the legitimate concerns that these generate among European citizens.

Taken together, these challenges concern nothing less than the security of Europe's citizens and Europe's place in a fast-changing world. Sovereign debt crisis notwithstanding, they will have to make their way back to the top of the European political agenda.

Index

Note: Page numbers in *italics* represent figures
Page numbers in **bold** represent tables

INDEX

For Product Safety Concerns and Information please contact our EU
representative GPSR@taylorandfrancis.com
Taylor & Francis Verlag GmbH, Kaufingerstraße 24, 80331 München, Germany